THE ART OF
M&A
VALUATION AND MODELING

A GUIDE TO
CORPORATE VALUATION

H. Peter Nesvold

Elizabeth Bloomer Nesvold

Alexandra Reed Lajoux

New York   Chicago   San Francisco   Athens   London
Madrid   Mexico City   Milan   New Delhi
Singapore   Sydney   Toronto

1 2 3 4 5 6 7 8 9 0   DOC/DOC   1 2 1 0 9 8 7 6 5

ISBN   978-0-07-180537-7
MHID   0-07-180537-0

e-ISBN   978-0-07-180538-4
e-MHID   0-07-180538-9

Library of Congress Cataloging-in-Publication Data

Nesvold, H. Peter, author.
    Art of M&A valuation and modeling : a guide to corporate valuation / Peter Nesvold, Elizabeth Bloomer Nesvold and Alexandra Reed Lajoux.
        pages cm
    ISBN 978-0-07-180537-7 (alk. paper) — ISBN 0-07-180537-0 (alk. paper)
        1. Consolidation and merger of corporations.   2. Corporations—Valuation.
        I. Nesvold, Elizabeth Bloomer, author.   II. Lajoux, Alexandra Reed, author.
        III. Title.
    HG4028.M4N4923 2016
    658.1'62—dc23   2015028852

To:

Lily Nesvold

Patricia Bloomer

The memory of Stanley Foster Reed

CONTENTS

SECTION III SAMPLE FINANCIAL MODELS   online[*]

[*]Available at www.ARTofMA.com

FOREWORD

With the publication of this book, McGraw-Hill Education rounds out a series that has flourished and grown for nearly 30 years. Our founding author, the late Stanley Foster Reed, launched the original, all-purpose volume, *The Art of M&A: A Merger/Acquisition/Buyout Guide*, in 1988 with two seemingly ostentatious goals: (1) to explain the complete life-cycle of an M&A transaction—from strategy, to valuation, financing, structuring, due diligence, integration, and even restructuring—and (2) to explore these topics purely through the Socratic method, itself a lost art that uses questions and answers to stimulate critical thinking and to illuminate ideas.

Since its humble beginning three decades ago, *The Art of M&A* series has outperformed even Mr. Reed's grand vision. The series now counts nine titles, one for each of the major chapters of the original text, involving more than a dozen experts and coauthors driving aggregate sales of more than 100,000 books. We believe this marks *The Art of M&A* series as the best-selling authority on mergers and acquisitions of all time. It's an extraordinary testament to Stanley Foster Reed's original vision.

The authors of this book—*The Art of M&A Valuation and Modeling*—represent the vitality of Mr. Reed's vision. The lead author, H. Peter Nesvold, now Executive Editor of the series, has been deeply involved in the series for nearly 15 years, with leading roles on four of the nine titles. A lawyer, accountant, and financial analyst by background, he brings unparalleled knowledge of complex corporate transactions and the capital markets to the effort. His coauthor, Elizabeth Bloomer Nesvold, is not only his wife and business partner, but also a successful investment banker and entrepreneur who, like Mr. Reed, has made a career out of devising and delivering upon seemingly ostentatious visions. Last and certainly not least, Alexandra Reed Lajoux, Founding Editor-in-Chief of the series, has been involved in each and every title since day one, both as a primary author and recruiter of new collaborators—thereby carrying the torch not only of her father's original vision, but also for M&A professionals industry-wide. "Alex," as she is known to many, has likely trained more M&A practitioners than any other commentator in the industry through her devotion to *The Art of M&A* series.

McGraw-Hill has also been a major part of the series. Ever since acquiring the series in 1998, the McGraw-Hill name has been associated with every title, supporting each updated edition and launching new spin-off volumes. We are proud to be associated with McGraw-Hill and the legacy of this series.

OK, enough with the nostalgia. Let's do a deal!

SECTION I
FUNDAMENTALS OF M&A VALUATION

CHAPTER 1

Cracking the Code: What's It Worth?

The White Rabbit put on his spectacles. 'Where shall I begin, please your Majesty?' he asked.
'Begin at the beginning,' the King said gravely, 'and go on till you come to the end: then stop.'

—Lewis Carroll, Alice's Adventures in Wonderland, *1865*

INTRODUCTION

As the King does for the White Rabbit, we find ourselves in the position of advising about where, and how, to begin a story—in our case, about where and how to begin the process of valuing a business. The valuation discussion does not only come up in the context of buying and selling a business. An owner should understand the worth of his or her business when borrowing money (particularly when a portion must be offered as collateral); when designing buy–sell agreements with employees; when determining the insurable value of selected corporate assets; and when crafting employee stock ownership plans. Likewise, financial managers should understand the valuation process so that they may better anticipate the reactions of investors, banks, and other capital allocators to key business decisions.

For some, the process of valuing a business might start and end with looking up its current stock price. But we should never confuse value and price. Two sages of equal wit each spoke to this point. Renowned author Oscar Wilde once noted, "The cynic knows the price of everything and the value of nothing." Famed investor Warren Buffett echoed this sentiment when he observed, "Price is what you pay; value is what you get."[1]

As the global economy continues to heal from the financial excesses leading up to the Great Recession of 2008–2009, the distinction between price and value is more critical than ever. After all, price is a subjective reading easily manipulated by asset bubbles, whereas value can be an objective measure established through time-tested methodologies. Yet too often, this concept—how to estimate the value of a business—remains foreign: a seemingly opaque process left to investment bankers and equity research analysts. Nevertheless, how to value a business is a practical problem that should be of specific concern to the managers, shareholders, and regulators who influence the operating policies of America's corporations. Without a basic grasp of the value of a particular business, the constituencies of that business lack the necessary tools to evaluate and support its success.

This book tackles an all-important question for a business's owners, investors, or advisors—what's it worth?—and provides a framework for arriving at an appropriate answer. Some elements of this framework are timeless; for instance, some valuation methodologies, such as those rooted in cash flow, have changed little over the decades. In contrast, other elements change constantly based on the economic and/or regulatory landscapes. Prime examples include valuation methodologies based on trading multiples and the impact of new tax code changes.

Moreover, the value of the asset depends partly on who owns it; that is, some owners may be uniquely positioned to generate revenue enhancements, or harvest cost savings, by combining the business with another within the owners' portfolios. Accordingly, the answer to that critical question—what's it worth?—may depend partly on whether the business is being valued as a standalone or as part of a larger transaction.

This book is divided into three parts. Section I explains how to value a business as a standalone. Chapter 1, which follows below, outlines valuation fundamentals, including some background into valuation multiples and discounted cash flow (DCF) analysis. Chapter 2 introduces the concepts of comparable companies and comparable transactions— arguably the most common valuation methodologies, given their ease of use. Finally, Chapter 3 delves further into DCF analysis, the granddaddy of all corporate valuation methodologies. For the most part, Section I of this book transcends mergers and acquisitions (M&A) and is relevant to most any capital allocation or corporate finance/investment decision.

Section II of this book introduces facts-and-circumstances consid-erations to evaluate in the context of a prospective merger or acquisition. Chapter 4 provides tools to consider if there is a meaningful gap in the perceived value of a business between a would-be seller and a prospec-tive buyer. Chapter 5 considers whether there are ways to create value through tax structure. Finally, Chapter 6 illustrates how a business's worth might change if the analysis shifts from a standalone valuation to a transaction model.

With the above perspective in mind, Section III of this book (avail-able exclusively online at the website www.ARTofMA.com) provides sample models that illustrate—using real-world examples—the concepts outlined throughout this book. Lastly, do not overlook the legal case sum-maries and glossary at the end of this text. Each entry contributes to a full appreciation of the "Art of M&A Valuation."

VALUATION FUNDAMENTALS

Are "valuation" and "price" interchangeable?

Value is the intrinsic worth of an asset, whereas price is what a buyer has actually paid for it. Recall the words of Warren Buffett above: "Price is what you pay; value is what you get." Prices change daily; value is more stable.

The key point is that the price paid for an asset, or a company for that matter, does not always reflect its underlying value—but rather the zone of agreement between a buyer and a seller at a given point in time. Confusing "valuation" and "price" is an easy trap to fall into—we inadvertently do it ourselves more often than we care to admit. However, it is important to at least keep in mind how the two are differentiated.

What exactly is a valuation multiple?

A *valuation multiple* is simply a means of expressing a firm's market value relative to one or more key financial metrics that presumably relate to that value. To be useful, those metrics—whether earnings, cash flow, or some other measure—must bear a logical relationship to the market value observed. That is, the financial metric should comprise a key driver of that market value.

Consider an example outside of the M&A context: real estate. How would a prospective buyer ascribe a value to a particular apartment in the Center City West section of Philadelphia? The first step might be to ask, how are other apartments in the area valued, and what are they worth? Some initial research would likely show that the value of an apartment in Philadelphia is typically related to its size, with the price per square foot representing the most common valuation multiple. According to the website Zillow.com, the average price per square foot for an apartment in Center City West is approximately $460.[2] However, is valuation as mechanical as applying a multiple to some financial metric? Is every 1,000-square-foot apartment in Center City West worth $460,000? The answer, of course, is no. Other factors will influence whether a buyer should pay $750 per square foot: How close is it to a desirable location such as Rittenhouse Square? How many bathrooms does the apartment have? Does the building have a doorman? Accordingly, the valuation multiple must be considered in the context of other datapoints.

Moreover, the type of valuation multiple used for one type of real estate investment might be completely irrelevant for another parcel. What if the opportunity were a 100-acre farm in rural Pennsylvania rather than an apartment in Philadelphia? How does this change the analysis? The first step is the same; the initial question is still, how are other farms in the area valued, and what are they worth? Moreover, the valuation might still be linked to the size of the parcel. For instance, the average value per acre for farm real estate in Pennsylvania is approximately $5,300, according to a recent survey by the United States Department of Agriculture (USDA).[3] So, does that mean that the 100-acre parcel is worth $530,000? Well, that depends.

A deeper dive into the USDA's data shows that the value drivers for Pennsylvania farmland are much different from the factors that matter in Philadelphia. For example, is the parcel cropland (worth, on average, $5,700 per acre, according to the USDA's survey) or pasture (worth, on average, $2,700 per acre)? If it is cropland, is it irrigated or nonirrigated? Are there buildings on the property? If so, how many, for what use, and in what condition?

In each case, multiples can provide a helpful starting point for analysis. But in these real-world terms, it becomes clearer why the appraiser must choose the appropriate sample set and still leave at least some room for interpretation.

What about valuation rules of thumb?

We've all heard them. A few years ago, supposedly knowledgeable people said, "Any good tech-based company is worth at least three times its annual sales." Or, "Never pay more than 80 percent of net worth."

These rules of thumb are tempting, but they can be treacherous. These statements are often wrong because they are based on past numbers and transitory trends of only a few deals on a local or industry basis. (As such, they frequently do not reflect the fact that similar companies in different parts of the country or even slightly different end markets can have very different levels of profitability. Consider construction equipment rental companies: a business in the fast-growing Atlanta market, which also benefits from near year-round good construction weather, will likely use its equipment fleet substantially more than a similarly sized business in a slower-growing, more seasonal market such as Detroit.)

Even worse, history is plentiful with valuation rules of thumb that really made no business sense. Here are just three examples:

- *Biotech.* In the 1980s, capital rushed into biotech concerns, the valuations of which were often based on a multiple of the number of PhDs who worked there. This rule of thumb eventually proved untrue, as the values of many of these companies fell, never to recover.
- *Telecommunications.* The Telecommunications Act of 1996 drew massive investment into competitive local exchange carriers (CLECs). One often-used valuation measure was the number of equipment switches these companies owned. Meanwhile, the manufacturers of such equipment were increasingly financing the sales of switches to the CLECs. In effect, a CLEC could borrow money from a manufacturer to buy a switch, which in turn increased the CLEC's perceived enterprise value by a multiple of the equipment purchased. It was circular thinking that never got out of the loop.

- *Websites.* During the "dot com" bubble of the late 1990s and early 2000s, many acquirers aggressively bought Internet websites at $100 per monthly unique user—the logic being that, once the buyer crafted a sustainable revenue model, each user had an annuity value analogous to a per-subscriber valuation for cable companies. This optimistic projection proved to be unsustainable.

In all three of these cases, the valuation rules of thumb emerged due to lack of current profitability and low visibility into future profitability. And in all three cases, reliance on the rule of thumb proved unwise.

What is discounting?

Discounting is the process of determining the present value of cash to be received in the future. Assuming interest rates and/or inflation rates above zero, cash today is worth more than it will be tomorrow. Discounting quantifies this premium.

In the sixth or seventh grade, your teacher probably taught you that a $1 investment, when *compounded* at 6% interest, will have a *future value* of $2 in 12.4 years, as that original $1 has earned an additional $1 in interest. What the teacher probably did not teach you was the reciprocal corollary: that $2 to be paid out 12.4 years from now, when *discounted* at 6%, has a *present value* of only $1 today. Most M&A investments revolve around projecting how much an investment will yield over some preset time horizon and factoring the uncertainties into the discount rate. The business of estimating *M&A investment risk* involves building into the discount rate the certainties and uncertainties of receiving a future stream of earnings or cash flows from your M&A investment. The lower the certainty, the higher the discount rate; the higher the certainty, the lower the discount rate.

What are hurdle rates?

A *hurdle rate* is the discount rate, usually set by the board of directors or other governance of a corporation, that must be applied to a projected earnings stream to determine whether the investment is likely to generate at least a minimally acceptable return. If the expected return does not exceed the hurdle rate, the investment is unlikely to be approved. Most companies set the hurdle rate as equivalent to their own cost of capital. Special situations then call for documented reasons to add points to the discount rate—for inexperience in the field, for high deviation rates on historical earnings for the target or its industry, or for other risk-related reasons.

For example, executives may develop different hurdle rates for entries into different industries that coincide with the comfort level of the board's personal "feelings" about the industry, which, upon investigation, may turn out to coincide with their familiarity with the industry. This approach appears rational but is an inappropriate proxy for risk, because those assessing the risk are not necessarily the ones who will be managing the acquisition.

What about time horizons?

Any analysis requires the selection of a *time horizon*, also known as the *forecast period*. The time horizon is the period—usually measured in years—over which the analysis will evaluate the company's expected cash flows. Most companies have standardized this period at 10 years. However, in industries that depend on shorter-lived styles or fads, such as toys or fashion, five to seven years is much more common. Public utilities traditionally spun their forecasts out for 20 years but have lately turned to much shorter time horizons as patterns of energy production, consumption, and conservation have changed. In parts of Eastern Europe and in the Middle East, currently struggling with economic or political uncertainty, traditional planning horizons no longer make sense. Tomorrow is charted on a deal-by-deal basis. This is where a few financial skills can really help a dealmaker. One of the benefits of "sensitivity analysis" is to discover the effects of different time horizons on a target company's net present value (NPV).

Unfortunately, there is a trend toward shortening the time horizon or forecast period under conditions of uncertainty that are not random. This shortening is a poor substitute for factoring in quantifiable risk. In many cases, with a little work, the uncertainties can be converted to probabilities that can be quantified without creating a jumble of forecast periods. You don't have to be a financial economist yourself to get this work done. Any accredited business school is likely to have a team of them ready, willing, and able to help—at an affordable price, or even pro bono.

COMPARABLE COMPANIES AND TRANSACTIONS

What is the comparable companies and transactions approach?

The *comparables* approach is a two-step valuation process, as explained in the next chapter. First, we compare the value of one company to other standalone companies. Second, we compare one transaction to how companies were valued in other transactions. Both of these comparisons involve a series of questions that involve valuation multiples.

What are the basic types of valuation multiples?

There are two basic types of valuation multiples: multiples that relate to a company's equity value and multiples that relate to a company's enterprise value.

- *Equity multiples* refer to the value of shareholders' ownership and/or claims on the assets and cash flow of a business. An equity multiple therefore expresses the value of this ownership relative to a financial metric that applies to shareholders only. The best example would be a company's net income (sometimes also referred to as its earnings), defining *net income* as the residual income left after interest payments to creditors, minority shareholders, and other nonequity claimants.
- *Enterprise value multiples* refer to the value of the entire enterprise, or the value of all claims on a business—both the equity value and *net debt* (gross debt less cash on hand), as well as other nonequity claimants. An enterprise value multiple therefore calculates the value relative to a financial metric that relates to the entire enterprise; prime examples are sales and earnings before interest, taxes, depreciation, and amortization (EBITDA).

Why would someone want to use valuation multiples to ascribe a value to a business?

There are three key reasons to use valuation multiples in the context of M&A analysis:

1. *Objectivity.* Valuation is partly a subjective process. Multiples can provide a useful framework for introducing a level of objectivity to the process. That is, multiples provide helpful information about relative value when used properly. At a minimum, valuation multiples can serve as the proverbial rule of thumb to double-check other valuation measures. For example, if a DCF analysis were to peg the value of a business at $100 million, the analyst could calculate earnings-based multiples (for example, the price of the company in relation to EBITDA, as in "five times EBITDA," commonly written as 5x EBITDA) and then ask how those multiples compare with similarly situated companies in the industry.

2. *Ease of use.* The very ease of calculation makes multiples an appealing and user-friendly method of assessing value. Multiples can help the analyst avoid potential misperceptions of other, more "precise" approaches, such as DCF. Valuations such as these can sometimes create a false sense of comfort unless they are triangulated with other valuation analyses.

3. *Relevance.* Valuation multiples focus on key metrics that investors use. Key examples include a business's revenue, operating income (also commonly known as EBIT, or earnings before interest and taxes), EBITDA, and earnings. Since investors in aggregate make the market—and thus dictate relative value—the most commonly used metrics and multiples will have the most impact.

What about the disadvantages of using valuation multiples? What should I keep in mind?

Despite their advantages, multiples have several disadvantages that one should consider when evaluating the worth of a particular company. Some

of the principal criticisms levied against multiples can be summarized
as follows:

- *Overly simplistic.* A valuation multiple is a deceptively
  complex variable; it seeks to distill a tremendous amount of
  information—including both known and unknown data—into
  a single figure or series of numbers. At times, this can be an
  overambitious objective! By combining many value levers
  into a single-point estimate, multiples may make it difficult
  to disaggregate the effect of different drivers. Consider the
  following real estate example: a 100-acre farm in Pennsylvania
  arguably is worth $530,000 based upon the average value per
  acre for farm real estate of $5,300. However, this single variable
  neglects to consider the location, condition, and potential uses of
  the property. Clearly, these variables can have a tremendous
  influence on the intrinsic value of the land. The lesson learned,
  then, is not to rely on just one, or even a handful, of valuation
  multiples to dicate value. Dig deeper.
- *Static.* A multiple represents a snapshot of a firm's value at
  a given point in time. However, clearly every business and
  industry has a lifecycle. Moreover, the economic backdrop is
  constantly changing, which typically will have a carryover
  effect on the worth of a particular enterprise. Valuation multiples
  often fail to capture the ever-changing nature of business and
  competition. The takeaway: consider how the market valued an
  asset over an extended period of time, not just on any given day.
- *Potentially misleading.* Multiples are primarily used to make
  comparisons of relative value. However, comparing multiples is
  an inexact art, as there are many reasons that multiples can
  differ. If we were to extend the farm example above, a $530,000
  valuation might be grossly high if the land is, in fact, pasture
  (which, at $2,700 per acre, might only be worth $270,000) or a
  bit on the low side if the parcel is cropland (which, at $5,700 per
  acre, might be valued at $570,000). There are even more subtle
  ways in which valuation multiples might differ between two

Figure 1-1 Advantages and Disadvantages of Valuation Multiples

Advantages	Disadvantages
• **Objectivity:** Can be robust tools that filter out subjective assumptions such as future growth rates. Can provide useful information about relative value.	• **Overly Simplistic:** Can combine multiple value drivers into a single point estimate. Difficult to disaggregate the effect of different value drivers.
• **Ease of Use:** Are relatively simple to calculate, particularly with widely available data. Their wide use makes them a "common language" for dealmakers.	• **Static:** Only measure value at a single point of time. Do not fully capture the dynamic nature of business and competition.
• **Relevance:** Are based on key metrics that investors use.	• **Potentially Misleading:** Can vary for many reasons, not all relating to true differences in value. Can result in misleading "apples-to-oranges" comparisons among companies.

seemingly similar businesses, not all of which relate to true differences in value. For instance, even modest changes in accounting policies can result in diverging multiples for otherwise identically operating businesses. For these reasons, the selection of truly comparable companies is critical. Where there are differences, the analyst may need to make adjustments to the implied multiples. Figure 1-1 summarizes the key advantages and disadvantages of valuation multiples.

How can the disadvantages of valuation comparison be mitigated?

In addition to looking at the company in relation to others at a single point in time, look at the company at present in relation to itself at multiple future points in time. This is the purpose of DCF analysis.

DCF ANALYSIS

Isn't it misleading to base a valuation on unknown future events? Isn't the past record more reliable?

Admittedly, it is tempting to use historical results, rather than future projections when valuing a business; there's more certainty to past financials.

However, when a business changes hands, the new owners are interested in what the company can do in the future, not what it did in the past.

Consider, for instance, a business that is in structural decline. Newspapers would be one example. A valuation that focuses on historical results would likely overvalue a paper's worth, as electronic-based distribution channels are currently eroding its profit margins. By the same token, using historical results might actually *undervalue* a distressed acquisition target, as trailing financial results may fail to account for the often significant operational turnaround that is expected. Indeed, it has been a basic valuation principle for many decades that projected, not trailing, earnings should be considered when a company anticipates significant improvement in the near term.[4]

Accordingly, valuation, particularly when it is cash flow–based, should reflect forward-looking projections, not historical results. To be sure, there is risk to every forecast. In the words of management guru Peter Drucker, "Erroneous assumptions can be disastrous." The forward-looking projections must be constructed diligently. Otherwise, it's garbage in, garbage out.

What exactly is DCF analysis?

DCF analysis is a widely used analytical framework for measuring the present value of multiyear cash flows. In its simplest application in the world of M&A, a DCF analysis estimates the value of a business based on projections of how much cash the business will generate in the future. These cash flows are "discounted" because a dollar earned in the future is worth less than a dollar earned today, given the time value of money. Tweaking the analysis, DCF also enables an acquirer to explore whether a particular target is likely to generate sufficient risk-adjusted returns.

Although this text discusses DCF in the context of M&A, the analysis is not solely limited to that application. Rather, the framework can apply to nearly any financial decision-making process: whether to buy a stock; whether to purchase a new piece of equipment; whether a piece of real estate is attractively priced; and so on. Accordingly, the analyses described throughout are relevant for many other applications.

How is a DCF analysis different from a multiples analysis?

Discounted cash flow looks at *one* company, and it looks into the *future*. It predicts how well the company is expected to do in terms of future free cash flow (money left over after paying necessities). It skips historical analysis in favor of basics: cash is cash, and cash is good!

Multiples analysis looks at *many* companies, and it looks at the *past*. It tells you what kind of ratios have held true for comparable companies in past years. Also, multiples analysis uses a variety of accounting numbers—times sales, times profits, etc.—that may or may not indicate true economic value.

Moreover, as discussed in greater detail in Chapters 2 and 3, DCF has some advantages over static, point-in-time approaches—such as multiples analysis—in that it adds more flexibility and more precision to the investment analysis.

Using all of these approaches in combination can be a helpful cross-check.

How does DCF stack up against other valuation approaches?

In many ways, cash flow–based valuation is the granddaddy of all valuation techniques. This is because, at the end of the day, all valuation measures are directly or indirectly focused on answering the same question: how much cash do I expect this business to generate during the relevant measurement period?

As its name suggests, DCF analysis is a form of analysis that anticipates a company's future net operating cash flow and discounts it to present value. The purist approach counts only "free" cash flow—that is, cash that is available to spend; it is calculated after capital expenditures and dividends are paid during the period.

Many analysts believe that the DCF method is the best way to value a company, but it is not the only way. A thorough valuation can look not only at cash flow but also at assets, earnings, and stock price—as well as a variety of ratios and methodologies based on these fundamentals and of course a discount rate to reflect cost of capital.[5]

CHOOSING A VALUATION APPROACH

How does an acquirer choose a valuation approach?

The kind of financial analysis the acquirer conducts—DCF, multiples from comparable companies or transactions, a combination of these, or another approach entirely—will depend in part on the strategic reason for buying the company. There are many possible reasons one company would want to buy another. Here are some primary ones:

- *Growth.* To lessen economic vulnerability and/or increase latitude for strategic choices by increasing the size of the company and thus potential revenues and/or profits. A growth-oriented acquirer may consider valuation multiples focusing on ratios that involve sales, such as EBITDA to sales.
- *Diversification.* To hedge against risk in current industries by investing in others. A diversification-oriented acquirer may choose DCF as a valuation model because it lends itself to comparability across industries.
- *Progress.* To accomplish strategic goals more quickly and more successfully by buying an operating company that is already doing what is envisioned in the buyer's strategy, or that could provide some missing piece of the buyer's strategic puzzle. A progressive acquirer will rarely value the target company by itself but will value the future combined company—typically with DCF, using postcombination scenarios.
- *Vertical synergy.* To achieve economies of scale or other economic benefits by buying a customer or supplier. An acquirer interested in this kind of financial synergy will recast the financial statements showing a different cost structure postmerger and then create a DCF statement from that.
- *Horizontal synergy.* To increase market share ("market power") or reduce competition by buying an actual or potential competitor. Since this kind of acquisition involves a company that is similar to the acquirer, both multiples and DCF are relevant modes of valuation.

- *Financial offset.* To smooth financial performance by combining companies with different cash flow cycles, tax profiles, and/or debt capacities. Here, the emphasis is not so much on the amount of cash flow in the future as on its timing, so multiples may be the natural choice.

- *Efficiency.* To realize a return on investment by buying a company with less efficient managers and making them more efficient or replacing them. This is a natural candidate for DCF analysis, because the acquirer is relying on a new and different scenario; current and historical multiples will be meaningless.

- *Bargain hunting.* To take advantage of a price that is low in comparison to current stock prices, or in relation to the cost the buyer would incur if it built the company from scratch. Regarding current stock prices, this is clearly a candidate for multiples (e.g., price/earnings, earnings per share). As for cost to build, this is a cost-based approach unrelated to multiples and DCF. This is not so much valuation as appraisal—a subject in its own right.

- *Control.* To assert control in an underperforming company with dispersed ownership by acting as an agent for the owners. Here any multiple or ratio involving stock price and/or dividends is most relevant, such as total shareholder return (TSR).

With these types of goals in mind, let us now take a deeper look at the two valuation approaches emphasized in this book: comparable companies and transactions and DCF. The next chapter focuses on comparables.

Evaluating Comparable Companies and Transactions

Odyous of olde been comparisonis, And of comparisonis engendyrd is haterede.

—John Lydgate, 1440

Tryin' to make it real—compared to what?

—Eugene McDaniels, 1967

INTRODUCTION

"It's all relative." Perhaps nowhere is this cliché truer than when it comes to business valuation. Although it is common to use a single measure as a proxy for company value—one speaks of a "$1 billion enterprise" based on annual sales or market value—accurate valuation requires comparisons. The key question of course is, what will be compared to what?

In the previous chapter, we presented an overview of different approaches to valuation and concluded that the most common methods were comparable approaches and DCF. This chapter will focus on the first; more specifically, we will explain how to calculate and use multiples commonly used in M&A analysis.

First, we compare one company to other companies. This process involves a long list of qualitative and quantitative decisions—which companies are truly comparable and why? Which financial metrics and valuation multiples are more common? How do differences in business quality impact valuation multiples? After all, any given company is composed of many elements, financial and nonfinancial, each of which can influence the business's valuation.

Second, we compare one transaction to other transactions. This method likewise requires a series of inquiries into the facts and circumstances behind the sample of transactions chosen. What was the price paid? What was the timing of payments, and were those payments guaranteed or contingent upon some future event? These terms are as important, if not more so, than the headline valuation. It raises an industry adage—"You can name the price, if I can name the terms."

Therefore, this chapter will provide the fundamentals of comparability itself—both corporate and transactional. Let's get started.

COMPARING ONE COMPANY WITH OTHER COMPANIES

What is comparable companies analysis?

The *comparable companies* approach to valuation is the most widely used methodology in corporate finance. It involves contrasting the financial metrics and valuation multiples of a peer group of companies (generally publicly traded) to those of the business being appraised, known as the *target*. The foundation of this approach is the concept that the market should ascribe similar valuations to businesses with similar characteristics. To select the appropriate peer group—also called the *universe of comps*, or just *comps* for short—the analyst must understand the target's business. Comparable companies should be comprised of companies that are similar to the target; that is, the comps should be from a similar industry, of approximate size, with similar growth trajectories, and so on.

The analyst will calculate the peer group's average margins, financial returns, growth prospects, and—most importantly—valuation multiples to arrive at a group mean and median. The analyst will then apply these metrics to those of the target to arrive at an approximate valuation. This process underscores a key difference between comparable companies and DCF as valuation techniques: whereas DCF evaluates companies on an individual basis, the comparable companies approach considers valuation relative to the target's peers.

Importantly, the valuation determined through comparable companies analysis does *not* reflect any premiums or discounts that might apply—such as the control premium a buyer typically pays in an M&A transaction or the discount that either the public or private capital markets might apply to a bankrupt entity to reflect the future operating uncertainty.

However, the evaluation will provide a useful starting point for the M&A analysis, or a confirmational datapoint for a more exhaustive DCF model.

Why are publicly traded stocks typically used as the comps? Why not private companies?

The comparable companies analysis typically uses publicly traded stock prices to drive the process because public companies generally provide the most transparent valuations. Privately held businesses, in contrast, typically do not publish their financial statements and do not trade on stock exchanges, yielding limited public data. In addition, a publicly traded company's current stock price is generally viewed as one of the best pricing metrics because it represents a balance of the subjective views of numerous investors on various factors affecting the company's future performance. In this sense, the comparable companies methodology provides an up-to-date judgment on the company's risk profile, competitive pressures, cyclicality, and business prospects.

Which financial metrics and valuation multiples do M&A analysts typically focus on?

The answer partly depends on a particular company's industry and stage of development, among other factors.

As a practical matter, investors or acquirers in different industries may scrutinize entirely different financial metrics. As described in greater detail later in this chapter, an acquirer of an early-stage technology company might focus on revenue, rather than earnings—particularly if the target has incurred heavy upfront costs and is not yet profitable but is now on a tremendous growth trajectory. In contrast, the potential buyer of a company in a mature industry, such as newspapers, might be more concerned with cash flow, and less about revenue, as the would-be purchaser may be more concerned with sustainability than growth.

Likewise, a commodity-driven business, like a gold mine or natural gas producer, might typically be valued as a multiple of its reserves. That may be because the market might choose to focus primarily on the business's current production capacity and the bankable value of what the producer has in the ground and assume that production will cease once the reserves are depleted. However, one would not necessarily expect an auto manufacturer to be valued as a multiple of its production capacity, but rather as a multiple of EBITDA or some other more standard financial measure.

These extremes aside, there is a reasonably finite list of financial metrics and valuation measures from which acquirers are likely to start. We elaborate on several of these later in this chapter.

From a valuation standpoint, the most popular valuation multiples involve the following:

- EBITDA,
- Earnings or earnings per share (EPS),
- Sales or revenue,
- Cash flow, and
- Book value.

Profitability can likewise be benchmarked many different ways. However, the most common measures include gross margins, operating and/or EBITDA margins, pretax margins, and net margins. Other key metrics that acquirers will examine include the company's growth trajectory—whether measured in unit sales, revenue, earnings, or some other figure—and the target's financial returns—such as return on equity (ROE), return on invested capital (ROIC), or return on assets (ROA).

The preceding examples, while popular, only scratch the surface of possible financial ratios. Looking at the balance sheet and income statement (as itemized in Appendix 2A), we see that there are some 53 financial realities that companies must report—32 for the balance sheet and 21 for the income statement. In theory at least, each of these can be compared with each of the others, both within the same statement and across statements. Mathematically, therefore, this yields *2,756 possible ratios*. Adding the dimension of time (rate of change) only multiplies the possibilities!

Lastly, the buyer might look at variables that fall beyond the company's financial statements—such as its sales per employee or (as noted above) mining reserves. Much depends on the facts and circumstances of a particular situation. Like we said at the beginning of the chapter, *it's all relative!*

Which is better: Measuring valuation as a multiple of EBITDA or earnings?

As outlined above, it largely depends on the particular industry. However, the fact is that the price-to-earnings (P/E) ratio is an equity metric—that is, it only looks at the equity portion of the company and ignores debt and preferred shareholders—whereas enterprise value divided by EBITDA (EV/EBITDA) is an enterprise metric. As such, a company's leverage can dramaticaly influce its P/E. All else equal, two identical companies with slightly different capital structures can have markedly divergent P/E ratios. This can cloud the valuation process.

EV/EBITDA is capital structure neutral. The mix of equity and debt does not change the EV calculation, but it can dramatically skew a company's P/E. Ultimately, then, it doesn't matter how you slice the pie between debt and equity—total enterprise value remains unchanged.[1] Accordingly, EV/EBITDA generally results in more comparable multiples among various companies.

When might P/E represent a better valuation yardstick than EV/EBITDA?

The question that the analyst should consider is whether interest expense is an operating expense or a *financing expense* of the target company. An *operating expense* is an expense incurred in carrying out an organization's day-to-day activities. For example, interest is a cost of doing business for companies such as banks, leasing companies, and other financial institutions. These businesses borrow money at one rate and lend it out at a higher rate. As such, interest expense is directly related to operations. For these companies, P/E is the better valuation measure.

A *financing expense* is an expense triggered by how a particular company is capitalized—that is, how much debt it chooses to carry. One illustration would be an auto parts manufacturer; the amount of debt—and therefore interest expense—a company carries is a balance sheet decision and really has no impact on operations. In a case such as this, EV/EBITDA is preferable.

The other instance in which P/E might be a better measure is in industries that carry negligible amounts of debt. Prime examples include tech companies and those with highly volatile business models, such as biotech firms. In these situations, the extra effort of calculating EV/ EBITDA might not add any additional useful information and therefore isn't worth the extra step.

With so many potential valuation and financial metrics to consider, how do I narrow the alternatives to those that are the most important to my target's industry?

This question reminds us of an old phrase: "paralysis by analysis." With so much data readily available these days, one must fight the temptation to be drawn into seemingly endless amounts of analysis. The consequences of getting too caught up in infinite spreadsheets extend beyond a migrane headache (although let's not discount the severity of that one!). The potential acquisition of a business at an attractive valuation may prove to be a fleeting opportunity. He who hesitates is lost.

So how do we jump-start the process? From a practical standpoint, there are three sources of information that we historically have found to be useful starting points—once the analyst has identified the relevant industry and peer group:

- *Sell-side analyst reports*. Most major investment banks and brokerage firms employ entire departments of equity research analysts that publish reports on stocks in specific industry sectors. (In fact, one of the authors of this book spent a dozen years as a sell-side analyst covering the machinery, transportation, and automotive industries.) Once highly guarded publications, sell-side analyst reports are becoming increasingly available to retail investors through various websites (or, frankly, by simply researching the analysts' names and contacting them directly). In particular, ask for "intiation reports," "industry primers," or "deep dives"—these terms are analyst jargon for the firm's most comprehensive reports. See how the analyst critiques and values the businesses in his or her sector. Inevitably, these insights will advance your research quickly.

- *Company 10-Ks, annual reports, sustainability reports, and investor presentations.* As is commonly known, all publicly traded companies are required to publish annual reports (on Form 10-K) containing a minimum level of financial disclosures as well as a Management Discussion and Analysis (MD&A) section detailing risks. Many companies supplement their 10-Ks with an additional annual report telling the company's story in more detail, using illlustrations aimed at retail investors. In addition, a growing number of companies provide in-depth information on their nonfinancial performance—either within their annual reports (thus called an "integrated report") or in a separate report (often called a "sustainability report").[2] All such reports are posted on the company's website under investor relations, along with transcripts from recent earnings calls or analyst presentations, which management has used to communicate its business fundamentals to current and potential investors in the stock. Taken together, these reports can be a gold mine of information.

- *Industry benchmarking surveys.* Finally, the M&A analyst might track down trade associations and/or consulting firms that specialize in the relevant sector for benchmarking surveys. Benchmarking involves comparing a given company's process and/or performance metrics to industry norms or best practices from within or outside the given industry. Trade associations often provide benchmarking surveys, either for free or at a relatively modest price, as a member benefit. Consulting firms, in contrast, sometimes create such surveys, generally for a price, to demonstrate their industry expertise and attract clients. One example is IHS, a publicly traded company that sells industry-specific forecasts and strategy tools. In any event, the M&A analyst can learn volumes from how these industry experts measure companies in a given sector.

Figure 2-1 summarizes the most common multiples used for selected sectors and provides the rationale behind each selection.

Figure 2-1 Common Multiples Used in Selected Sectors

Sector	Multiples Used	Rationale
Cyclical manufacturing	P/E, relative P/E	Consider using normalized earnings
Growth firms	PEG[1] ratio	Big differences in growth rates
Young growth firms with losses	Revenue multiples	Few other choices
Infrastructure	EV/EBITDA	Early losses, substantial D&A[2]
REITs[3]	Price/Cash flow to equity[4]	Large depreciation charges on real estate
Financial services	Price/Book value	Works better if book value is marked to market
Retailers	Revenue multiples	Margins equalize sooner or later

[1]Price/earnings to growth
[2]Depreciation and amortization
[3]Real estate investment trusts
[4]Cash flow to equity, also known as CFE, is defined as net income plus depreciation

Source: Professor Aswath Damodaran, New York University.

Which companies are comparable?

As noted above, in constructing a comparable companies analysis, the analyst typically chooses a peer group of firms from the same industry as the target. These firms should also have similar fundamental characteristics, such as revenues, profitability, credit quality, and so on. While this analysis should ideally target direct competitors, it is often necessary to include a broader array of firms as a practical matter. One example would be where there are only a handful of publicly traded peers. The analysis should also adjust the capital structures of each comparable company in order to more accurately compare them with the corporation being valued (see Figure 2-2).

Figure 2-2 Comparable Companies Checklist

Look for similarity in:

• Industry

• Size (revenues)

• Profitability

• Rate of growth

• Credit quality

• Capital structure (debt/equity and related ratios)

• Business model

It's easy to overlook the last category in Figure 2-2: business model. However, that should not discount its significance. The Delaware Chancery Court tackled the issue of differing business models in *ONTI, Inc. v. Integra Bank,*[3] a frequently cited 1999 case. The *ONTI* court agreed with plaintiffs that the initially similar physician practice management companies being compared were, upon close inspection, too different because one was less equipment intensive and derived more revenues and profits from pharmaceuticals.[4]

How many comparable companies should the analysis use?

While there is no formal requirement, practical experience suggests that the analysis should involve approximately four to eight comparable companies to form a representative group for performing the valuation analysis. If few or no companies exist that are both comparable and publicly traded, then the analyst might want to broaden how he or she is defining the industry.

Consider, for example, the potential purchase of a regional chain of vitamin stores. If the analyst defines the industry sector that narrowly—retailers of vitamins—the analyst will only find two public comps: Vitamin Shoppe, Inc. (VSI) and Vitacost.com Inc. (VITC). That's not really enough to create a thoughtful comparable companies analysis. What's more, Vitamin Shoppe, with a market capitalization of more than $1 billion, might be too large to be truly relevant as a valuation comp, depending on the size of the target. However, if the M&A analyst were to broaden the industry definition to specialty retailers—particularly those that are both regional and in the small- or micro-cap segment of the market—several more options open up: indeed, a quick online screen yields well over a dozen candidates with market caps ranging from $100 million to $500 million.

Ultimately, if the broadened industry definition still yields too few results, the comparable companies valuation methodology fails, and the analyst should apply other methods instead. For example, in *In re Radiology Assoc., Inc. Litigation,*[5] the bankruptcy court held that differences between proposed comparable companies were so large that any comparable companies comparison was meaningless.

After identifying the list of comparable companies, the comparable valuation multiples are applied to the company being valued to establish a relative valuation range. Multiplying the mean or median P/E ratio of the comparable companies by the earnings of the company being valued to establish a relative valuation can be helpful to pinpoint a specific valuation but may be misleading. A better approach is to consider the relative strengths and weaknesses of the target.

Over what time period should multiples be measured?

Ideally, the time period selected for multiples should be long enough to correct for cycles that occur in the elements being measured. In some industries, such as those that are consumer driven (e.g., restaurants), this cycle might coincide with the macroeconomic cycle. In other industries, such as so-called short-cycle markets like semiconductors, there can be multiple inventory stocking and destocking periods within a single macroeconomic cycle. As always, the answer depends on the facts and circumstances of a particular situation. However, there are a couple of criteria to keep in mind:

- Any multiple that includes stock price as an element should be measured during a period that was not distorted by a bull or bear market. A valid period could be the most recent market cycle from its start to end points, typically a three- or four-year period, though this may vary.[6]
- Any multiple that includes revenue or earnings as an element should be measured over a time period long enough to correct for cycles of boom and bust in the company's industry (e.g., four years in the construction industry or seven years in aerospace).[7]

Why might multiples vary across seemingly similar businesses?

There are a number of ways of answering this question, but arguably there are four primary reasons why multiples may vary: (1) the businesses might have varying levels of quality; (2) the companies might use different accounting approaches; (3) the firms might be encountering short-term or cyclical fluctuations in financial performance; and (4) the market might simply be mispricing the two enterprises. We elaborate on each of these four reasons below.

How do differences in business quality impact valuation multiples?

All else equal, higher-quality businesses deserve higher valuation multiples. Invariably, there will be qualitative differences in the underlying drivers of a firm's valuation—management experience and depth, the business's opportunity set, its specific strategy, and so on. Converting these qualitative factors into measurable statistics is challenging, although four metrics worth considering are the business's ROIC, cost of capital, rate of growth, and duration of growth.

What about variations in accounting? How do they impact valuation?

Differences in accounting policies that do not affect cash flow do not impact the intrinsic value of the business. However, differences in accounting policies *can* impact the business's reported sales, earnings, financial returns, and so on. From a practical standpoint, then, these policy differences can drive a range of reported financial results that have a carryover, optical impact on valuation multiples. Unless these variations in accounting are normalized, the differences in valuation multiples can paint a misleading picture of relative valuation.

Consider, for example, two companies—A and B—with identical revenue, operating expenses, tax rate, share count (e.g., shares outstanding), and stock prices. In fact, the two businesses are identical operationally but have one accounting difference. Both companies carry $50 million of goodwill on their balance sheets; however, Company A does not amortize it, whereas Company B expenses this item over 10 years (or $5 million annually). How might this one accounting difference impact the companies' relative valuation?

Figure 2-3 illustrates the outcome. Company B's amortization expense of $5 million results in $35 million of operating income compared to Company A's $40 million. There is no impact to cash, mind you, as goodwill amortization is a noncash expense. If we progress down the income statement through book taxes and shares outstanding, Company A has $2.40 of EPS compared to Company B's $2.10. The stock market, however, isn't fooled in this case by the difference—shares of both companies are trading at $35. *In effect, the market is looking through these accounting differences and ascribing the same value to both stocks.* A natural question might be, why is this so? After all, why should two stocks with comparable growth prospects trade at the same price if one has an EPS of $2.40 while the other has an EPS of $2.10? The answer is cash flow. Amortization is a noncash accounting expense. Either way, the two companies are delivering the same amount of cash to shareholders. However, the implied P/E multiples are meaningfully different—Company A is trading at 14.6 times (14.6x) earnings, while Company B is trading at 16.7x. If an M&A analyst had not dug into the details, he or she might have concluded that Company B is worth 14% more than its counterpart based on a high-level P/E analysis. However, this premium is actually mere accounting fiction; it would be wrong to conclude that Company A is cheaper than Company B.

Figure 2-3 Variations in Accounting May Affect Valuation Multiples[1]

	Company	
	A	B
Revenue	$100	$100
Operating expenses	(60)	(60)
Amortization	–	(5)
Operating income	40	35
Taxes @ 40%	(16)	(14)
Net income	**$24**	**$21**
Shares outstanding	10	10
Earnings per share	$2.40	$2.10
Share price	$35	$35
P/E multiple	**14.6x**	**16.7x**
Valuation "premium"		14%

Is Company B really trading at a 14% premium to Company A?

[1]$ in millions, except per-share data

How commonly do accounting differences impact a firm's reported financials and, consequently, valuation multiples?

Accounting differences are not a one-off issue. Studies have identified more than 250 different factors that can drive variations in a company's profit measurement.[8] As was the case in the example used in Figure 2-3, these accounting differences can also impact valuation multiples. Although not all differences in profit measurement are material enough to move the needle, accounting differences are clearly not a trivial issue.

How might an analyst adjust a company's finanical results in response to accounting differences?

There are practically an infinite number of accounting decisions that the management of any particular company can make. While it is virtually impossible to completely eliminate the impact of different accounting methodologies, there is still much that the analyst can do to mitigate their impact and produce data relevant to M&A analysis. In particular, there are two steps the analyst can take when these differences have the potential to unreasonably influence the valuation results: (1) restate accounting data in a common format; and (2) focus on key metrics that are less affected by accounting differences.

What are some of the most common accounting adjustments that analysts make?

Accounting adjustments can be acutely industry sensitive—for instance, accounting standards for companies in the energy industry differ substantially from those in the insurance industry, the biotech space, and the transportation sector. However, there are a few key issues that can be analyzed across industries: depreciation, extraordinary items, and leases. Although these items may be more common in some industries than others, they are calculated in the same way across the board (with some global differences as noted below). Other, more complex issues to consider include deferred tax assets, pensions and postretirement health benefit plans, and provisions such as those for doubtful accounts.

- *Depreciation.* How a business depreciates its property, plant, and equipment is a prime example of how there can be significant differences in accounting policies. There are several standard methods of computing depreciation expense, including fixed percentage, straight line, and declining balance methods. Moreover, it is entirely reasonable for two different firms to adopt different economic lives for similar assets. Any of these variables can drive a meaningful difference in a company's annual depreciation expense. Study each company's depreciation policies. If possible, adopt a standardized methodology across each company, and calculate whether the change to net income would be material for each. If the data do not permit a standardized methodology, the analyst should at least keep these differences in mind when building the valuation model.
- *Extraordinary items.* Nonrecurring gains and losses are given a variety of names such as extraordinary, exceptional, unusual, or one-time. Unfortunately, the type of item included in this category, as well as its presentation in the income statement, varies. All such "exceptional" items should be excluded from EBIT and adjusted net income figures. These items include gains and losses on capital transactions and all truly one-off operating items, such as the cost of restructuring.
- *Leases.* There can be material differences in lease accounting across different companies, even those that are similarly situated. These differences are particularly important in capital-intensive industries with heavy use of leasing, such as airlines, construction, equipment manufacturing, and real estate. The primary area to consider is the classification of a capital lease (or finance lease, called Type A) versus an operating lease (called Type B) under U.S. generally accepted accounting principles (GAAP) accounting. In a capital lease, the underlying asset is considered purchased; the transaction gives rise to an

on-balance sheet debt obligation with a corresponding interest charge. In an operating lease, in contrast, the underlying asset is considered rented and does not necessarily create a liability. Under new U.S. leasing standards (which became final in June 2014), leases with a term of more than 12 months must make a balance sheet disclosure. Comparability would improve, particularly with respect to balance sheet and enterprise value ratios, by consistently capitalizing all lease obligations. The biggest challenge is that disclosure can be inconsistent, adding subjectivity to some adjustments. As a result, many analysts do not automatically adjust for leases unless leasing is highly material. Evolving standards for lease accounting complicate the situation as U.S. and global accounting standards move toward convergence through a joint project on lease accounting, which is ongoing.[9]

What are the main differences between U.S. and global accounting for leases?

The Financial Accounting Standards Board (FASB) and the International Accounting Standards Board (IASB) are still working on this discrepancy, as described below. However, the differences are narrowing.[10]

- For *lessor* accounting, the two boards recently confirmed that a lessor should determine lease classification on the basis of whether the lease is effectively Type A (a financing or sale) or Type B (an operating lease). A lessor would make that determination by asking whether the lease transfers substantially all the risks and rewards from owning the leased asset. In addition, the FASB, which creates GAAP accounting rules, decided that a lessor should not be allowed to recognize profit and revenue for any Type A lease that does not transfer control of the underlying asset to the lessee.[11]
- For *lessee* accounting, the FASB decided on a *dual* approach, with lease classification determined in accordance with the principle in existing lease requirements (that is, determining whether a lease is effectively an installment purchase by the

lessee). Under this approach, a lessee would account for most existing capital/finance leases as Type A leases (that is, recognizing amortization of the right-of-use, or ROU, asset separately from interest on the lease liability) and would account for most existing operating leases as Type B leases (that is, recognizing a single total lease expense). Both Type A leases and Type B leases result in the lessee recognizing an ROU asset and a lease liability. This is a different outcome than under international accounting standards, which use a *single* approach for lessee accounting. Under the international approach, a lessee would account for all leases as Type A leases (that is, recognizing amortization of the ROU asset separately from interest on the lease liability). See below for an illustration.

Which financial metrics are less affected by accounting differences?

As noted above, it is generally impossible to eliminate all accounting differences between two companies—particularly when the analyst does not have complete access to the internal books of one or both businesses. Consequently, the M&A analyst should supplement the adjusted valuation multiples above with multiples that are less likely to be distorted by accounting assumptions. The be-all and end-all financial measure is cash flow: after all, either the cash is there or it is not. After that, measures such as EBITDA and, to a lesser extent, sales are commonly used for valuation multiples.

- *Cash flow.* Cash flow is a helpful basis for valuation because cash, when calculated properly, is entirely independent of accounting assumptions. Indeed, this is one key reason why DCF is generally considered the best valuation methodology. However, even this metric should be interpreted with care, as cash flows naturally vary from year to year, and any single year's results may not be indicative of a company's true earnings potential. To some degree, this volatility is mitigated if the analyst uses the next 12 months' forecasted cash flows as the basis for valuation. This does require that the analyst construct cash flow estimates for each company that is used in the comparables group. It goes without saying that predictions of the future can fall prey to error and bias.[12]

- *EBITDA.* EBITDA is often used as a proxy for cash flow and is arguably the most common measure of financial performance and value that purportedly overcomes the challenge of accounting differences. This is partly true, particularly when it comes to varying accounting assumptions used for depreciation, amortization, and deferred taxes. However, there are other accounting problems with EBITDA as a valuation methology, particularly when EBITDA is presumably being used as a proxy for cash flow. That is, EBITDA ignores capital expenditures and cash taxes. The cost of these items certainly *does* have an impact on value. More subtly, however, EBITDA shares many of the challenges that proliferate with GAAP—revenue and cost recognition, pension accounting, and so on.

- *Sales.* Sales, or revenue, has some appeal for valuation, as it speaks to a company's sales volume and, potentially, market share. Also, it is probably the second-least vulnerable financial metric after cash flow. This is because line items at the top of the income statement, such as sales, generally have fewer assumptions underpinning them. However, even these are open to at least some accounting interpretation—as is evident from the FASB's ongoing project on revenue recognition. Furthermore, revenue says nothing of the company's profitability and cash flow–generating capabilities. Sales, in a vacuum, therefore may be of relatively minimal importance to the valuation discussion. As such, revenue multipes are less popular than EBITDA multiples and are often used only as a last resort if some of the other, more relevant, profit measures are unavailable or unreliable.

How do fluctuations in financial performance impact valuation multiples?

A valuation multiple based on a firm's profits is only meaningful if the profitability measure used is representative of the true earnings power of the business over time. What if, for instance, the target booked a large, windfall gain from multiyear litigation? Likewise, what if the target had experienced a substantial operating loss from a union strike? Clearly, the analyst would not want to put a mutiple on these sums, as they are unlikely to recur each year. Rather, the analyst might make adjustments to a target's financial results to reflect unusual or nonrecurring gains or expenses such as these.

Sometimes, however, the fluctuation in a company's financial performance might reflect a cyclical downturn in earnings. Consider the impact to aluminum company Alcoa from a slowdown in auto sales, housing starts, or some other macroeconomic variable. Even a modest downturn in auto sales might have a disproportionate impact on Alcoa's earnings in a particular year, given Alcoa's relatively high fixed costs and, thus, operating leverage. Clearly, auto sales are not Alcoa's sole earnings driver; other variables will also impact results. The point, however, is that some companies—even entire industries—are more vulnerable to others to shorter-term fluctuations in demand.

So, does that mean that Alcoa's intrinsic value should mirror the peaks and valleys of a volatile factor such as auto sales? Most analysts would agree that the answer is no. If it did, a buyer could just wait for an inevitable blip in demand, swoop in to acquire businesses like Alcoa on the cheap, wait 12 to 24 months for demand to rebound, and then sell the company. If only it were that easy! A multiple is only meaningful if the profit on which it is based is indicative of the target's future profit potential. Where this is not the case, the analyst should smooth out earnings over a reasonable period of time (three to five years often works).

Is it possible that inconsistencies in valuation multiples might simply reflect market mispricings?

Yes. If the analyst cannot reconcile differences in multiples by the companies' relative business quality, accounting differences, or profit/cyclical fluctuations, then it is at least possible that the market may be mispricing the asset. Indeed, market inefficiencies such as these are what nearly every active manager of publicly traded stocks and bonds seeks.

Furthermore, the M&A market, which involves control, is a less efficient market than the publicly traded securities market as a whole, so it is even more likely that, yes, mispricings can, and do, happen. (For more about the role of control premiums, see the discussion of comparable transactions analysis in the following section.) Just as identifying mispricings is the rallying cry of most asset managers, so too is it the objective of many M&A practitioners. In our experience, if the work is exaustive and accurate, and a business still appears mispriced, it probably is. This is what we work for! It is the M&A analyst's task to identify such mispricings; the analyst's skill is in distinguishing between differences from underlying fundamentals—which are therefore justifiable—and those from market inefficiencies.

Can you use the comparable companies approach for distressed companies?

Comparable companies analysis is not easy for a distressed entity, because the trailing earnings and cash flow for a business in bankruptcy will be low (perhaps even negative) relative to its normalized earnings power. However, this might only be a temporary dip—at least until the company is able to stabilize operations and/or its balance sheet. Accordingly, it may be difficult to apply comparable company multiples to the distressed entity's most recent results. Instead, it is frequently necessary to apply the multiples to projected financial results (one to two years is typical) and, if applicable, discount the implied valuation back to the present. If applying the comparable companies analysis to projected financial results, be sure to calculate forward multiples using projected financial results of comparable publicly traded companies.

Are there other times when a particular comp should not be used?

Yes—beware of valuation outliers. Sometimes, a valuation multiple might look unusually high when the denominator is very small relative to the numerator. A good example might be the P/E of an emerging-growth Internet company with a stock price of $50 per share but an EPS of only a small amount, say, $0.25 per share. The P/E ratio in this case would be 200x. Think about that—on its surface, it would appear that the market is willing to capitalize 200 years' worth of the tech company's current earnings! Of course, what the market is more likely doing is looking through the near-term EPS of $0.25 and anticipating significant earnings growth in the future. If, for instance, the tech company were on a path to improve earnings tenfold over the next five years, a $50 stock price would essentially be discounting $2.50 of EPS for a more reasonable 20x P/E five years out.

Still, this does little to help our universe of valuation comps today. When an output value is very large relative to the peer group, try to determine the reason, mark the multiple as "NM" (not material) in your spreadsheet, and exclude the outlier from the calculation of summary statistics.

What does a comparable companies analysis look like?

Let's consider an example from an old-line industry: How might an M&A analyst build a comparable companies peer group for a potential acquisition target in the railroad industry? The first step would be to develop a list of industry comps and gather their relevant valuation and financial metrics.

Figure 2-4 outlines the six independent and publicly traded "Class I" railroads in North America. (Class I is a regulatory designation made by the Surface Transportation Board, a governmental regulatory body housed within the U.S. Department of Transportation.) These railroads include Canadian National, Canadian Pacific, CSX Corporation, Kansas City Southern, Norfolk Southern, and Union Pacific. (The seventh and final

Figure 2-4 Peer Group's Key Measures of Value[1]

Company and Ticker	Stock Price 6/5/14	Diluted Shares	Market Cap.	Net Debt	Enterprise Value	Book Value
Canadian National (CNI)	$60.77	821.8	$49,940	$7,368	$57,308	$12,805
Canadian Pacific (CP)	179.75	169.7	30,510	4,223	34,733	7,264
CSX Corp. (CSX)	29.79	981.8	29,247	8,627	37,874	10,445
Kansas City Southern (KSU)	106.41	110.4	11,748	1,493	13,241	4,215
Norfolk Southern (NSC)	100.49	305.6	30,711	7,960	38,671	11,812
Union Pacific (UNP)	200.34	447.6	89,664	8,320	97,984	22,416

[1]$ in millions, except per-share data
Source: FactSet

Figure 2-5 Peer Group's Summary Income Statement Items[1]

Company and Ticker	Revenue		EBITDA		EPS	
	2014e	2015e	2014e	2015e	2014e	2015e
Canadian National (CNI)	$11,301	$11,932	$4,774	$5,141	$3.05	$3.43
Canadian Pacific (CP)	6,487	7,026	2,796	3,164	7.88	9.38
CSX Corp. (CSX)	12,263	12,821	4,701	5,198	1.85	2.19
Kansas City Southern (KSU)	2,657	2,895	1,133	1,293	4.66	5.44
Norfolk Southern (NSC)	11,654	12,362	4,533	4,895	6.56	7.46
Union Pacific (UNP)	23,355	24,419	9,968	10,661	10.81	12.11

[1]$ in millions, except per-share data
Source: FactSet

Class I railroad, Burlington Northern, is owned by conglomerate Berkshire Hathaway.) As a starting point, then, Figure 2-4 summarizes the equity capitalization, enterprise value, and book value of each comp. (Note: All financial results for Canadian National and Canadian Pacific have been converted from Canadian dollars (CAD) into U.S. dollars (USD) at the then-prevailing exchange rate of 0.937 CAD to 1.000 USD.)

Figure 2-5 contains three key line items—revenue, EBITDA, and EPS—from the 2014e and 2015e projected income statements of all six independent Class I railroads.[13] These estimates are widely available from sell-side analyst reports. Figures 2-4 and 2-5 might not contain a substantial amount of numbers, but they can lead to some insightful analysis, a portion of which is summarized in the figures that follow.

First, we look at the peer group's projected growth, margins, and returns. Figure 2-6 calculates the expected revenue, EBITDA, and EPS growth from 2014e to 2015e across the six independent Class I railroads. In reviewing the results, it can be helpful to notice how widely dispersed the data are. Consider, for instance, that the range of expected EBITDA growth is relatively high: Kansas City Southern is expected to see EBITDA growth of 14.1% in 2015e, a little more than twice Union Pacific's 7.0% improvement. It will be a key responsibility of the M&A analyst to understand why. (Union Pacific faces increasingly difficult year-ago comparisons, whereas Kansas City Southern is outgrowing the industry due to its exposure to Mexico's fast-expanding industrial production base and, therefore, freight demand.) Another datapoint that jumps out is how profitable the railroad industry is—with average EBITDA margins

Figure 2-6 Peer Group's Projected Growth, Margins, and Returns[1]

Company and Ticker	2014–15 Growth (%)			EBITDA Margins		Net Margins		ROE[2]
	Revenue	EBITDA	EPS	2014e	2015e	2014e	2015e	
Canadian National (CNI)	5.6%	7.7%	12.5%	42.2%	43.1%	22.2%	23.6%	19.6%
Canadian Pacific (CP)	8.3%	13.2%	19.0%	43.1%	45.0%	20.6%	22.7%	18.4%
CSX Corp. (CSX)	4.6%	10.6%	18.4%	38.3%	40.5%	14.8%	16.8%	17.4%
Kansas City Southern (KSU)	9.0%	14.1%	16.7%	42.6%	44.7%	19.4%	20.7%	12.2%
Norfolk Southern (NSC)	6.1%	8.0%	13.7%	38.9%	39.6%	17.2%	18.4%	17.0%
Union Pacific (UNP)	4.6%	7.0%	12.0%	42.7%	43.7%	20.7%	22.2%	21.6%
Mean	6.3%	10.1%	15.4%	41.3%	42.8%	19.1%	20.7%	17.7%
Median	5.8%	9.3%	15.2%	42.4%	43.4%	20.0%	21.5%	17.9%

[1]$ in millions, except per-share data
[2]Return on equity (ROE) calculated as 2014e net income/2014e book value
Source: FactSet

of more than 40%. (Who would have guessed that a stodgy old industry like *railroads* would have better margins than most software companies?!) Datapoints such as these can provide insight into the quality of a particular company or market segment.

Next, we use the data in Figures 2-4 and 2-5 to calculate each company's valuation multiples. In Figure 2-7, we briefly tally five common valuation methodologies: EV/EBITDA, P/E, and each company's PEG ratio, price-to-sales ratio, and price-to-book value. We also include P/E to ROE—a more obscure metric used more commonly in the financial sector for companies involved with insurance or specialty finance.

Figure 2-7 Peer Group's Valuation Multiples[1]

Company and Ticker	EV/EBITDA		P/E		PEG[2]	Price to 2014e:		P/E to ROE
	2014e	2015e	2014e	2015e		Sales	Book Value	
Canadian National (CNI)	12.0x	11.1x	19.9x	17.7x	1.6x	4.4x	3.9x	1.0x
Canadian Pacific (CP)	12.4x	11.0x	22.8x	19.2x	1.2x	4.7x	4.2x	1.2x
CSX Corp. (CSX)	8.1x	7.3x	16.1x	13.6x	0.9x	2.4x	2.8x	0.9x
Kansas City Southern (KSU)	11.7x	10.2x	22.8x	19.6x	1.4x	4.4x	2.8x	1.9x
Norfolk Southern (NSC)	8.5x	7.9x	15.3x	13.5x	1.1x	2.6x	2.6x	0.9x
Union Pacific (UNP)	9.8x	9.2x	18.5x	16.5x	1.5x	3.8x	4.0x	0.9x
Mean	10.4x	9.5x	19.3x	16.7x	1.3x	3.7x	3.4x	1.1x
Median	10.8x	9.7x	19.2x	17.1x	1.3x	4.1x	3.4x	1.0x

[1]$ in millions, except per-share data
[2]PEG ratio calculated as 2014e P/E/2014e–2015e projected earnings growth
Source: FactSet

In our experience, the most common valuation multiples in the railroad industry are EV/EBITDA and P/E. As illustrated in Figure 2-7, the group was trading on average at 10.4x and 9.5x 2014e and 2015e EBITDA, respectively, and at 19.3x and 16.7x 2014e and 2015e earnings, respectively. These are helpful datapoints that we can apply to a valuation target with similar financial and operating characteristics. Importantly, however, there is a relatively wide range of valuation multiples: in terms of EV/EBITDA, the richest valuation in the group (Canadian Pacific) trades at a 53% premium in 2014 to the lowest valuation (CSX). This carries over to P/E, as CP trades at a 42% premium to CSX.

So what explains this relatively wide dispersion of valuation multiples? As described earlier in this chapter, there are a variety of factors that might be at play: varying levels of quality, different accounting standards and policies, short-term or cyclical fluctuations, and/or market mispricings. From a qualitative standpoint, one argument might be that CSX trades at a discount to the group average because it has disproportionate exposure to Central Appalachian coal, which is under regulatory pressures and, it would seem, is a shrinking industry. Canadian Pacific, in contrast, is in the midst of an operational turnaround, plus has exposure to Bakken oil—a high-growth segment of the energy industry. Accordingly, Canadian Pacific has a stronger growth profile than CSX, as reflected in the relative valuations.

Putting this qualitative perspective aside, what about the fact that railroad industry earnings are cyclical? Figure 2-7 is really only a "point-in-time" valuation—it shows us how the market valued the six independent, publicly traded Class I railroads as of June 4, 2014. What might industry valuations look like if we were to stretch out the analysis over a longer period of time to smooth out the peaks and troughs in earnings?

Figure 2-8 tackles this point. Here we look at the forward P/E for all six of the publicly traded Class I railroads from 2000 through 2014. For the sake of perspective, we have also added CSX's forward P/E to this graph to show the company's relative valuation over that time. What this figure suggests is that, over time, the railroads have traded at about 14x forward earnings (versus 17x to 19x as of June 4, 2014, as illustrated in Figure 2-7). As a supplemental datapoint, then, the M&A analyst might consider 14x forward EPS as the "normalized" multiple to apply to a railroad's "normalized" EPS.

Figure 2-8 The Railroad Industry's Forward P/E from 2000 Through 2014

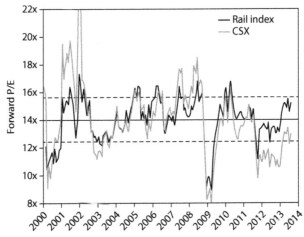

Source: FactSet

Moreover, we note that CSX has historically traded in line with the group but in recent years has lagged and traded at a discount.

The discussion above addressed CSX's discount from a qualitative perspective (i.e., the railroad's changing business mix). Figure 2-9 takes a quantitative approach to reconciling valuation. The left-hand graph plots EV/EBITDA valuation for each industry participant against the company's EBITDA margin. The right-hand graph plots each EV/EBITDA multiple against the company's size (as measured by net income). The results are revealing if we look at the statistical correlation expressed as a percentage (or R^2) (that is, the square of the correlation coefficient, which shows the proportion of the variabilty of CSX that can be explained by the variability of its peers).

One takeaway from this simple analysis is that the market appears to ascribe a higher multiple to "high-quality" railroads (i.e., those with the highest margins), as illustrated by the chart's R^2 of 77.9%. Size, in contrast, appears to have relatively limited impact on valuation: the R^2 between these two variables is only 21.8%.

Figure 2-9 raises one final thought: imagine we could acquire CSX or Norfolk Southern—which have the industry's lowest margins and therefore trade at the lowest multiples—and enhance the business's operations,

Figure 2-9 Comparison of Railroad Industry Valuations

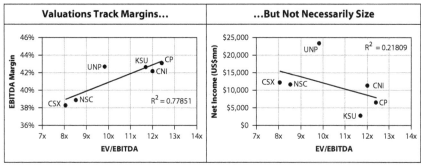

Source: FactSet

thereby driving margins (and earnings) higher. We could later sell the target at a higher valuation multiple, based on increased margins and earnings. Therein lies the lure of M&A!

Where can I obtain a sample comparable companies analysis?

Visit www.ARTofMA.com to download some of the models presented in this book.

COMPARABLE TRANSACTIONS ANALYSIS

What about comparable transactions? How can they be used to value a business?

At the root of *comparable transactions analysis*, also known as *precedent transactions analysis*, is that an analyst can estimate the value of a business based upon the prices paid by acquirers of similar companies in similar circumstances. This analysis provides useful information on valuation multiples that acquirers have paid for companies in the past in a specific sector.

The purpose and process are similar to what an acquirer would undertake in the case of a comparable companies analysis. Recall that the foundation of the comparable companies approach is the concept that businesses with similar characteristics should have similar valuations in the marketplace. This logic carries over to precedent transactions analysis—similar companies

should sell at similar multiples—so the M&A analyst can approximate valuation for a particular target by researching the multiples paid in comparable
deals. In effect, historical multiples represent an index of recent market prices
paid by other acquirers and accepted by sellers. From a potential seller's
perspective, these multiples suggest a price range within which buyers have
been willing to transact. For potential buyers, the multiples represent price
ranges that have been acceptable to sellers. At times, sharing this information
can help bridge expectation gaps between the two sides.

The biggest difference between comparable companies and comparable transactions is the control premium embedded in transaction
prices. As described earlier in this chapter, the comparable companies
analysis generally does not reflect the control premium that a buyer typically pays in an M&A transaction. This control premium typically means
that transaction multiples (i.e., those implied by a comparable transactions analysis) will generally be higher than trading multiples (i.e., those
implied by a comparable companies analysis).

Strategic considerations for the future combined companies often
take precedence over standalone valuation and cause companies to pay
more than the company would attract from general investors. For example,
in scenarios in which the buyer and seller have substantial geographic and
product overlap, there may be greater prospects for cost synergies. This
allows the buyer to increase its purchase price. Similarly, companies will
often pay more in a competitive bidding situation to ensure a strategic asset
does not fall into the hands of a competitor. Buying a company may also
be a way of reserving a future opportunity that may or may not occur—an
approach that can be valued as a "real option."[14]

Accordingly, a thoughtful comparable transactions analysis will provide at least some insight into what premium past acquirers have been
willing to pay to gain control of a target.

Earlier you said that comparable companies analysis typically considers only publicly traded businesses. Is that true for comparable companies, as well?

Not necessarily. Recall that transparency was the key reason why comparable companies analysis typically uses public comps; the stock market

ascribes a specific value on a stock at any given time, discounting a tremendous amount of economic and industry data into a single-point price. Also, the Securities and Exchange Commission (SEC) requires publicly traded companies to publish a minimum level of financial detail to public investors, making the data collection process a little easier for an M&A analyst.

M&A transactions involving two privately held businesses can be just as relevant to a given situation as deals involving two publicly traded companies. As before, though, the level of price transparency can pose challenges—it can be difficult to obtain sufficient financial data for private deals. In contrast, where at least one of the parties to a deal is public, there is likely to be a press release or quarterly filings on Form 8-K with at least high-level financial data. Often, the only data available in smaller acquisitions by public companies are the purchase price and target's revenue. However, even this can offer at least some perspective on valuation—despite the shortcomings of price-to-sales multiples, described earlier in this chapter.

As a practical matter, then, the data underlying M&A transactions involving at least one public company will be easier to obtain. Consequently, it would not be unusual for a precedent transactions analysis to be skewed toward those involving either a publicly traded buyer or seller.

What are the advantages of incorporating comparable transactions into the M&A valuation process?

Similar to its valuation cousin, comparable companies, the precedent transactions analysis is helpful because it is based on publicly available data and reflects real-world situations. Just as a comparable companies analysis is meaningful because it shows how the financial markets value publicly traded stocks, so too is the comparable transactions analysis helpful because it illustrates past transactions that successfully closed at certain valuation levels.

A thorough comparable transactions analysis yields a secondary, but equally important, benefit to the M&A practitioner: by researching who paid what for which companies or assets, the M&A analyst is building valuable market research into which industry players are the highly acquisitive consolidators versus those companies focused primarily on organic growth and into the underlying market demand for different types of acquisition targets. For instance, the frequency of transactions, trend of multiples paid, structure of transactions, and so on can help suggest whether M&A demand is building or waning in a particular sector.

What should I be wary of when building a precedent transactions analysis?

Unfortunately, there are some limitations to using comparable transactions to estimate the value of a target. Here again, precedent transactions share several of these disadvantages with their comparable company bretheren. Arguably, the biggest question to ask is whether the public data on past transactions is "clean" or whether it might be limited and/or misleading. Consider the following questions in any transaction comps that you might consider including in your M&A universe:

- What was the state of the financial markets at the time of the deal? Was the stock market particularly strong or weak? Could that have had an impact on the price paid?
- Where were we in the business cycle when the transaction closed? Were the target's earnings peakish, normal, or at trough levels? Did the target recently report any one-time gains or losses that might have skewed reported earnings? How might these factors have been accounted for in the takeout price?
- What was the sale process? Did the acquirer source the transaction through its proprietary deal flow, or was it a competitive auction run by an investment bank?
- How competitive was the M&A market for businesses like this at the time of the deal? Was there some scarcity value attributable to the asset? At the other end of the spectrum, was this a distressed sale or some other form of motivated seller?
- How strategic was the target to the acquirer? What cost savings and/or revenue synergies were discounted into the deal? Are these assumptions representative of most deals in the industry, or was this deal special?

- Were there unique structuring details to this transaction that we should consider? Was there future, contingent consideration that we should add back? Was there a unique tax angle, such as net operating loss carryforwards that represented hidden value?
- How much time has lapsed since the deal? Understandably, recent M&A transactions may more accurately reflect the values that buyers are currently willing to pay than would acquisitions that happened in the distant past. In addition to the fact that business cycles are always changing, industry fundamentals are similarly in constant evolution.

The key takeaway is that precedent transactions are rarely comparable. Nearly every deal represents a unique set of circumstances. It is the role of the M&A analyst, then, to tear into the details behind each deal and understand at least the high-level strategy behind each deal. This will help explain *why* the deal happened and, consequently, how representative the transaction might be as a clean "deal comp."

Which transactions are comparable?

We faced a similar challenge earlier in this chapter when we thought through which companies are comparable enough to be grouped together as a peer group. *In re Sunbelt Beverage Corp. Shareholder Litigation,* a decision by Chancellor William B. Chandler in the form of a letter to counsel, offers a cautionary tale in company valuation using comparable transactions.[15] In this case, the plaintiff contended that members of the Sunbelt board of directors violated their fiduciary duties in cashing them out at an unfair price ($45.83 per share), based on a flawed comparison of other transactions. Like the *ONTI* case mentioned earlier with respect to comparing companies, it is clear that a target's size and industry may not represent narrow enough criteria when selecting which transactions are truly comparable. As one commenter noted, it is not enough to simply apply the median implied multiple from a set of transactions involving companies in the same general industry: "A comparable transaction analysis is much more likely to be a meaningful indicator of value, and to therefore withstand serious scrutiny, if the unique attributes of each transaction are fully understood and accounted for in applying the data to the subject company."[16]

As above, comparable transactions should share a number of characteristics: similar industries, fundamental characteristics (margins, credit quality, etc.), and size. In addition to these factors, which are shared by the comparable companies analysis, deal comps should also consider transaction-specific characteristics, such as those described in the preceding question. The M&A analyst should understand the background to the deal and why it occurred. In addition to the questions listed above, the analyst should know whether the buyer was strategic or financial (with financial buyers more likely to pay a "pure" multiple), domestic or international, and whether the acquirer sourced the transaction through a full-blown auction process (which tends to drive up prices) or through proprietary channels (likely resulting in a more negotiated, middle-of-the-road multiple).

Figure 2-10 contains a checklist of variables to consider in gauging the comparability of two M&A transactions.

You mentioned cost savings and revenue synergies a couple of times. How exactly do they impact transaction multiples?

We will discuss cost savings and revenue synergies in greater detail in Chapter 6, "Building a Transaction Model." Cost savings are typically the

Figure 2-10 Comparable Transactions Checklist

Look for similarity in:

- Industry group
- Size (revenues, assets, market cap)
- Timing
- Business mix (products, markets served, distribution channels, etc.)
- Geographic location
- Profitability
- Rate of growth
- Credit quality
- Capital structure (debt/equity and related ratios)
- Business model

biggest value driver in most M&A transactions, although the magnitude can vary dramatically from situation to situation.[17] The point of raising cost savings in this chapter is to emphasize that you should comb through press releases, investor presentations, and other sources to understand what might have been discounted into the M&A transaction. This will help you to normalize the implied transaction multiple.

In the event that the parties have not quantified the expected cost savings in the public disclosure, but you are reasonably confident that they were a key driver of the deal's pricing, there are a few rules of thumb that you can try to see if they normalize the multiples. For instance, we have found that many investment bankers in industrial deals will assume cost savings of approximately 3% of revenue. In other cases in which there are material back-office and production savings, we have also seen advisors assume that 20% to 25% of costs are eliminated. Like everything else in M&A, however, we caution that these rules of thumb should not be viewed in a vacuum—they should be considered in the context of the facts and circumstances of the specific situation.

What about revenue synergies? How do they factor into deal pricing?

We often read about potential revenue synergies in M&A announcements. In the classic case, the acquirer anticipates a healthy amount of cross-selling between the buyer's and seller's customer lists. In other circumstances, the purchaser might have strong distribution but limited product, whereas the seller has strong product and weak distribution. It seems fairly intuitive.

We are often skeptical of these assumptions. To be sure, such situations can and do arise. However, they often look better on paper than they do in practice. For instance, we recall a specific case in which a manufacturer of aluminum wheels for heavy-duty trucks bought out a manufacturer of brake kits for the same kind of truck. Both suppliers made components for the same *type* of truck, but for different original equipment manufacturer (OEM) customers. In theory, combining the two businesses seemed like a home run: cross-sell into each other's customers, and, potentially, even eliminate some redundant sales resources. The problem, however, was that the purchasing managers for wheels and brake kits at the OEM customers were two completely different people! So the fact that the wheel manufacturer sold into "Joe at Peterbilt" really had no benefit to the brake kit manufacturer, since he really needed to talk to "Mike at Peterbilt." This company ultimately filed bankruptcy, and while the transaction itself did not cause insolvency, the debt load from the acquisition certainly didn't help matters—the point being, we caution against overly optimistic revenue expectations.

Indeed, while revenue synergies often populate M&A press releases, rarely do you read about potential revenue *attrition*. That is, how much revenue do the combined companies expect to *lose* to competitors as a result of this deal? Although not discussed frequently, revenue attrition is seen at least as often as revenue synergies.

One memorable example is the merger between Roadway Corporation and Yellow Corporation in the early 2000s. Both companies operated in the highly consolidated less-than-truckload (LTL) market, in which there were only about a half-dozen providers with national capabilities at the time. Most freight customers (known as "shippers" in the transportation industry) maintain supplier contracts with two different LTL truckers—partly to keep a competitive balance for pricing, and partly in the event labor at one of the trucking firms goes on strike. So, what if your two LTL truckers happened to be Yellow *and* Roadway? Well, chances are you would fire one of them and redirect a substantial amount of your business to another provider. In that particular deal, we recall modeling a very substantial amount of revenue attrition—20%, if memory serves correct.

To be sure, the Yellow–Roadway deal is an extreme example. The specific amount of potential revenue attrition really depends on the industry, amount of overlap, etc. But it probably doesn't hurt to model a "worst case" 10% loss of revenue, the majority of which would likely take place in year one. At the very least, modeling a 5% hit is prudent in your transaction stress test.[18]

Which party generally pays more for an acquisition: strategic buyers or financial sponsors?

At the risk of making broad generalizations, the conventional wisdom is that strategic buyers can generally pony up more for a target because they perceive greater synergies and/or cost savings. In addition, financial sponsors are generally more price sensitive because they will typically target a five-year annualized return of 20% to 25% before making an investment. Strategic buyers may also face hurdle rate requirements from their boards of directors—perhaps 15%, 20%, or more. However, a strategic buyer, all else equal, has more leeway to deviate from these return criteria for a target that's, well, "strategic."

Of course, there are exceptions. If a financial sponsor is consolidating a particular segment, it might have all the same cost savings opportunities as a strategic buyer. Also, the sponsor might consider a particular target as a "platform deal" of a certain size that creates follow-on acquisition opportunities. Some financial sponsors will use these points to rationalize paying up for a deal—and, in some cases, rightly so.

One other comment: it's no surprise to financial sponsors that strategic buyers can afford to pay more. This has some influence on the behavioral aspects of the M&A cycle. For instance, financial sponsors are more likely to buy into segments that are out of favor—where EBITDA, deal multiples, and competition for acquisitions are all depressed. Also, financial sponsors will often pay all cash, whereas a strategic buyer might need to incorporate a large amount of stock as transaction consideration. This can be a deal advantage to the financial buyer when the sellers are highly focused on liquidity. Lastly, some financial sponsors will understandably point out to a seller that a strategic buyer can pay more because it's likely to take out costs (i.e., fire people). The prospect—whether fairly or unfairly cast—of an industry competitor potentially dismantling an entrepreneur's life work can motivate some prospective sellers to select a financial buyer, even at a lower price.

So what's the process for constructing a comparable transactions analysis?

As noted above, the process is similar to that used in a comparable companies analysis. We can summarize this process in five steps:

1. Research the universe of M&A deals involving companies in similar industries and of approximate size as the potential target.
2. Refine this universe to a list of ideally five to ten acquisitions.

3. Calculate the implied valuation multiples, based on the most commonly used metrics in the target's particular industry. As was the case with comparable companies, this list will typically involve EV/EBITDA, P/E, price to cash flow, and potentially price to sales.
4. Strip out the transaction-specific factors that might skew the multiples in other deals.
5. Apply the resulting multiples to the target to broadly estimate its change-of-control value.

Where should I look for transaction details?

If you have access to a database such as Bloomberg, Zephyr, Merger-market, FactSet, Capital IQ, or Reuters, this step is easy. If you do not have access to these types of resources, you will have to find annual reports, conduct Google searches, or track down sell-side analyst reports to gather your data.

What does a precedent transaction analysis look like?

Much of the process is similar to the comparable companies analysis outlined earlier in this chapter. As a result, we will not go into the same level of detail for precedent transactions. However, we live by the old saw that a "picture is worth a thousand words." Figure 2-11 summarizes eight hypothetical deals in the transportation/logistics industry and what the output might look like. The most common datapoints to include are the following:

- Names of the buyer and seller in each deal;
- For public sellers, pricing, including offering price per share and percentage premium over recent closing prices;
- The equity value and enterprise value at the offering price;
- The implied EV/EBITDA and P/E multiples (which, in this case, we calculated as last 12 months (LTM), current year, and next year);
- The mix of transaction consideration (not shown here, but occasionally included in notes); and

Figure 2-11 Summary of Precedent Transactions[1]

Acquirer	Target	Pricing Data for Public Sellers		Enterprise Value	Enterprise Value Multiples			Equity Multiples		Contingent Consideration
		Per-Share	One-Day Premium		Sales	EBITDA	EBIT	Earnings	Book Value	
Delta Logistics	Mom & Pop Trucking	N/A	N/A	$230	1.5x	4.3x	5.6x	8.3x	1.0x	$20 million in Year 4
Eagle Freight	U Store It Ltd.	$34.00	18%	$1,267	1.2x	8.0x	10.4x	15.4x	1.2x	N/A
Expedited Process	Fox Enterprises	N/A	N/A	$356	1.6x	3.5x	4.6x	6.7x	0.9x	$15 million over three years
XTP Delivery	Keytouch Logistics	N/A	N/A	$337	1.4x	4.0x	5.2x	7.7x	1.1x	None
Delta Logistics	Global Freight	$45.50	21%	$773	1.7x	5.0x	6.5x	9.6x	1.1x	N/A
Eagle Freight	Big Sky Leasing	$77.25	35%	$2,227	1.2x	8.5x	11.1x	16.4x	1.3x	N/A
United Express	Ivy Track	N/A	N/A	$135	1.7x	4.5x	5.9x	8.7x	1.0x	$25 million in Year 5
Delta Logistics	Forever Freight	$36.70	26%	$665	1.3x	6.0x	7.8x	11.5x	1.2x	N/A
	Mean		25%	$749	1.5x	5.5x	7.1x	10.5x	1.1x	
	Median		24%	$511	1.5x	4.8x	6.2x	9.1x	1.1x	

[1] $ in millions, except per-share data

Source: FactSet

- For an accurate view of pricing, whether there was an earnout or some other contingent consideration. (As an aside, transactions involving public sellers do not have contingent consideration. It would be too difficult mechanically to allocate subsequent payments to formerly public shareholders long after the deal has closed.)

Why do takeout multiples in one market segment or geographic region sometimes appear conservative compared with precedent transactions in other geographic regions?

The concept that M&A transaction multiples can vary widely across different market segments and geographic regions is sometimes a bit surprising, given how global the financial markets and economic forces are. Nonetheless, these variations can, and do, happen. A prime example is the relatively substantial gap between bank acquisition multiples in Canada versus the United States in the 1990s and 2000s.

When these wide ranges in valuation multiples materialize, it is helpful to consider whether there are structural differences in the various regions or market segments. For instance:

- Does one market face a more difficult regulatory environment? The more likely it is that industry regulators might challenge a deal, the more likely it is that the deal will crater, which can narrow the list of potential buyers. To compensate, many acquirers will ultimately reduce takeout multiples.
- Does one market represent a mature oligopoly, while the other is in the early stages of consolidation? In a mature market, there will likely be more targets than acquirers, thus reducing price competition. In contrast, a market in the early stages of consolidation may offer many possible suitors for quality targets, thus providing the targets more leverage. This competition pushes takeout multiples up and, as a consequence, risks nudging postdeal value creation down.

- Are targets in one geographic market more profitable and/or better capitalized than in the competing market? This may have two impacts on M&A valuations: (1) the stronger industry dynamics of the "better" region might attract more buyers and, therefore, increase competition for deals; and (2) the publicly traded acquirers in that "better" region might have higher stock prices and, therefore, a lower cost of capital. This can allow them to "stretch" more for acquisition prices.

What if there are too few (or no) transactions that are comparable or the only comparables are dated?

This is a real-world problem. A key difficulty with the comparable transactions approach is the limited availability of financial data regarding past deals involving one or more private companies. That said, it is always possible to do an analysis of transactions that are not exactly comparable and to give a discount or premium to adjust their values. Ultimately, however, the precedent transaction approach is generally used in conjunction with other valuation techniques, including DCF and comparable companies analysis. As a result, leaving comparable transactions out of a valuation report is certainly permissible.

Can comparable transactions be used in valuing distressed companies?

The comparable transactions approach (similar to the comparable companies approach discussed earlier) is not ideal for distressed transactions unless it is comparing two distressed entities.

Where can I obtain a sample comparable companies analysis?

Visit www.ARTofMA.com to download some of the models presented in this book.

CONCLUSION

Comparing companies, and comparing transactions, can be challenging—particularly as no two companies, and no two transactions, are exactly alike. Therefore, valuations should include other approaches to be complete. Another commonly accepted approach is the DCF method. The next chapter offers a primer of this all-important subject.

APPENDIX 2A

A List of Required Line Items for Balance Sheets and Income Statements of Companies Covered Under Federal Securities Laws

Source: Electronic Code of Federal Regulations (e-CFR)[19]

The following two appendices, Appendices 2A–1 and 2A–2, list required line items for public company financial statements. We are listing them here because financial analysis generally requires an understanding of each of these items, as well as their relationship to one another, both within a company and compared with other companies.

TITLE 17—Commodity and Securities Exchanges

Chapter II—Securities and Exchange Commission

Part 201—Form and Content of and Requirements for Financial Statements...[20]

APPENDIX 2A-1

Elements of the Balance Sheet

§210.5-02 BALANCE SHEETS.[21]

The purpose of this rule is to indicate the various line items and certain additional disclosures which, if applicable, and except as otherwise permitted by the Commission, should appear on the face of the balance sheets or related notes filed for the persons to whom this article pertains (see §210.4-01(a)).

ASSETS AND OTHER DEBITS

Current Assets, When Appropriate

1. *Cash and cash items.*
2. *Marketable securities.*
3. *Accounts and notes receivable.*
4. *Allowances for doubtful accounts and notes receivable.* The amount is to be set forth separately in the balance sheet or in a note thereto.
5. *Unearned income.*
6. *Inventories.*
7. *Prepaid expenses.*
8. *Other current assets.*
9. *Total current assets, when appropriate.*
10. *Securities of related parties.*
11. *Indebtedness of related parties—not current.*
12. *Other investments.*
13. *Property, plant and equipment.*
14. *Accumulated depreciation, depletion, and amortization of property, plant and equipment.*

15. *Intangible assets.* Shall be explained in a note.

16. *Accumulated depreciation and amortization of intangible assets.*

17. *Other assets.*

18. *Total assets.*

LIABILITIES AND STOCKHOLDERS' EQUITY
Current Liabilities, When Appropriate

19. *Accounts and notes payable.*

20. *Other current liabilities.*

21. *Total current liabilities, when appropriate.*

Long-Term Debt

22. *Bonds, mortgages and other long-term debt, including capitalized leases.*

23. *Indebtedness to related parties—noncurrent.* Include under this caption indebtedness to related parties as required under §210.4-08(k).

24. *Other liabilities.*

25. *Commitments and contingent liabilities.*

26. *Deferred credits.*

Redeemable Preferred Stocks

27. *Preferred stocks subject to mandatory redemption requirements or whose redemption is outside the control of the issuer.*

Non-Redeemable Preferred Stocks

28. *Preferred stocks which are not redeemable or are redeemable solely at the option of the issuer.*

Common Stocks

29. *Common stocks.*

Other Stockholders' Equity

30. *Other stockholders' equity.*

Noncontrolling Interests

31. *Noncontrolling interests in consolidated subsidiaries.*
32. *Total liabilities and equity.*

APPENDIX 2A-2

Elements of the Income Statement

§210.5-03 INCOME STATEMENTS.

1. *Net sales and gross revenues.*

2. *Costs and expenses applicable to sales and revenues.*

3. *Other operating costs and expenses.*

4. *Selling, general and administrative expenses.*

5. *Provision for doubtful accounts and notes.*

6. *Other general expenses.*

7. *Non-operating income.*

8. *Interest and amortization of debt discount and expense.*

9. *Non-operating expenses.*

10. *Income or loss before income tax expense and appropriate items below.*

11. *Income tax expense.*

12. *Equity in earnings of unconsolidated subsidiaries and 50 percent or less owned persons.*

13. *Income or loss from continuing operations.*

14. *Discontinued operations.*

15. *Income or loss before extraordinary items and cumulative effects of changes in accounting principles.*

16. *Extraordinary items, less applicable tax.*

17. *Cumulative effects of changes in accounting principles.*

18. *Net income or loss.*

19. *Net income attributable to the noncontrolling interest.*

20. *Net income attributable to the controlling interest.*

21. *Earnings per share data.*

[45 FR 63671, Sept. 25, 1980, as amended at 45 FR 76977, Nov. 21, 1980; 50 FR 25215, June 18, 1985; 74 FR 18615, Apr. 23, 2009]

CHAPTER 3

Introducing Classic DCF Analysis

Life must be understood backwards. But…it must be lived forwards.

—*SØren Kierkegaard,* Journals, *1843*

INTRODUCTION

The value of any company, while foretold by the past, exists in the future: it must be "lived forwards." But how? The short answer is DCF. Business value is ultimately expressed in monetary form (i.e., cash now or later), so cash and value are inseparable.

According to the DCF method of company valuation, an analyst can make a reasonable prediction of how much unencumbered cash the company will generate within some significant future period. This requires calculating the company's future net operating cash flow and discounting it to the present. This method will come up sooner or later when negotiating the price and the timing of acquisition payments.

This chapter provides the fundamental tools to conduct this classic analysis. First, we provide some necessary background information. Second, we explain how to forecast free cash flow. Third, we describe how to calculate a discount rate. Fourth, we outline how to estimate a firm's terminal value. Finally, we describe sensitivity analyses that the analyst might consider running. Many of these tools are available for download at our website, www.ARTofMA.com.

FUNDAMENTALS OF DCF ANALYSIS

Help! I just glanced at the models available on your website and already feel overwhelmed. Where do I even begin learning DCF?

On the surface, DCF analysis might appear to be rather complicated. This is especially true if one merely jumps into a template model and begins dropping in assumptions without customizing the analysis to a particular situation. If DCF is approached that way, it is easy to get mired in myopia, focusing on learning where to plug in the inputs rather than learning how to interpret the outputs or testing various assumptions.

A novice analyst who figures out where to put the inputs can be drawn into a false sense of confidence, measuring success by merely mastering the inputs and then focusing on some of the outputs that pop out, such as the internal rate of return (IRR). Many practioners call this "plug and chug"—an idiomatic expression in investment banking that suggests that an analyst merely pulled a standard DCF model template off the shelf, blindly entered the assumptions (i.e., "plug"), and quickly moved on to the next task (i.e., "chug"). For these reasons, we recommend that an analyst start with a clean Excel spreadsheet—and not a template—whenever time permits.

Moreover, the reality is that DCF analysis is relatively straightforward, involving a series of tables or schedules that are generated through a number of mathematical equations. The most complicated financial calculations consist of the math behind the discount rate, which requires fewer assumptions but is even more critical because the model's ultimate output—a company's valuation or IRR—is most sensitive to the discount rate used.

So there's no "standard" DCF model?

Conceptually, all DCF models share a common theme: they discount future cash flows to estimate their present value. In practice, there certainly are a number of commercial DCF models on the market—each with different levels of precision and flexibility—that can be bought off the shelf. At the same time, there is an infinite assortment of proprietary spreadsheets created in Microsoft Excel that have been developed by individuals and companies to accommodate their personal preferences or analytical requirements. This proliferation of models, coupled with the absence of a dominant industry model, creates a confusing array of analytical techniques and models that are used in pricing or analyzing acquisition targets.

In addition to the array of financial models, individual analysts might enter inputs and make adjustments that distort the final DCF outputs, either deliberately or accidentally. As discussed later in this chapter, even minor changes to the model can have major consequences to the valuation. Furthermore, due to the lack of definitive standards and terminology in some industries, one must be careful to explore the meaning of the various terms that are used in the DCF. Thus, it is extremely important to get definitional and mathematical clarity when analyzing DCF outputs.

What are the primary inputs into a DCF model?

To run a basic DCF model, a number of basic assumptions must be made to "drive" the calculations. These include the target's cash flows over a certain period of time, the target's projected capital structure, the appropriate discount rate, and the target's so-called terminal value. How, precisely, the analyst arrives at these assumptions depends on a large number of variables: the target's particular industry, the stage of the company's lifecycle, market conditions, the acquirer's requirements, capital structure, and so on.

The number of input variables and the level of detail will also vary, depending on a deal's complexity and the nature of the decision for which the DCF analysis is being conducted. Consequently, forgoing a "plug-and-chug" template model benefits the analyst not only because the analyst will understand the inner workings of the model better, but also because the model can better be customized to the specific target.

How do I build a DCF analysis?

A basic DCF analysis is comprised of four major steps, each of which in turn involves a number of assumptions and calculations. These are illustrated in Figure 3-1 and include the following:

- *First, forecast the target's free cash flow.* This involves identifying the components and drivers of free cash flow; building out the complete set of historical financial statements; determining the appropriate forecast horizon, as well as operating assumptions and scenarios; and layering in potential synergies and cost savings (if building a transaction model).

- *Second, estimate the cost of capital.* To do so, the analyst develops a target capital structure; estimates the cost of equity capital and cost of debt capital; and then calculates the weighted-average cost of capital.

- *Third, determine the target's terminal value.* One method involves taking the last year of projected financials and applying a multiple, whether EV/EBITDA, P/E, or a growing perpetuity. More on this later.

- *Fourth, calculate and interpret the results.* The analyst discounts each annual cash flow, as well as the terminal value, to the present. It's helpful, as we will discuss, to perform sensitivity analyses to better understand which variables have a disproportionate influence on valuation. Importantly, the analyst must consider and interpret the model's output, as well as the sensitivity analyses, in a broader context (i.e., does the valuation make sense?). Lastly, the analyst considers ways of enhancing value through tax, legal, or other structuring techniques.

What are the benefits of DCF analysis?

A key advantage of DCF analysis over the valuation techniques introduced in Chapter 2—comparable companies and comparable transactions—is that DCF evaluates companies on an absolute basis, whereas other methodologies consider valuation relative to the target's peers. That

Figure 3-1 Overview of the DCF Analysis Process

Forecast Free Cash Flow	Estimate the Cost of Capital	Estimate the Terminal Value	Calculate and Interpret the Results
• Identify the components of free cash flow • Build out historical financials • Determine forecast horizon, assumptions, and scenarios • If building a transaction model, consider potential synergies and cost savings • Prepare the forecast	• Develop a target capital structure • Estimate the cost of equity • Estimate the cost of debt • Calculate the weighted-average cost of capital	• Select an appropriate means of capitalizing the cash flow in the final year of the forecast period • Consider EV/EBITDA, P/E, free cash flow perpetual growth, etc.	• Discount the annual cash flows and terminal value to the present • Perform sensitivity analyses • Interpret results with decision context • Consider ways of enhancing value through tax or legal structures

is, the alternatives to DCF are relative valuation measures, which use multiples to compare stocks and/or transactions within a sector. The upshot to relative valuation metrics, such as EV/EBITDA, P/E, and price to sales, is that they are easy to calculate; the downside, however, is that they can fall short if an entire sector and/or market is overvalued or undervalued. A thoughtfully designed DCF model, in contrast, should stand on its own and steer you clear of opportunities that look inexpensive—but only against overvalued peers.

A second and equally valuable benefit of DCF analysis is that the approach is rooted in cash flow, rather than more subjective financial measures, such as EBITDA, earnings, and even sales. As discussed in Chapter 2, these noncash line items are all subject—to varying degrees—to accounting interpretation. For instance, a company's reported earnings may change dramatically based on what depreciation or amortization assumptions the business uses. Figure 2-3 in the preceeding chapter illustrates how a minor change to a company's amortization schedule changed its net income by 14%. EBITDA, likewise, can change based on how inventories are tracked, among other assumptions. Cash, in contrast, is independent of accounting assumptions. Either the cash is there or it is not.

Consider, for instance, a manufacturer of injection-molded plastics in an environment of rapidly rising oil and resin prices. The manufacturer's EBITDA may look markedly different depending on whether the company tracks inventories on the basis of last in, first out (LIFO) or first in, first out (FIFO). Even sales figures depend on when and how the company recognizes revenue. For instance, does the above manufacturer recognize a sale upon shipment to a distributor, or is the product shipped considered contingent stock, with title passing only upon a follow-on sale to a retailer? These seemingly minor differences in accounting assumptions can result in dramatic differences to the company's income statement and, therefore, valuation multiples.

Lastly, the DCF framework is flexible enough that it can be used to value a company as a standalone operation or in the context of a business combination. In the case of a standalone valuation, the analyst can forecast the cash flows for two separate businesses over a certain period of time, layer in the terminal values, and arrive at estimated values for each business as is. Then, the analyst can develop a proforma forecast for the cash

Figure 3-2 Advantages of DCF Analysis

- Absolute, rather than relative, valuation
- Rooted in cash flow, a more objective basis than earnings-based measures
- Highly flexible in application

flows of the *combined* businesses—that is, including cost savings, revenue synergies, tax savings, and other transaction benefits—layer in a terminal value, and calculate the expected value of the combined businesses. If the present value of the combined businesses exceeds the combined value of the constituent companies on a standalone basis, the deal creates value and should proceed to the next stage in the process. Figure 3-2 summarizes the advantages of DCF analysis.

What are the drawbacks of DCF analysis?

Just as DCF certainly has its merits, so too does it have its share of short-comings. Some readers will be familiar with the phrase "garbage in, gar-bage out." The output to a model is only as strong as the quality of its inputs. A DCF model really boils down to three broad assumptions: free cash flow forecasts, terminal value, and discount rate. Depending on the analyst's beliefs around how the company will operate and how the indus-try will advance, DCF valuations can fluctuate widely. If the model's inputs—cash flows, terminal value, and discount rate—miss the mark materially, so will the resulting analysis. Garbage in, garbage out.

Even when the assumptions are reasonable at the time, small changes can result in material changes to valuation. One such example is illustrated in the discussion accompanying Figure 3-18 later in this chapter, where a change of one percentage point in the future expected growth rate has approximately a 10% impact to valuation. Imagine! Granted, the example we use is an extreme one—but the point is that, like all other valuation analyses, no one approach is sacrosanct. The output from one analysis should be compared to those from other analyses to better understand the vulnerabilities of the conclusions.

Similarly, the DCF approach is enormously sensitive to the discount rate that is used. Because the discount rate can be influenced by many subjective factors, the valuation method is criticized at times as being ripe for manipulation. For instance, one of the first steps in calculating a discount rate is selecting a peer group of comparable publicly traded companies to establish "beta," a component of the weighted average cost of capital calculation defined later in this chapter. Which companies are, or are not, included in this peer group is entirely the decision of the individual conducting the analysis.

Another issue with DCF analysis is that the terminal value may be too large a portion of the total value (e.g., 90%). If the terminal value is too large in proportion to the overall value, then the DCF analysis may be meaningless because the interim cash flows that the DCF is supposed to be valuing have become insufficiently relevant. In particular, the higher the perpetuity growth rate discounted into the analysis, the higher the terminal value.

Consequently, it is good practice to constantly update one's assumptions in a DCF model. DCF analysis is a moving target that demands constant rethinking and modification. No model is set in stone; the analyst must adjust inputs and assumptions upon any meaningful development, such as a negative trend in earnings, the financial distress of a customer or vendor, or even a material change in interest rates. If expectations change, valuations change. This might not necessarily be the case, at least to the same degree, with valuation approaches that look at companies on a relative basis. Figure 3-3 summarizes the disadvantages of DCF analysis.

Which inputs into the DCF model can influence the output the most?

This is an important question, particularly given the discussion above about "garbage in, garbage out." The fact is, it depends—on the industry, on the company, what growth assumptions are reflected in the model, and

Figure 3-3 Disadvantages of DCF Analysis

- Sensitive to cash flow projections, which may be inherently difficult to predict
- Validity of the discount rate depends on assumptions for beta and the market risk premium
- Terminal value may be distorted by incorrect estimations

so on. However, of the three key inputs into a DCF model—cash flows, discount rate, and terminal value—a company's annual cash flows during the forecast period will typically have the least influence on the final valuation. The biggest driver is typically either the terminal value assumed or the discount rate used.

So when is the terminal value a bigger driver of the valuation than the discount rate? The longer the forecast period, the less impact the terminal value will generally have. Most DCF analysis will involve a forecast period of about five to seven years. When the forecast period is less than five years, the risk that the tail may wag the dog starts to increase.

How can I ensure that the assumptions I'm using in my DCF model are reasonable?

Many variables in a DCF analysis are interrelated, with many of the outcomes, such as IRR, highly sensitive or elastic in response to changes in a number of key variables. Several steps can be taken to address this caveat:

- *Input validation.* The analyst should spend considerable time researching the set of assumptions and their relevance to the particular target being analyzed.
- *Sensitivity analysis.* In addition to crunching a core set of numbers, the analyst should explore the stability of the outputs and metrics generated by a DCF in response to changes in assumptions, scenarios, or "states of nature." We touch on this more in the "Forecasting Free Cash Flow" discussion below.
- *Monte Carlo simulations.* While sensitivity analysis is helpful, in some cases the use of "best-case" and "worst-case" scenarios may provide misleading indications of risk. This is due to the fact that the scenario approach fails to recognize the interdependencies and probabilities that a worst-case or best-case scenario could be realized. That is, in many cases the joint probability of all things going bad, or all things going well, at the same time is infinitesimally small, and thus the use of worst-case or best-case scenarios provides false cues. The use of

Monte Carlo simulations through specialized applications or spreadsheet add-ins can improve the quality of decision support provided by static DCF analysis.

- *Attribution analysis.* A final form of analysis that can help qualify the outputs generated by DCF models is the application of attribution analysis. Briefly, this technique focuses on identifying the key input assumptions that have the most impact on the outputs and performance measures. Once the critical assumptions have been identified, they can be subjected to more scrutiny through additional research.

How far out should I forecast annual cash flows before ascribing a terminal value?

As noted above, the analyst should ideally forecast out at least five years—or else the terminal value comprises a disproportionate percentage of the enterprise value. Five to seven years is probably the most common horizon, although plenty of models look out 10 years. However, the ultimate test comes down to visibility; the analyst should forecast future cash flows as far out as there is a reasonable degree of confidence and until the business has matured and settled into slower growth.

This is not to say that the analyst must have 100% conviction in the forecast. After all, nobody has a crystal ball, and so each flow will be an estimate. However, there should be some reasonable basis to each year's view, with an explanation for how the analyst arrived at the particular forecast. Consequently, the acquirer's ability to make effective forward-looking projections is critical—or else the DCF will be particularly vulnerable to error.

Earlier you said that many analysts see the DCF method as the best way to value a going company. Why is DCF so popular?

An M&A analyst has a lot to gain from mastering DCF. The analysis can serve as a sanity check to the valuation that the analyst's multiples analysis produces.

Let's assume that, after a full multiples analysis, an acquirer is inclined to value an auto parts manufacturer at 7x next year's EBITDA of $100 million, for a $700 million enterprise value. Where did the 7x multiple come from? "Well," the acquirer may respond, "the peer group was trading at 6x EBITDA, and this particular manufacturer is growing 15% to 20% faster than those peers." Is this a reasonable valuation? What if the peer group was overvalued at the time of the multiples analysis? Or what if industry sales were below trend? Such factors might temporarily skew the peer group's valuation multiples to a figure that is either too high or too low.

Complementing this multiples analysis with a DCF model will help the acquirer think through how quickly the target must grow to achieve its $700 million valuation. DCF analysis requires the acquirer to think through such factors as where we are in the auto cycle, annual price-downs from OEM customers, obsolence risk, unionized labor costs, etc. The acquirer must also consider the discount rate, which depends on the risk-free interest rate, the acquirer's cost of capital, and so on. These considerations should enhance the likelihood that the acquirer is ascribing a realistic price tag to the target. In this way, the DCF framework can help acquirers identify where a company's value is coming from and whether the proposed purchase price is justified.

Can DCF be used to value company divisions and subsidiaries, and how important is it to do this?

It is possible to perform DCF analysis on individual business units, but it can very much be a do-it-yourself job. Unit-level cash flow statements are not required under current accounting rules, although this has arisen as a suggestion in discussions of FASB Accounting Standards Codification Topic 280, Segment Reporting. The current accounting rules require separate income statements for company units but do not require cash flow statements, which must be estimated based on other data.[1]

Eventually, accounting standard setters may require this if the demand continues to grow. In a 2014 study, Ernst & Young showed that divestment is alive and well as a company strategy—not only for diversified companies but for all businesses. "Leading companies employ consistent practices around portfolio reviews ensuring successful divestments aligned to the strategic priorities of the business," the study observed.[2]

The value of divestment or breakup is particularly high in the case of companies that have diversified too far beyond their strategic core. While diversification makes sense for a financial portfolio, it can be risky for an operating company. Some become not so much conglomerates as *agglomerates*—an assortment of disparate operations, each paying a fee for what often proves to be headquarters hindrance rather than headquarters help. The benefits of association—synergies such as the smoothing of cash flows effected by joining countercyclical operations—are often more than offset by the headquarters stultification of the entrepreneurial process so necessary for successful growth. The agglomerators are discovering that their disparate operations will generally do better as standalones if they cannot be integrated with similar operations.

FORECASTING FREE CASH FLOW

What exactly is free cash flow?

Free cash flow is the cash that a company throws off during a particular measurement period after all cash expenses have been paid. Free cash flow represents the actual amount of cash that a target has left from its operations that could be used for investing or financing activities. Examples of such activities include paying dividends and buying back stock.

In predicting future cash flows can I just use current cash flows and grow them from there?

M&A deals typically involve millions, if not billions, of dollars at risk. In our view, this is not the time for back-of-the-envelope work.

Ideally, the process of forecasting cash flows starts with the M&A analyst building a full set of three-part financial statements, including the income statement, balance sheet, and statement of cash flows. Although it is tempting to start with the target's most recent EBIT or EBITDA and run a quick top-down cash flow analysis, as described below, the analyst risks missing the true insight that can be gleaned from building a full model from the ground up.

In our experience, the only way an analyst can really understand how a company operates is by digging into the detail of forecasting revenues, margins, working capital, and so on—using perspectives from the target's historical results. Building a full model also forces the analyst to consider economic and industry cycles, as well as shifts in product mix and customer base. Understandably, there are times when only a high-level analysis is required, making a full set of financials seem like a waste of time. But those who choose this route should be aware that the results are unlikely to accurately represent the target's financial future.

How do you calculate free cash flow?

There are two ways of calculating free cash flow: the top-down approach and the bottom-up approach. Figures 3-4 through 3-7 supplement the definitions that follow.

The *top-down approach* (Figure 3-4) starts with the target's EBIT; it adds back depreciation and amortization, which are noncash expenses, to arrive at EBITDA. The analyst then adds or subtracts changes in working capital (depending on whether working capital was a source or use of cash during the period) and subtracts capital expenditures. This arrives at *free cash flows to the unlevered firm* (FCFF). FCFF are the cash flows, generated by the target, that are available to both debt and equity holders. From here, the analyst substracts financing expenses—both interest and preferred dividends—to calculate *free cash flows to the common equity* (FCFCE). This is the residual cash flows available to common shareholders after required financing expenses are paid to creditors and preferred shareholders.

Figure 3-5 illustrates a top-down calculation of free cash flow for an auto parts manufacturer.

In contrast, the *bottom-up approach* (Figure 3-6) starts with the target's reported net income (i.e., GAAP earnings) and adds back noncash expense and other flows. For instance, the bottom-up approach either adds or subtracts to net income (depending on the aggregate flows) such noncash expenses as depreciation, amortization, and deferred taxes, as well as changes in working capital. The resulting figure is the target's cash flows from operations. From here, the analyst adds back the tax-effected interest expense (i.e., interest expense less the tax shield) and subtracts

Figure 3-4 Defining Free Cash Flow—Top-Down Approach

Financial Statement Line Item	Comments
EBIT	
Add depreciation and amortization	*Includes all depreciation and amortization subtracted from EBITDA to arrive at EBIT.*
EBITDA	
Subtract (add) increases (decreases) in working capital	*Includes changes in accounts receivable, inventory, prepaid expenses, accounts payable, accrued liabilities, etc.*
	In some cases, it may be appropriate to include as working capital the minimum amount of cash necessary for operational purposes.
Subtract capital expenditures	*Going forward, should include one-time, non recurring cash flows to the extent they are planned.*
Equals free cash flows to the unlevered firm (FCFF)	***Cash flows available to both debt and equity holders.***
Subtract cash interest paid	*May differ from interest expense due to non cash interest charges.*
Add interest tax shield	*Calculated by multiplying marginal tax rate by interest expense.*
Add (subtract) increases (decreases) in debt, preferred stock, and minority interest	*Increases in non common equity sources of capital, net of principal repayments, result in greater cash for common equity holders.*
Subtract preferred dividends	*Any cash payments to non common equity claimholders result in less cash to common equity holders.*
Equals free cash flows to the common equity (FCFCE)	***Cash flows available only to common equity holders. Assumes that all cash flows to the common equity are distributed (i.e., not reinvested) to ensure that retained earnings are not double-counted.***

Figure 3-5 Calculating Free Cash Flow—Top-Down Approach ($000s)

Financial Statement Line Item	Amount
EBIT	**$12,880**
Add depreciation and amortization	2,576
EBITDA	**15,456**
Changes in working capital	(1,546)
Subtract capital expenditures	(2,190)
FCF to the unlevered firm	**11,721**
Cash interest paid	(586)
Add interest tax shield	234
Changes in debt, preferred stock, and minority interest	–
Preferred dividends	–
FCF to the common equity	**$11,369**

Figure 3-6 Defining Free Cash Flow—Bottom-Up Approach

Financial Statement Line Item	Comments
Net income	*Net income as reported.*
Add (subtract) non cash expenses (income)	*Includes depreciation and amortization, deferred taxes, and other non cash items but excludes noncash interest expense.*
Subtract (add) increases (decreases) in working capital	*Includes changes in accounts receivable, inventory, prepaid expenses, accounts payable, accrued liabilities, etc.* *In some cases, it may be appropriate to include as working capital the minimum amount of cash necessary for operational purposes.*
Equals adjusted cash flow from operations	
Add interest expense	*Includes non cash interest expense. As long as you assume that initial excess cash and all interim cash flows are distributed to shareholders (i.e., no cash other than minimum cash balances accumulates in the forecast period), it is appropriate to exclude interest income on excess cash balances from the free cash flow calculation.*
Subtract interest tax shield	*Calculated by multiplying marginal tax rate by interest expense. If the company has net operating losses NOLs or is not expected to be a taxpayer within the forecast horizon, there should be no interest tax shield.*
Subtract capital expenditures	*Going forward, should include one-time, non recurring cash flows to the extent they are planned.*
Equals free cash flows to the unlevered firm (FCFF)	***Cash flows available to both debt and equity holders.***
Subtract cash interest paid	*May differ form interest expense due to noncash interest charges.*
Add interest tax shield	*Calculated by multiplying marginal tax rate by interest expense.*
Add (subtract) increases (decreases) in debt, preferred stock, and minority interest	*Increases in non common equity sources of capital, net of principal repayments, result in greater cash for common equity holders.*
Subtract preferred dividends	*Any cash payments to non common equity claimholders results in less cash to common equity holders.*
Equals free cash flows to the common equity (FCFCE)	***Cash flows available only to common equity holders. Assumes that all cash flows to the common equity are distributed (i.e., not reinvested) to ensure that retained earnings are not double-counted.***

Figure 3-7 Calculating Free Cash Flow—Bottom-Up Approach ($000s)

Financial Statement Line Item	Amount
Net income	**$7,376**
Add (subtract) non cash expenses (income)	7,728
Changes in working capital	(1,546)
Adjusted cash flow from operations	**13,559**
Add interest expense	586
Subtract interest tax shield	(234)
Subtract capital expenditures	(2,190)
FCF to the unlevered firm	**11,721**
Subtract cash interest paid	(586)
Add interest tax shield	234
Changes in debt, preferred stock, and minority interest	–
Subtract preferred dividends	–
FCF to the common equity	**$11,369**

capital expenditures to arrive at FCFF. The bridge from FCFF to FCFCE is identical under both the top-down and bottom-up approaches, so we won't repeat ourselves here.

Figure 3-7 illustrates a bottom-up calculation of free cash flow for the same auto parts manufacturer discussed earlier.

Which approach for calculating cash flow is preferable: top-down or bottom-up?

Mathematically (and as illustrated in Figures 3-5 and 3-7), the two approaches should generate the same FCFF and FCFCE. (If they do not, your model is wrong!) Thus, it doesn't *really* matter which method the analyst selects; it's a matter of personal preference.

As a practical matter, however, we would suggest that the choice might partly depend on whichever valuation multiples the acquirer is most focused on, for example, EV/EBITDA or P/E (as described in Chapter 2). If the valuation discussion is generally focused on a multiple of EBITDA (i.e., 7x EBITDA for an auto parts manufacturer), most of the discussion will revolve around that financial metric. In this case, we generally prefer to use the top-down approach because it has EBIT or EBITDA neatly at the top of the column.

If, in contrast, the valuation multiples are focused largely on earnings or net income, then it probably makes more sense to use the bottom-up approach because it leads with net income. A good example might be a specialty lender, for which interest is a "real expense." Such companies are more likely to sell for a multiple of book value or a multiple of earnings, rather than a multiple of EBITDA, since interest is actually an operating expense in such cases.

OK, I understand the mechanics of how cash flows are calculated. How do I go about evaluating whether they are reasonable?

Projecting cash flow is the most difficult and usually the most subjective part of constructing a DCF model. It requires addressing a myriad of questions, including the following:

- Is the forecast substantially different from management's projections? If so, why?
- Has the company been able to meet its projections in the past?
- What are the industry's prospects?
- How secure is the company's competitive position?
- Is this business cyclical? If so, do the projections properly take this into account?
- What are the company's growth or expansion plans?
- What are the working capital and fixed asset requirements to achieve these plans?
- Is the business seasonal? If so, what are the seasonal working capital needs?
- What events (such as strikes, currency fluctuations, foreign competition, loss of suppliers, and so on) could affect the projected results?
- Does the company have any excess assets or divisions that can or should be sold?
- How long would it take to make these sales, and how much money would they generate?
- Are there any other potential sources of cash?
- What can go wrong in all this, and does the company have any contingency plans?

The above list is far from exhaustive, and it can take anywhere from a few hours to several weeks or months of due diligence to get a good feel for the cash flow. Once this has been done, the acquirer will be able to reasonably estimate the total financing needed at the closing date and prospectively for a five- to ten-year period thereafter.

How do you avoid undue optimism in cash flow projections?

At least two sets of projections should be made: the *base case* and a *reasonably worst case*. The base case tends to have some optimistic thinking in it, and the reasonably worst case is one in which management believes it has a 90% chance of meeting its targets. The buyer's decision to pursue a deal and the amount of money he or she targets to borrow is dependent on that 90% case. If the buyer relies on the reasonably worst-case projection, everything need not fall exactly into place for the target to meet its debt obligations.

CALCULATING THE DISCOUNT RATE

What is a discount rate?

Recall that the fundamental concept behind the DCF method is that the value of a business is the sum of all future cash flows of that business, discounted back to the present. Because a dollar in the future is worth less than a dollar today, future cash flows are discounted using a *discount rate*. The formula to calculate the value of future cash flows is summarzied in Figure 3-8.

Consider an example. If you were to offer me a guaranteed payment of $100 one year from today, what would be the value of that payment

Figure 3-8 Present Value Formula

$$PV = \frac{FV}{(1 + i)^n}$$

Where:

PV = Present value of the future payment
FV = Future amount of the money that must be discountec
i = Discount rate used
n = Number of periods (typically in years)

today (known as the *present value*)? If we were to assume a 10% discount rate, the present value of that payment would be $90.91. Mathematically, the equation would look like the following:

$$PV = \frac{\$100}{(1+10\%)^1} = \$90.91$$

In contrast, if we were to assume a 12% discount rate, the present value would be only $89.29. Note the inverse relationship between the two: a *higher* discount rate results in a *lower* present value, whereas a *lower* discount rate drives a *higher* present value.

$$PV = \frac{\$100}{(1+12\%)^1} = \$89.29$$

Sometimes it is more intuitive to think about a discount rate being the corollary to an interest rate. For example, let's assume I have a $100 debt that comes due one year from today. If I were to put $90.91 in the bank today at a fixed interest rate of 10%, the account would be worth $100 in the future. But let's say I shop around a bit and find a competing bank willing to offer me a 12% rate. How much must I deposit today to have $100 in a year? Only $89.29; the higher interest rate requires a lower present value.

The examples above calculate the present value of only one future payment. My DCF model has several years of future cash flows. How does that work?

This is typical of most DCF models—the analyst is calculating the *net present value*, or *NPV*, of a stream of future cash flows. In effect, the value of each period's cash flow is discounted to today.

Let's revisit the first example above. Let's assume a guaranteed payment of $100 every year for three years, starting one year from today. If we were to assume a 10% discount rate, the analysis would like the following:

$$NPV = PV_1 + PV_2 + PV_3 = 100/(1.10)^1 + 100/(1.10)^2 + 100/(1.10)^3 = \$90.91 + \$82.65 + \$75.13 = \$248.69$$

So, what is the correct discount rate to use in a DCF analysis?

There really is no "correct" rate to use. Selecting which discount rate to use is a subjective process. But if we were to rephrase the question as, what is the *appropriate* discount rate to use, there would probably be (at least) two ways to answer this question: the academic approach and the practical approach. As with most things academic, it is important that the student understand the theory behind the textbook answer. By understanding the theory, the student has a better appreciation for when to tweak the rules. For nothing in M&A is as much an art as valuation.

The textbook DCF analysis uses a firm's aftertax, nominal *weighted average cost of capital*—more commonly referred to as its *WACC*—to discount the aftertax, nominal unlevered free cash flows to the firm. WACC is the weighted average of the debt and equity costs of capital (including preferred stock), using market value weights for capital structure components.

How do I calculate a company's WACC?

The weighted average cost of capital is calculated as shown in Figure 3-9.

The cost of equity capital is the return a firm theoretically pays to its shareholders to compensate for the risk such shareholders undertake by investing their capital. Likewise, the cost of debt capital is the return a firm pays to its creditors for a loan. Both the cost of equity and cost of debt are typically expressed as a rate of return. So, the shareholders of a particular company might target a 20% annual return before investing in a company,

Figure 3-9 WACC Formula

$$WACC = K_E(E/V) + K_D(1 - T)(D/V) + K_P(P/V)$$

Where,

K_E = Cost of common equity capital
E/V = Ratio of market value of common equity to total firm value
K_D = Cost of debt capital
T = Corporate marginal tax rate
D/V = Ratio of market value of debt to total firm value
K_P = Cost of preferred equity capital
P/V = Ratio of market value of preferred equity to total firm value

whereas lenders might only need an 8% return. The cost of equity capital, in this case, is 20%, while the cost of debt capital is 8%.

We can extend this example to calculate the company's WACC. Assume the company described above is 20% debt financed and 80% equity financed. For the sake of simplicity, we will assume the equity is common, that is, no preferred shares. As noted above, this particular company has a cost of common equity capital of 20% and a cost of debt capital of 8%. Its marginal tax rate is 40%. To reiterate the formula above:

$$WACC = K_E\,(E/V) + K_D\,(1 - T)\,(D/V) + K_P\,(P/V)$$

Where:

K_E = 20% (cost of common equity capital)

E/V = 80% (ratio of market value of common equity to total firm value)

K_D = 8% (cost of debt capital)

D/V = 20% (ratio of market value of debt to total firm value)

T = 40% (corporate marginal tax rate)

Accordingly, the company's WACC is 16.6%:

$$WACC = 20\%\,(80\%) + 8\%\,(1 - 40\%)\,(20\%) = 16.0\% + 0.6\% = 16.6\%$$

This makes sense if I'm doing a standalone valuation. But what if I'm combining two companies? Whose WACC should I use?

In valuing an M&A target, the analyst should use the WACC of the target company rather than the WACC of the acquirer.

How do I calculate a company's cost of debt capital?

Estimating a company's cost of debt capital is relatively straightforward when the company already has debt outstanding and the capital structure is static; the interest rate charged on the existing debt should be an accurate proxy, provided that the rate is arm's length and not below market (i.e., from an intercompany or shareholder-provided loan).

The current interest rate on the debt might not be an accurate proxy if circumstances have changed since the time the company secured the debt. Have macroeconomic conditions improved or worsened? What about the company's financials? Has its industry fallen out of favor? If the debt is publicly traded, these factors are likely discounted into the debt's effective yield. If, however, the debt is privately held, the stated interest rate may be misleading. Accordingly, it is important that the analyst consider changes in both macroeconomic and microeconomic factors.

What about changes in the target's capital structure? How does that impact its WACC?

WACC does not take into account a dynamic capital structure; therefore, the analyst should generally assume a constant capital structure (i.e., the target's existing leverage or the industry average). For a company with a rapidly changing capital structure (i.e., a leveraged buyout [LBO]), it may be appropriate to use a different WACC in each year of the forecast as financial leverage changes.

Consider, for instance, a private equity firm that's evaluating a target with a debt-to-capital (debt-to-cap) ratio of 20% and current borrowing costs of 8%. The target's borrowing costs would likely increase meaningfully from 8% currently if the private equity firm were to increase the target's debt-to-cap ratio to 80%. As the private equity firm repays the loan, the target's borrowing costs would presumably decline—which would drive the WACC lower. As an aside, this changing capital structure may impact not only the cost of debt capital, but also the cost of equity capital. That is, capital providers demand higher returns for riskier investments or they will place their capital elsewhere. As a company's risk increases (decreases), its cost of capital increases (decreases)—from both a debt and equity standpoint.

What about a company's cost of equity capital?

While a company's present cost of debt capital is relatively easy to estimate by its current interest rate, the company's cost of equity is more difficult to estimate because the cost of equity is unobservable. However, equity capital is still a cost despite the fact that it might not have a fixed and stated price that a company must pay. Equity investors will have an expected return on the capital they invest in the company; if the company cannot meet this expected return, the company's stock price will go down. This declining stock price may be obvious if the company's shares are publicly traded. In the case of a privately held company, this deteriorating equity value may not be apparent until management seeks to raise new equity capital.

There are multiple models—derived both in academia and practice—for estimating a company's cost of equity capital. The granddaddy of these is the *capital asset pricing model*, or *CAPM*, which estimates a company's cost of equity based on the risk-free rate plus a company-specific premium for equity risk. To be sure, CAPM is a deeply rooted methodology, although at times the analyst might choose to blend the CAPM results with one or more other methods; these include the Gordon Model (which is based on dividend returns and an eventual capital return from the sale of the investment) and/or the Bond Yield Plus Risk Premium (which incorporates a subjective risk premium added to the company's long-term debt interest rate).

How do I estimate a company's cost of common equity using CAPM?

The formula for the cost of common equity is defined in Figure 3-10.

The fundamental idea behind CAPM is that an investment must reward investors in two ways: time value of money and risk. The time value of money is represented in the formula by the risk-free rate (R_F); this compensates investors for allocating capital to any investment over a period of time. Risk is captured in the formula by estimating the premium that the investor requires for taking on a specific investment opportunity.

Figure 3-10 Cost of Common Equity Formula

$$K_E = R_F + \beta\, [R_M - R_F] + S$$

Where,

R_F = Risk-free rate
β = Beta of the security
R_M = Market risk premium

This premium is calculated by taking a risk measure (ß, or beta) that compares the returns of the asset to the market over a period of time and to the market premium ($R_M - R_F$).

Of the three variables—the risk-free rate, beta, and the market risk premium—beta is probably the least intuitive. As noted above, *beta* is a measure of the risk of a particular stock or other investment. It measures the stock's relative volatility, that is, how much a stock's price is expected to rise or fall as the stock market rises or falls:

- *Beta equal to 1.0.* A stock with a beta equal to 1.0 would be expected to track the overall stock market in lockstep—if the market rises (or falls) by 10%, the stock would be expected to rise (or fall) by 10%.

- *Beta higher than 1.0.* A beta of more than 1.0 implies that the stock would be more volatile than the overall market. For example, a stock with a beta of 1.5 would be 50% more volatile than the market. If the market rises (or falls) by 10%, the shares would be expected to rise (or fall) by 15%.

- *Beta lower than 1.0.* A beta lower than 1.0 (but greater than 0.0) implies that the stock would be less volatile than the market. Accordingly, a stock with a beta of 0.8 would be 20% less volatile than the market. Accordingly, if the market rises (or falls) by 10%, the shares would be expected to rise (or fall) by 8%. Companies with betas lower than 1.0 tend to be stable; a milk or bread producer might be one example. Demand for such consumer staples is unlikely to swing dramatically from year to year, even as external conditions change.

Beta values are calculated and published regularly (e.g., Bloomberg) for all stock exchange–listed companies. The problem here is that uncertainty arises in the value of the expected return because the value of beta is not constant, but rather changes over time. For relatively stable, mature companies, we suggest using a stock's five-year historical beta with monthly observations. For targets that are in dynamic, high-growth industries, or for recently restructured companies, consider using a shorter period—e.g., two years using weekly observations.

The biggest drawback to using beta as a risk measure is that it implicitly assumes that all of a company's risk can be distilled down to only one market factor. This is rarely the case. However, this drawback echos Sir Winston Churchill's views on democracy—that it's the worst form of government, but for all the alternatives. Nevertheless, those who feel strongly about beta's biggest drawback might consider developing a multifactor model to increase the formula's relevance to a particular situation.

From a practical standpoint, how do I calculate the three inputs for my CAPM model?

This is a key question, because seemingly minor changes in a CAPM model can drive substantial changes in a company's cost of equity capital. Accordingly, the assumptions that an analyst uses in a CAPM model are subject to our favorite adage: garbage in, garbage out. Choose wisely.

- *Risk-free rate.* The widely accepted basis for the risk-free rate is the current yield on the government bond whose duration most closely matches the time horizon in the DCF model. For instance, a 10-year DCF would typically use the current yield on 10-year U.S. Treasuries as its basis for the risk-free rate. As will likely become clearer below, this assumption is the least subjective of all those in the CAPM process and likely to be the source of the least debate when it comes to the valuation of a particular company.

- *Beta.* If the company that you are valuing is publicly traded, simply use the published beta for its stock. For companies that are privately held, or have short operational histories, restructured operations, or leverage that departs significantly from the industry average, it may be appropriate to use an industry average beta rather than an individual company beta—provided good comparable companies are available. In calculating the industry average beta, use the market cap weighted average unlevered beta for a group of comparable, publicly traded companies. Lastly, the proliferation of industry-specific exchange-traded funds (ETFs) adds a new option; consider using the ETF's beta if the fund's underlying components are representative of the valuation target.

- *Market risk premium.* As noted above, the market risk premium is an estimate of the excess returns an investor can expect to receive as compensation for bearing equity risk (i.e., investing in the market portfolio rather than a risk-free instrument). The market risk premium is calculated by taking an average of datapoints over time in order to incorporate a large sample of events and mitigate measurement error. The appropriate time frame over which to calcuate the market risk premium is a matter of debate. On the one hand, a long horizon helps smooth out short-term fluctuations, whereas on the other hand, a short horizon is arguably more relevant in current circumstances. This is an academic debate that could rage on for years. Our approach is a bit more pragmatic: the market risk premium should be based on the same duration as that used to calculate the risk-free rate. Lastly, for those analysts who are looking for a "quick and dirty" starting point for arriving at a reasonable market risk premium, we would recommend Duff & Phelps' helpful text, *Valuation Handbook—Guide to Cost of Capital*, which is updated annually. Since February 28, 2013, Duff & Phelps has suggested an equity market risk premium of 5.0%.[3] That seems about right.

What if the valuation target is substantially smaller than its public peers? Does this change the analysis in any way?

Yes, we add a *size premium* (also sometimes known as a *small company premium*) to the CAPM-derived discount rate. Accordingly, the CAPM formula is restated as $K_E = R_F + ß [R_M - R_F] + S$, where S is the size premium.

The theory behind the size premium is that smaller companies are often more capital constrained and/or do not have the scale and competitive advantages of larger competitors. Investors in smaller companies, the logic goes, will require a higher return on equity investments into such companies to compensate for these added risks. The higher the size premium, the higher the cost of equity, and consequently the lower the DCF value, all else equal.

Figure 3-11 Size Premiums by Quartile and Decile ($000s)

Quartile Group	Size Premium (Quartile)	Decile Group	Size Premium (Decile)	Size of Largest Company. in Decile
Large cap (1 and 2)	N/A	1	–0.38%	$314,623
		2	0.81%	15,080
Mid cap (3-5)	1.20%	3	1.01 %	6,794
		4	1.20%	3,711
		5	1.81%	2,509
Small cap (6-8)	1.98%	6	1.82 %	1,776
		7	1.88%	1,212
		8	2.65%	772
Micro cap (9-10)	4.07%	9	2.94 %	478

Source: Ibbotson SBBI Valuation Yearbook (2011).

To calculate historical size premiums, the analyst should construct portfolios of publicly traded stocks by size. The size premiums are computed as the average returns for each size portfolio less the average of the returns predicted by CAPM for the stocks in each portfolio. The results are then divided into quartiles, quintiles, deciles, etc. Figure 3-11 summarizes the results of this analysis as published by data vendor Ibbotson in 2011.[4] (Ibbotson further divided the tenth decile into four size categories: 10w, 10x, 10y, and 10z.)

As can be seen from Figure 3-11, companies with small market capitalizations command larger-size premiums, whereas companies with large market caps command modest-size premiums. One way of using this table is to apply no size premium to companies with market capitalizations above $6.8 billion. Discount rates for companies with market caps between $1.8 billion and $6.8 billion would include a 1.20% size premium. Similarly, discount rates for companies between roughly $478 million and $1.8 billion would include a 1.98% size premium. And discount rates for companies with market capitalizations below $478 million would include a 4.07% size premium.

Figure 3-12 illustrates these results graphically. Notice that the relationship is not entirely linear. Moreover, the substantial size premiums

Figure 3-12 Size Premiums by Decile

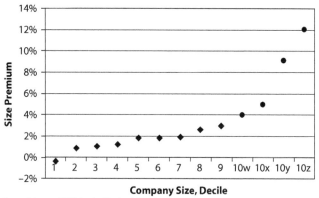

Source: Ibbotson SBBI Valuation Yearbook (2011).

observed for very small companies lead many to question whether the lower end of the sample set contains an unusual number of statistic outliers. One argument, for instance, is that the lowest end of the market contains the largest number of financially distressed firms. As described earlier, capital structure is a key component of how portable assumptions in CAPM are. Accordingly, we would generally be inclined to disregard the results for 10y and 10z.

We believe that it is important to understand the theory behind the process. However, many practitioners also value general rules of thumb. To this end, we have found over the years that the most common small company premium we've seen is roughly 25%; that is, the appraiser might increase a CAPM-driven discount rate of, say, 13.6% by 25% to 17.0%. This benchmark is not based on any scientific survey, mind you; just historical perspective. As such, use it with discretion.

What if the valuation target is privately held? How is this reflected in the valuation?

This touches on a subject that is closely related to a target's size premium—namely, whether an illiquidity premium is appropriate. An *illiquidity premium* is the additional return that an investor requires when a particular security cannot be easily converted into cash.

For example, assume an investor is evaluating the purchase of stock in one of two companies that are identical except for one factor: the shares of the first company are publicly traded, whereas the shares of the second company are privately held. The shares of the second company are said to be *illiquid* because there's no active market for the investor to subsequently sell the shares, should the investor later decide to exit. Accordingly, the investor will not be willing to pay as much for the shares of the second company.

From a practical standpoint, a company's size and liquidity are generally interrelated. The larger the company, the more liquid its equity; the smaller the company, the less liquid its equity. From a CAPM standpoint, the discount rate of an illiquid target increases to reflect its illiquidity premium.

My target is a lower-middle-market, privately held business. Should I apply both a size premium and an illiquidity premium?

Many commentators argue that an appraiser should add premiums to a small private company's discount rate to reflect both its size *and* lack of liquidity. From a practical standpoint, however, be careful that you are not double-counting the same factor and adding premiums that are too high.

For example, Figure 3-11 calculates historical size premiums for companies across a wide range of market capitalizations—from mega-cap to micro-cap. However, somewhere embedded in the size premiums is each stock's liquidity, that is, the size premiums shown reflect not only each company's size, but also how liquid the shares are. Micro-cap stocks are less liquid than mega-cap stocks; investors will understandably require a higher return on an equity investment in an illiquid stock to compensate for the added risk of not being able to pull the capital out when needed. However, this risk is generally reflected in the size premium calculated, unless the analyst has created a two-factor model.

Accordingly, adding an illiquidity premium *in addition to* the size premium calcuated in Figure 3-11 would likely involve some double-counting. This would potentially lead to a discount rate that is unreasonably high and an unusually low valuation under CAPM. Make sure your final outcome "feels" right.

ASCRIBING A TERMINAL VALUE

Why does DCF analysis use a terminal value?

A company is unlike you and I—while it is an entity that is "alive" in the eyes of the law, the simple truth is that a business is not a person; it goes through cycles, and ultimately it may mature, but it *theoretically* has an infinite life. Accordingly, a business valuation that is rooted in cash flows should reflect the present value of those cash flows forever.

This is an excellent example of why theory does not always carry over into reality: it is simply impractical to forecast a company's cash flows into infinity. Frankly, it is hard enough to predict next year's flows, let alone those 10, 20, or 30 years from now. However, if we do not include the value of long-term cash flows, we are, in effect, assuming that the company will stop operating at the end of the projection period. Typically, this is not the case.

Consequently, the DCF approach to valuation involves estimating cash flows over the forecast period and then estimating a *terminal value* to capture the value at the end of the period. This terminal value is intended to approximate the discounted, lump-sum value of the target's cash flows after the forecast period—that is, when the business has matured and settled into middle age.

How do I calculate a company's terminal value?

There are three primary ways of estimating a firm's terminal value: liquidation value, the exit multiple approach, and the constant growth model:

- *Liquidation value.* This calculation assumes the liquidation of the target's assets in the final year of the DCF analysis by estimating what the market would pay for the firm's assets at that point. The liquidation value approach is most useful when the target's assets are separable and marketable. However, by assuming a firm will cease operations and liquidate its assets at the end of the DCF analysis, this approach is limited as it does not reflect the earning power of the target's assets.

- *Exit multiple approach.* The exit multiple approach is the easiest to implement but involves traces of the comparable companies approach. This approach uses a multiplier of some income or cash flow measure, such as net income, EBITDA, or free cash flow, which is generally determined by looking at how the market values comparable companies. Recall that a key benefit of DCF analysis is that it focuses more on a company's absolute value and less on relative value. Accordingly, in order to keep the terminal value "pure," the basis of the terminal value multiple should have some basis beyond trading multiples. Also, if the multiple relates to enterprise value, don't forget to subtract the projected debt. Figure 3-13 illustrates the exit multiple approach to estimating terminal value.

- *Constant growth model.* Some commentators consider the constant growth model to be the soundest technically. However, it does require the analyst to make judgments about when the firm's growth rate will decline to a mature level and what its sustainable rate is. At a minimum, the constant growth model should be used to check the reasonableness of the exit multiple assumption for the terminal value.

Analytically, the terminal value calcuation for a company generally looks like the formula for a growing perpetuity: the expected cash flow

Figure 3-13 Exit Multiple Approach to Estimating Terminal Value

Assume that Target is expected to generate $15 million of EBITDA in Year 10. Target is expected to have $20 million of debt at that time. Multiplying $15 million of EBITDA by a projected EV/EBITDA multiple of 8.0x produces a terminal enterprise value of $120 million. Subtracting $20 million of debt results in $100 million of terminal equity value.

Terminal value:

EBITDA	$15 million
EV/EBITDA Multiple	8.0x
Enterprise Value	$120 million

Less:

Debt	$20 million
Equity Value	$100 million

Figure 3-14 Terminal Value Model Assuming Constant Growth

$$\text{Terminal value} = \frac{\text{Expected cash flow next period}}{(r - g)}$$

Where,

r = Discount rate
g = Expected growth rate

next period, divided by the firm's discount rate, less the expected growth rate of those cash flows. This formula is illustrated in Figure 3-14.

Intuitively, the analogy to a perpetuity makes sense. After all, the concept of terminal value is rooted in the view that the life of a company is infinite—much like a perpetuity that pays dividends forever. So what would an investor pay for a perpetuity that pays $100 per year, assuming that investor cost of capital is 10%? The answer, of course, would be $1,000, as illustrated in Figure 3-15.

What if the annual payment from the perpetuity were to start at $100 and grow 2% annually thereafter? Again assuming a 10% cost of capital, the value of the perpetuity would increase to $1,250, as demonstrated in Figure 3-16.

As described in the discussion that follows, a firm's terminal value follows the same logic.

How do I estimate a company's constant growth rate?

Many companies can maintain high growth rates for extended periods, but they will all approach stable growth at some point in time. The primary

Figure 3-15 Perpetuity Value Assuming No Growth in Cash Flows

$$\text{Perpetuity value} = \frac{\$100}{10\%} = \$1,000$$

Figure 3-16 Perpetuity Value Assuming 2% Growth

$$\text{Perpetuity value} = \frac{\$100}{10\% - 2\%} = \$1,250$$

questions, as noted above, are when the company will see its growth rate mature and what the longer-term assumed growth should be.

In terms of timing, the M&A analyst might want to choose among three different alternatives:

- That there is no high growth remaining, and that the company is already in constant growth mode.
- That there will be high growth for a period of time, at the end of which the growth rate will drop to the constant growth rate. This is known as a *two-stage model*.
- That there will be high growth for a period of time, at the end of which the growth will decline gradually to a constant growth rate. This is known as a *three-stage model*.

What factors determine a company's growth rate, and how should I factor these into the terminal value model?

There are almost as many drivers to a firm's growth rate as there are to valuation itself. However, there are a handful of factors that rise to the top in terms of importance:

- *Size of the firm.* As a company becomes larger, the harder it becomes for it to maintain the high growth rate it once enjoyed. This is the law of big numbers in action.
- *Current growth rate.* Despite the disclaimers plastered over nearly every stock market–related advertisement, the past *can* be a reasonable predictor for some things. In our experience, there is at least a loose correlation between a company's current growth rate and its future growth rate. Of course, it is up to the analyst to understand if this growth is due to some temporary factor. However, it is not an unreasonable starting point to assume that a company currently expanding at 30% can probably grow faster for longer than a business currently growing at 10%.

- *Barriers to entry and/or structural advantages.* It's difficult, if not impossible, to think about a company's longer-term growth rate without referencing factors such as Michael Porter's five competitive forces and/or barriers to entry. Consequently, the question of how long growth will last and how great it will be can be reframed as a test of the relevent barriers to entry, including how strong they are and how long they are likely to remain in place.

- *Lifecycle of the firm and its industry.* As described in greater detail below, every industry—and every market participant in that industry—has a lifecycle. Where an industry or company is in this cycle will partly depend upon the barriers to entry and/or structural advantages just discussed. However, there are other reasons why a particular company in an otherwise thriving industry might fade away; key examples include the company's reinvestment rate and management execution.

This final point—low reinvestment and/or poor execution in an otherwise growing market—is key, as it can happen more often, and on a grander scale, than one might think. For instance, it may surprise some younger readers that the most popular fast-food chain after McDonald's used to be a company called Burger Chef. Not only was Burger Chef a dominant player in the fast-food industry, it held the first patent to the flame broiler (now associated with Burger King) and pioneered the value combo, the "Works Bar" (now most commonly seen at Roy Rogers restaurants), and even the "Funmeal" (preceeding McDonalds' Happy Meal by many years). Eleven years after opening its first location, Burger Chef sold in 1968 to General Foods, which ultimately was unable to support the company's growth. The chain sold in 1982 to Canadian-based Imasco, the parent company of Hardee's. Most Burger Chef locations were rebranded shortly thereafter, with the once-iconic name disappearing completely by the mid-1990s.

Lastly, and on a more technical note, we would add that the constant growth rate cannot be higher than the growth rate of the economy in which the firm operates. For the avoidance of doubt, if you use nominal cash

Figure 3-17 DCF for a Business Already in Constant Growth Mode

$$\text{Enterprise value} = \frac{\text{Expected cash flow next period}}{(r - g)}$$

Where,

r = Discount rate
g = Expected growth rate

flows and discount rates, the growth rate should be nominal in the currency in which the valuation is denominated.

How do I conduct the DCF analysis if a company is already in its stable, constant growth mode?

The valuation process, in this case, is easier than in a full-blown DCF: the enterprise value of the business is simply the terminal value component of the broader DCF analysis. That is, it's the expected cash flow for the next period, divided by the discount rate, less the expected growth rate. This is illustrated in Figure 3-17.

Consider, for instance, a manufacturer in a slow-growth industry—perhaps No. 2 pencils—with forward-year cash flows of $10 million, a growth rate of 4% per annum, and a 12% discount rate. The enterprise value of the business, then, would be $125 million, calculated as illustrated in Figure 3-18.

As an aside, the example in Figure 3-18 illustrates why the assumed growth rate can have a tremendous impact on enterprise value. For instance, every one percentage point change in the growth rate of the above pencil manufacturer has approximately a 10% carryover impact to valuation. That is, if the manufacturer was expected to grow at a rate of 2%, rather than 4%, the firm's valuation would plummet to $100 million, a rather striking 20% haircut.

Figure 3-18 DCF for a No. 2 Pencil Manufacturer

$$\text{Enterprise value} = \frac{\$10 \text{ million}}{(12\% - 4\%)} = \$125 \text{ million}$$

Are there circumstances that do not warrant using a terminal value?

The biggest exception to the preceeding discussion is a so-called "run-off" business or "wasting" asset: one that does, in fact, have a finite life. Some industries simply go into secular decline, whether due to changes in technology, regulation, or social preferences. One solution to this challenge is to use a negative assumption in the constant growth rate model above. The resulting terminal value would be lower than it would be if the business were growing and would reflect the perception that the business will disappear over time. In circumstances in which the business is expected to disappear in less than, say, 10 years, it might be better not to assume any terminal value, but rather to forecast the annual cash flows through the expected time horizon and discount each back individually.

When do these situations arise? Envision the proverbial buggy-whip manufacturer in the automotive era or the typewriter repair service during the proliferation of personal computers. Changes such as these continue today: certainly, digital communications have already pressured once-substantial industries such as newspaper publishing, record stores, and video rental stores.

In fact, we remember advising on the divestiture of a publisher of custom newsletters in the late 1990s on behalf of a preeminent venture capital firm that had once had aspirations of rolling up the custom publishing industry. During the sale process, one prospective acquirer—which specialized in digital marketing services—ascribed an usually low purchase price, citing mounting industry pressures, such as email marketing, and really only valued the customer list. The ultimate buyer was a commercial printing business; at the time, we thought the buyer had gotten the company at the rock-bottom price of 5x EBITDA. Valuation notwithstanding, in hindsight it was a magnificent sale from the standpoint of the seller: digital marketing ended up decimating the newsletter publishing industry within one business cycle.

We like to think of such an example as the exception, not the rule. At the risk of turning existential, it is more likely than not that nearly every company, and almost every industry, that we encounter today will eventually fade away as others come into focus.[5] But keeping the focus on our true task—valuing businesses today—the real hurdle is considering whether changes in technology, the regulatory environment, or end-user preferences might have a material impact on the business or the industry over a reasonably foreseeable investment horizon. If anything, we tend to err on the side of conservatism, given the changes we have seen over our careers.

CONDUCTING SENSITIVITY ANALYSES

What is a sensitivity analysis?

As the term suggests, a sensitivity analysis is used to ascertain the impact of changes to a model's inputs on the predicted outcome. In other words, it is a way to predict the outcome—or range of outcomes—of a decision if a situation turns out to be different compared to a key prediction. Several methods of conducting sensitivity analyses are built into Microsoft Excel's "what-if" analysis tools.

Why should I conduct a sensitivity analysis?

Despite best intentions, forward-looking assumptions may not always hold true. In fact, there's an old saying among financial analysts: the question is not whether your forecast is wrong, it's *how* wrong it is and in *what direction*. Nobody has the proverbial crystal ball, so of course forecasting errors will occur. The use of sensitivity analysis, through a scenario manager, is a great way to incorporate several different performance possibilities into your financial model. This allows the analyst to "stress-test" the financial results; the reality is that expectations can, and usually will, change over time. Because the future cannot be predicted with certainty, it is never a good idea to take your financial model's results and claim, either to your boss or to your client, that these results are final. This is where the sensitivity, or "what-if," analysis comes into play.

What can a thoughtful sensitivity analysis of my DCF analysis tell me?

A thorough sensitivity analysis will allow you to do the following:

- Test the robustness of the results of the DCF model in the presence of uncertainty;

- Increase the understanding of the relationships between input and output variables in the model;
- Focus attention on those variables that have the most impact on the valuation;
- Search for errors in the model (by encountering unexpected relationships between inputs and outputs); and
- Simplify the model by fixing model inputs that have no effect on the output or by identifying and removing redundant parts of the model structure.

Which inputs to my DCF model should I subject to a sensitivity analysis?

While the answer ultimately depends on the facts and circumstances of a particular situation, we suggest a rigorous testing of the following inter-related assumptions: (1) discount rate, (2) long-term growth rate, and (3) terminal value. We illustrate this process in greater detail in Section III (available online at www.ARTofMA.com), which includes a full DCF model.

CONCLUSION

When it comes to the pros and cons of DCF, we resurrect the words of Winston Churchill as a fitting analogy to the dilemma: "Democracy is the worst form of government except all those other forms that have been tried from time to time." DCF is not perfect. But it is better than the alternatives because it focuses only on cash flow and disregards accounting-based forms of earnings. Because of this, we believe DCF is a superior valuation methodology. However, any party proffering a DCF-based valuation would be well advised to be able to defend all of the assumptions reflected in the model.

The next chapter of this book will show how to bridge expectations with contigent consideration.

ADVANCED TOPICS IN M&A VALUATION

CHAPTER 4

Bridging Expectations with Contingent Consideration and Related Tools

There is everything you know and there is everything that happens. When the two do not line up, you make a choice.

—*Mitch Albom,* For One More Day

INTRODUCTION

Valuation, at its core, is a subjective process. Setting a value on a company means making judgments about its future, which can never be known with perfect certainty. Financial forecasts inherently reflect the modeler's expectations about the economy, the industry, and the company with all its moving parts: What will become of the company's products and services and those who supply, make, and buy them? All of these predictions help move the buyer toward a final number.

In most cases, buyers and sellers have asymmetrical information: after all, the buyer is on the outside looking in, whereas the seller has intimate knowledge of the inner workings of the business—with all its risks, but more importantly, all its potential opportunities. It may not come as a surprise, then, that gaps in valuation most commonly arise when a potential buyer is overly pessimistic while a potential seller is unduly optimistic.

In other circumstances, there may be significant uncertainties associated with the business shared by both sides. These uncertainties may include the outcome of a significant lawsuit, regulatory approval of a major drug, the retention of certain businesses after the deal is announced, and so on. This situation is particularly likely to occur if there are outstanding material issues at the end of due diligence, there is significant uncertainty about the company's future prospects, there is pressure to get a deal closed quickly, and/or the parties have trouble agreeing on the purchase price.

Fortunately, techniques have evolved over time to bridge these clashing expectations and shared uncertainties. Buyers and sellers can use contingent consideration and related tools to bridge differing expectations and to hedge against unknowns. Contingent consideration can align the interests of the buyer and seller, harmonize valuation expectations, afford the buyer some flexibility in terms of how to finance the deal, and shift some postdeal risks and opportunities to the seller, incentivizing the seller to remain involved in the business after closing. This chapter will explain how this tried and true deal-closing tool can work.

SALVAGING THE DEAL THROUGH CONTINGENT CONSIDERATION

If a buyer and seller cannot agree on valuation, are there any ways to salvage the deal?

Yes. There's an old saying, "You can name the price if I can name the terms." Buyers and sellers in disagreement over value should not get too focused on price; if they do, they will miss out on the other key aspect of the deal: the structure. Just as in the realm of employee compensation incentives and perquisites can sweeten pay, so too in the realm of deal-making you have potential flexibility in terms of how much you pay, when, and under what conditions. The best example of this point is contingent consideration—which can be an effective means of compromising in negotiations to get a deal closed rather than having both sides walk away. Contingent consideration promises the seller a better final sale price if its projections are achieved, thus protecting the buyer from overpaying if the seller's projections are inaccurate.

How does contingent consideration work when buying a company?

Contingent consideration involves a future payment from the buyer to the seller based on the outcome of future events. The seller receives only a portion of the purchase price at close, with the agreement that the buyer will pay more if certain conditions (i.e., contingencies) are met. Contingent consideration can help address multiple obstacles holding up a potential transaction by doing the following:

- Closing the gap in expectations for the business between the buyer and the seller;
- Allowing the buyer to share the postdeal risk with the seller by making some of the consideration contingent upon future performance;
- Allowing the seller to participate in the upside posttransaction; and
- Incentivizing the seller to remain involved with and help drive the ongoing success of the business.

For example, a typical contingent consideration provision in an M&A agreement could provide that, if the target company's EBITDA for the measurement period is greater than an agreed-upon amount, the selling shareholders will be entitled to receive additional consideration for their stock. In some cases, the contingent consideration may be placed in an escrow account and then either released to the seller, if and to the extent the contingency is resolved in the seller's favor, or returned to the buyer.

The primary form of contingent consideration discussed in this chapter is the earnout. We also delve into seller takeback financing and compensation-related incentive plans, as both serve similar functions of bridging valuation expectations.

How common is the use of contingent consideration in M&A transactions?

Contingent consideration is a mainstay of the M&A world, although its use is admittedly cyclical. The American Bar Association (ABA) conducts a helpful biannual survey, the Private Target M&A Deal Points Study, which tracks various deal points over time. These points include not only the use of contingent consideration, such as earnouts, but also indemnification baskets and escrow.

Figure 4-1 Percentage of M&A Transactions with Earnouts, 2005–2013

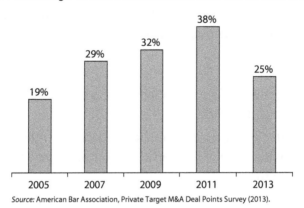

Source: American Bar Association, Private Target M&A Deal Points Survey (2013).

Let's look at earnouts. According to the ABA, earnouts were involved in 19% of transactions tracked in 2005. This percentage steadily increased as the economic environment deteriorated—rising to 29% in 2007 and peaking at 38% in 2011. More recently, that percentage declined to 25% in 2013.[1] This trend is illustrated in Figure 4-1.

In our view, two factors drive the cyclical nature of contingent consideration: (1) Valuation gaps between buyers and sellers widen as economic uncertainty increases, particularly as buyers become more risk averse. (2) Competition for deals heightens during stronger economic times. In a seller's market, buyers are urged to front-load consideration in order to win the deal. It's classic supply and demand at work!

How much of the transaction proceeds should be structured as contingent consideration?

This amount varies dramatically based on the facts and circumstances of a particular case. According to one study of 103 transactions involving contingent consideration, the percentage of potential deal value that was contingent ranged from 3% to 94%![2] The more useful datapoints from the study, however, were the mean and median of 41% and 39%, respectively.[3] Probably the most important factors influencing these figure are the earnings visibility of the target and how reasonably (or unreasonably) one side to the deal is behaving.

How can a seller in a contingency payment deal make sure the buyer will comply with the business plan?

The buyer might be asked to promise to fulfill a number of conditions, ranging from strategic to legal. For example, the seller could require the buyer to:

- Engage only in the kinds of business contemplated at the time of the sale; and/or
- Limit capital expenditures, lease payments, borrowings, and investments with affiliates and third parties to agreed-upon amounts.

The new owner could also be required to promise to refrain from:

- Merging or selling all or substantially all the business's assets, or any portion thereof in excess of a specified value, without the seller's consent;
- Acquiring other businesses; and/or
- Making changes in the acquisition agreement, subordinated debt instruments, or other material documents.

Is it possible to use contingent consideration in all deals?

Some sellers will be reluctant to accept contingent consideration purely because it is, well, contingent. Recall the old saying that a bird in hand is worth two in the bush. Moreover, such contingencies may, at times, be linked to outcomes that are outside the seller's control. Some sellers will accept a competing bid, even if it's for lower total consideration, if the second bid is paid all in cash, all at close.

In other cases, there may be practical or legal reasons why contingent consideration is not a good solution. One example is an acquisition of a publicly traded company. Imagine the logistical challenge of trying to track down all those public shareholders several months—or even years—after the deal closes!

Also, there are times to be exceedingly careful about using—and perhaps even avoiding—contingency payments, such as when there are accounting complexities or when a business is sold through a tax-free reorganization. The key issue here is continuity of interest, a necessary condition for tax-free treatment.[4] Subsequent contingent payments must be factored in to meet safe harbor rules to maintain the tax deferral. Further, contingent payments are generally incompatible in certain bankruptcy transactions, such as sales classified as § 363 sales under the U.S. Bankruptcy Code, which normally requires that qualified bids involve cash only. We elaborate on these issues at the end of this chapter.

Must the contingent consideration be put in escrow at close? Can it simply be paid by the buyer when due?

There is no set rule, and it really will come down to a negotiation. There may be tax implications, so a tax advisor should be consulted.[5]

In many cases, the seller will request that the contingent consideration be placed in an escrow agreement if there is any question as to the financial stability of the buyer. If the contingency is resolved in the seller's favor, the escrow is released to the seller. If the contingency is resolved in the buyer's favor, the consideration is returned. In other cases, the parties may agree that nothing is placed in escrow and that the buyer will compensate the seller when (and if) necessary.

Before accepting such an arrangement, a seller should consider several factors. Are there multiple buyers that may be difficult to chase down? Does the buyer face any potential solvency risk? (Funds placed in escrow may potentially be bankruptcy remote, whereas a future promise to pay may be considered an unsecured claim in bankruptcy.) Consider also the reputation of the buyer and how subjective the "test" is—the less trusting the seller is of the buyer, or the more subjective the contingency is, the more the seller should consider insisting upon an escrow.

EARNOUTS

What exactly is an earnout?

An *earnout* is a method of compensating a seller based on the future financial performance of a company; the buyer owes the seller additional

Figure 4-2 Key Considerations in Structuring an Earnout

• Form of consideration
• Measure of performance
• Measurement period
• Maximum limits
• Timing of payments

payments if the business's results exceed agreed-upon levels. Another type of earnout may provide that certain debt given to the seller as part of the acquisition price is "anticipated" and paid out early out of earnings exceeding agreed-upon levels. Earnouts are probably the most common way to structure contingent consideration; in fact, the terms "contingent consideration" and "earnout" are sometimes used interchangeably.

Earnouts require consideration of various factors: the form of consideration that the contingent payment will take (cash, stock, or in the case of takeback financing, notes), the measurement of performance (net income, operating income, cash flow, or some other factor), the measurement period, maximum limits (if any), and the timing of payments (Figure 4-2).

Why would the parties use an earnout?

The parties may disagree on the value of the business because they have different opinions about the projected profit stream. Often, the buyer is relying on the seller's projections of future cash flow in setting the price. Most sellers wish to maximize value and thus may present financial forecasts that appear particularly rosy—even in light of recent weakness. This scenario is so common that it has its own nickname in M&A: *hockey stick projections*. (In fact, a buyer quipped in one recent negotiation, "I never met a set of seller projections that I didn't like.") To visualize the analogy, picture an upright hockey stick; the company's earnings have been moving sideways in recent years, but suddenly are expected to rebound shortly after the buyer acquires the business. How convenient! Figure 4-3 illustrates this analogy.

The buyer and seller may disagree on the seller's ability to realize the projected results. The buyer should be willing to pay a higher price for

Figure 4-3 The Dreaded "Hockey Stick" Projections

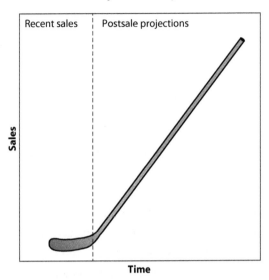

greater cash flow if the projected cash flow is realized by continuing the seller's prior business practices and, for example, waiting for a cycle to turn and for pricing and volume to recover. However, if the buyer expects to implement significant cost savings or synergies to improve the profitability of the business, then the buyer may feel that the seller does not deserve to share in the rewards of the buyer's efforts. Indeed, the buyer may even feel that he or she is fixing boneheaded mistakes that the seller has been making for years, so the seller should not reap any benefit from improvements made by the buyer.

An earnout permits the buyer to pay a reasonable price that takes into account the risks of the financial projections plus a premium if and when improved cash flow is eventually realized postclosing. It also allows the seller to realize the full value of the business if the path to ever-increasing profitability is as straightforward as was represented to the buyer.

Two industries in which we typically see the highest percentage of deals with earnouts are the life sciences and technology. Deals in both of these industries involve a disproportionate number of emerging-growth companies and those with new (and often unproven) technologies.

Earnouts can also be useful when buying a strategic business unit or product line from a large company. These divestitures are often called *corporate orphans* or *carve-outs*. For these transactions, because there are likely no separate audits, direct and indirect transfer costs can distort financial results, and estimates of postclosing overhead requirements may be unclear, it is extremely challenging to verify in due diligence the level of profitability that the business will generate under the buyer's ownership. Therefore, the best solution may be to sell the business with an earnout to discover whether it is profitable, and if so, how profitable. Indeed, the buyer may prefer that some insiders remain because they will know where all the bodies are buried, will be aware of untapped upside, and may have themselves artificially depressed earnings.

Which types of events are commonly used when structuring an earnout?

At a high level, contingent consideration is typically structured around one of four types of future events: (1) the *top-line performance* of the business (i.e., revenue targets); (2) the *bottom-line performance* of the business (i.e., income targets); (3) the business's balance sheet results; or (4) some nonfinancial target or milestone.

What is an example of a "top-line" earnout?

In a top-line earnout, the buyer and seller agree on sales targets for a future period, typically between two to five years. The seller will receive additional payments only if sales reach those targets. In such an arrangement, the seller often remains involved with the company with some sort of employment or consulting contract and is motivated to help the company generate the desired results.

What is an example of a "bottom-line" earnout?

A bottom-line earnout is similar to a top-line earnout, but it involves some measure for earnings. A common example would be a purchase price adjustment based on the operating income of the business for the next three years. In any event, the buyer and seller must agree on how to define and measure specific future outcomes—presumably in a manner that appropriately shares the relative risks and rewards.

What is an example of a balance sheet contingency?

Consider the sale of a business with substantial seasonality or other volatility in its working capital. One example would be a purchase price adjustment based on a company's closing date balance sheet and/or net working capital. For example, the seller might present the buyer with a projected closing date balance sheet at the time of the signing of a definitive purchase-and-sale agreement. At closing 60 days later, the seller would update this projected balance sheet with actual results as of the time of closing, and any difference would be netted against the purchase price.

What are some examples of nonfinancial milestones?

Nonfinancial milestones vary based on industry and company type. Examples include:

- Technical milestones, such as meeting a software development deadline;
- Premarket clinical trials for a biotechnology business;
- The issuance of a patent from the U.S. Patent and Trademark Office; and
- The favorable adjudication or settlement of an outstanding lawsuit.

Figure 4-4 illustrates an earnout based on both nonfinancial and financial milestones.

Which earnout structure is most common?

While the answer varies by industry, top-line earnouts are generally the most common. As illustrated in Figure 4-5, one study by the financial advisory firm Duff & Phelps found that 60% of the earnouts in its sample

Figure 4-4 Earnout Milestones

Argon Pharmaceuticals agrees to acquire a promising upstart, Inland Technologies, for $100 million and four milestone payments, as outlined below.

Milestone	Payment
First patient enrolls in a Phase III clinical trial	$25 million
FDA[1] approves the New Drug Application	$10 million
European regulatory authority approves a marketing authorization application	$5 million
Revenues for any 12-month period reach $100 million	$10 million

Note in this particular case, there are no deadlines ascribed to each milestone. Also, the milestone payments in aggregate represent $50 million, or a 50% premium to the $100 million upfront payment. This reflects the fact that Inland Technologies is still in the early stages of its lifecycle.

[1]FDA: U.S. Food and Drug Administration

were tied to top-line metrics, 37% to the bottom line, and the rest to a balance sheet item or nonfinancial milestone.

Why are top-line earnouts so common?

Top-line earnouts are often easier to define and administer with clarity. Sellers may perceive that it will be easier for them to impact, drive, and control postacquisition performance on top-line metrics rather than

Figure 4-5 Top-Line Earnouts Are Generally the Most Prevalent

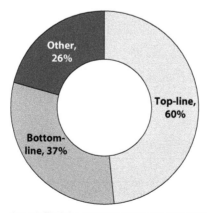

Source: Duff & Phelps, 2012 Contingent Consideration Study.

bottom-line metrics. Likewise, buyers may perceive that growth in areas such as revenues or number of customers will build long-term value in the business and/or strengthen the synergistic value with other parts of the buyer's business.

How long do most earnouts last?

Much depends on the industry and the nature of the target's business. However, for perspective, Figure 4-6 illustrates the findings of one study, which found that 51% of transactions in the sample had earnouts of two years or less.

What pitfalls should I keep in mind?

While earnouts can mitigate risks for both the buyer and the seller, they also have great potential for engendering subsequent disputes about the contingent payment. Disputes often arise when the seller suspects that the buyer is using different accounting techniques or is artificially depressing revenue or earnings during the earnout period to diminish the payment, or is not funding the business sufficiently or operating the business in a manner to allow it to reach the earnout milestones. To prevent these potential disputes, the buyer and seller should draft a clear, concise, and complete

Figure 4-6 Typical Duration of Earnout Provisions

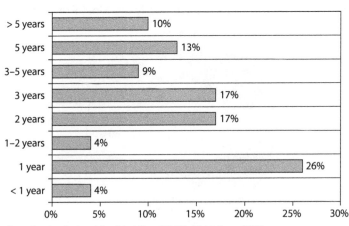

Source: American Bar Association, Private Target M&A Deal Points Survey (2013).

earnout formula before consummating a transaction. In addition, the parties should agree in advance on how these types of problems should be treated if they arise (e.g., indemnification, dispute resolution, or the use of specific accounting mechanisms).

In addition, earnout arrangements demand considerable monitoring and measuring of the target's performance, extracting both time and resources from the buyer, seller, and managers. The time spent on these tasks may distract management from effectively and/or optimally running the business. Buyers also face the risk that the payout formula will overcompensate the sellers if there is a change in the buyer's postclosing business plan or if it makes another acquisition—changes that otherwise may have little to do with the target's original value. This is one reason why a cap is often negotiated into the earnout.

What guidance do you have on setting earnout targets?

It probably comes as little surprise at this point that specific earnout targets will vary greatly case by case. Ultimately, earnout targets should align the interests of both buyers and sellers; dealmakers need to determine what is best for their particular situation. In some cases, this might be based on their industry; in other cases, it might be more narrowly tailored to the facts and circumstances of their particular situation (e.g., a distressed sale process that leaves little time for due diligence).

Most buyers typically push for the earnout to be linked to some bottom-line metric, for example, EBITDA, operating income, or pretax earnings. After all, it's the bottom line that matters most! However, many sellers will argue for the contingency to be linked to a top-line metric, such as revenue, net sales, or gross bookings. The best argument to support this view is that, once the deal is closed, the buyer may become the party who controls costs—particularly line items such as allocated corporate overhead.

Particularly in industries where revenue can easily be increased by sacrificing profit margins, it may be desirable to include a profitability component for the earnout, perhaps in conjunction with a revenue component. In such cases, the buyer should be explicit about its commitments to investment and expense targets when structuring a bottom line–based earnout metric in order to reduce the risk of disputes down the road.

In yet other circumstances, the earnout might be tied to the achievement of certain technical, research and development (R&D), or regulatory milestones. This option is particularly popular in life sciences transactions, where the value of the business may hinge dramatically on progress toward regulatory approval of a drug or technology.

Why are earnouts difficult to administer?

Although simple in concept, earnouts raise a number of definitional problems. For instance, if the earnout is linked to the company's generating $10 million of operating income in the 12 months following the sale, the buyer and seller must agree on the definition of the term "operating income" and what is—and what is not—included in its calculation. The buyer will want to be sure that such income comes from continuing operations and not extraordinary or nonrecurring events. For instance, what if a plant were to experience a casualty loss due to a hurricane or flood and is not fully covered by insurance? Does any out-of-pocket expenditure count against operating income for the purposes of the earnout? (And what if the buyer had increased the deductible postclosing to save money?) Furthermore, the earnout may require that the acquired company be operated separately and consistently with past practice. If the buyer wants to combine certain of its operations or modify them, such changes will be difficult to factor into the levels of earnings to be achieved, particularly if they are not decided upon until after the sale.

What concerns will the seller have in an earnout?

The seller is interested in ensuring that changes in the operation of the company after the sale do not affect the company's ability to attain the targeted earnings. The seller may thus seek assurances that the company will continue to be operated in a fashion consistent with past practice and will not be charged with new administrative overhead expenses. The seller may also focus on depreciation, interest charges, and intercompany transactions with the buyer's company.

The seller may seek some flexibility for the target to achieve selected postacquisition targets. Consider, for instance, an earnout based on the target's delivering $10 million of EBITDA in each of the next three years. If the company were to earn $8 million, $10 million, and $12 million in the first three years following the sale, the seller may feel entitled to receive the total contingent payment, even though EBITDA did not exceed $10 million in the first year. Accordingly, the parties may agree on a sliding scale or averaging approach and a maximum overall payment. Another option to consider is a multiperiod earnout with a catch-up provision, which allows the seller to recoup earnouts not earned in, say, the first year, by significantly outperforming targets in later years. Such provisions can keep incentives high in situations for which improved performance is still possible but has been delayed temporarily.

The parties must also determine when the buyer will make contingent payments to the seller. Typically, the debate is whether payments are made after each year's earnings are reported or in a lump sum at the end of the period, and whether prior years' payments are recoverable based upon performance in future years. If the period is three years, for example, the buyer may try to recoup the payment from the seller in Year 1 if the financial results in Years 2 and 3 fall below expectations. But the seller, naturally, may feel that the suboptimal performance of the business in Years 2 and 3 was the fault of the buyer's mismanagement, not the condition of the well-run company that the seller delivered at closing.

What implications does an earnout have for the buyer's financial statements?

Under U.S. GAAP, the buyer must value the earnout, include it as part of the purchase price, and record the value of the earnout as a contingent liability on its balance sheet. This liability needs to be revalued every period until the earnout period has ended, and all changes in the value must flow through the income statement. This requirement, which became effective in late 2008, increased the complexity of the purchase price allocation process. This is not a "do-it-yourself" activity; engage an experienced accountant.

Why aren't earnouts even more common than they are?

Ultimately, no legal agreement can provide complete protection for both parties in earnout agreements; there are far too many variables. The buyer and seller must rely on either the provisions expressed in terms of the intent or good faith of the parties or on their reasonable business judgments. Therefore, each side may want to investigate the reputation and trustworthiness of the other. By the time the buyer and seller have gone through a turbulent acquisition closing with each other, they may find little comfort in earnout arrangements. For these reasons and others discussed later, many painfully negotiated (meaning that expensive fees were paid to lawyers) earnout agreements are bought out, renegotiated away, or simply stricken from the purchase agreement at or near the closing of the transaction.

Some acquirers will conclude that maximizing the target's business plan will be much more difficult than they had originally expected when they negotiated the terms of the deal with the seller. If so, they may resent sharing the fruits of their postclosing efforts and ingenuity with the seller (i.e., the party who marketed the company as having a particularly rosy outlook). Moreover, in determining the financial projections upon which the earnout is to be based, the buyer may not want to reveal his or her growth strategies to the seller for fear that the seller will back out of the deal and proceed to implement the buyer's good ideas. In other cases, where an earnout might initially look feasible, the buyer may determine that it needs all the upside potential to attract investors or lenders, leaving little to no upside to share with the seller via an earnout. Furthermore, during the sale process, the lead buyer may determine that although other potential buyers have dropped out, the company urgently needs to complete a sale (e.g., the business is in distress). In such circumstances, the buyer may feel that he or she has the seller between the proverbial rock (bankruptcy) and hard place (reduced purchase price) and can use the seller's impaired negotiating leverage to remove contingent payments like earnouts from the purchase agreement at or near closing.

From the seller's perspective, if the seller deduces the buyer's good ideas from the buyer's focus in due diligence and in negotiating the earnout, then the seller may decide to drop the earnout and demand more upfront cash to capture more of the value at closing. The seller may feel that although the buyer was initially hesitant to pay a full price—making the earnout an acceptable compromise—due diligence has calmed the buyer's fears and made the buyer excited about the opportunity's upside, meaning that an earnout is no longer necessary. Also, the seller may assume that the buyer is "half-pregnant" after spending considerable resources on due diligence and legal fees and will not back away from the deal if the terms are sweetened to favor the seller. Separately, during due diligence, the seller may develop legitimate concerns about the buyer's ability to operate the company successfully and may not want the hassle of policing the earnout once the buyer is in command. For example, the buyer could overspend on R&D or advertising, reaping the benefits many years in the future but reducing the amount paid to the seller via the earnout by reducing reported earnings in the initial postclosing years. If the seller really wants a clean break so that he or she can move on to other endeavors, the last thing he or she will want is to ride herd on the proper application of the definition of direct expenses, which is often the essence of properly administering an earnout.

SELLER TAKEBACK FINANCING

You mentioned takeback financing. What exactly is that?

Contingent consideration is not the only way to bridge valuation expectations between a buyer and seller. If the seller is not willing to accept a contingent payment, the buyer might suggest some form of seller *takeback financing*. This is a type of financing in which the seller essentially defers payment for a set period of time—in effect, becoming a lender to the buyer to facilitate the purchase of the business. The biggest difference between contingent consideration and seller takeback financing is that takeback financing is unconditional.

The takeback financing will typically represent a junior collateral position, as many acquirers will likely have a senior source of funding other than the seller. In most seller takeback financing transactions, the buyer repays the seller with interest in accordance to mutually agreed-upon terms over a period of time. While the amount of this financing is technically not contingent upon the outcome of agreed-upon future events, the fact that seller takeback financing is typically deeply subordinated in the capital structure means that the ultimate payment is intrinsically interrelated with the credit, and thus the future financial performance, of the business. Related means of bridging valuation expectations with subordinated securities include preferred stock, warrants, and other contingent instruments.

Takeback or holdback financing can be structured in a number of ways (see also Figure 4-7):

- *Debt assumption.* The buyer pays a higher price but also takes on some debt that would normally remain with the seller (for example in an asset sale);[6]
- *Debt takeback.* The buyer pays a lower price, but the seller takes back some debt that would normally go to the buyer (for example in a stock sale);
- *Stock and/or earnings takeback.* The buyer pays a lower price, and the seller gets to keep some stock and/or retains a portion of the earnings stream; or
- *Holdback contingency.* The buyer and seller agree on a price, but the buyer pays only part of it up front; instead, the buyer puts the rest in escrow for a period of time postclosing, and the money is released only under certain conditions.

Holdback contingencies are often used in conjunction with certain representations and warranties regarding the business being sold. For instance, the buyer might want to have a full audit conducted as of the closing date. A portion of the purchase price proceeds might be placed in escrow in the event there is a material difference between the unaudited and audited results. An escrow or holdback might also be used

Figure 4-7 Selected Forms of Seller Takeback Financing

| * Debt assumption |
| * Debt takeback |
| * Stock and/or earnings takeback |
| * Holdback contingency |

when the buyer is concerned about potentially undisclosed liabilities, such as environmental issues. While many sellers will counsel buyers in such situations that the time to conduct thorough due diligence is before closing—not after—there can be circumstances that justify this approach.

Why might a seller consider takeback financing as a form of transaction consideration?

While a permanent fixture in the M&A landscape, seller takeback financing took on a more prominent role in the years following the financial crisis of 2008–2009. Conventional financing in periods of heightened economic uncertainty can be unusually costly, more difficult to obtain, and more time consuming to raise. From the seller's standpoint, using seller takeback financing can be an attractive means of selling the business quickly and at a higher overall valuation. Similar to the use of contingent consideration, we suspect that the use of seller takeback financing is cyclical and will decline at least modestly as credit conditions continue to ease.

What are seller notes, and why do some acquirers use them?

In one form of contingency payment, the seller takes back a note from the buyer in lieu of cash. Sometimes the note has a junior lien on the company's assets. If the note is subordinated to other debt, it is called a *seller's subordinated note* or simply a *seller note*.

If debt is taken back, it may be structured as a simple installment sale, or it may involve accompanying warrants. In either case, the claims of the seller are generally junior to those of other creditors, such as the senior lenders to the buyer.

In essence, a seller note is akin to a very large holdback. Typically, most acquisitions require that a portion of the cash paid be held back in an escrow account for a period of time. If the seller breaches representations or warranties in the purchase agreement, the buyer may look to the cash in the escrow account before needing to collect directly from the seller. Similarly, if there is a seller note, the buyer may cease payments on it as a remedy for breaches of representations or warranties by the seller. Therefore, because the seller knows that the seller note will give the buyer leverage in postclosing litigation or arbitration, the seller is more likely to be accurate and thorough in its disclosures during due diligence and legal documentation.

Can I use a seller note in the acquisition of a public company?

A seller note tends to be an impractical solution for paying stockholders of publicly held companies because of the delays and disclosures involved in getting a prospectus registered under federal securities laws to accompany the offer of debt or other securities.

Why do sellers consider takeback financing?

Sellers are generally reluctant to take back stock or debt that is junior to all other debt. Moreover, unless the acquirer's stock is publicly traded on a national stock exchange, takeback financing in the form of private company stock may not serve the seller's objectives of achieving full liquidity.

Still, a seller benefits from such subordinated financing by receiving an increased purchase price, at least nominally, and obtaining an equity kicker or its equivalent. The seller may well be aware, and should be prepared to face the fact, that the note or stock will realize its full value only if the acquired company prospers and that there is a real risk that this part of the purchase price will never be paid.

However, the upside potential that the seller can realize if the transaction is successful can be much greater than what it could receive if no part of its purchase price were contingent or exposed. There may also be cosmetic advantages to both buyer and seller in achieving a higher nominal price for the target company, even though a portion of that price is paid in a note or preferred stock with a market value below its face value. For example, if a seller has announced that it will not let its company go for less than $100 million but has overestimated its value, the seller may eventually be pleased to settle for $60 million cash and a $40 million 10-year subordinated note at 4% interest. The note will go onto the seller's books at a substantial discount. (The amount of the discount will be useful for the buyer to discover if he later wishes to negotiate prepayment of the note in connection with a restructuring or workout.)

What are the relative advantages and disadvantages of using preferred stock versus subordinated debt (through notes) for takeback financing?

Preferred stock has the advantage of increasing the equity listed on the balance sheet and thus helps protect a highly leveraged company from insolvency and makes it more attractive to senior and high-yield bond lenders. Also, increasing the amount of equity on the balance sheet can make the company look better during credit checks by vendors when they are reevaluating payment terms.

On the other hand, subordinated debt through notes also offers considerable advantages to the seller. Payments on the debt are due whether or not there are corporate earnings, unless otherwise restricted by subordination provisions. Also, taking back a note, rather than receiving preferred stock, bespeaks a greater degree of separation between the buyer and the seller and greater level of certainty that the amounts due will be paid. The seller has the ability to sell the paper it takes back, and it can get more for a note than for preferred stock. In addition, the seller may be able to obtain security interests in the acquired company's assets (junior to the liens of the acquisition lenders, of course), whereas no such security interest accompanies preferred stock.

From the buyer's point of view, a note has the major advantage of generating deductible interest payments rather than nondeductible dividends. Also, preferred stock has the important disadvantage of preventing a buyer from electing a type of corporate form (such as an S corporation) that enables favorable tax treatment in select circumstances. For both reasons, be sure that if a note does emerge, it is not subject to reclassification as equity by the Internal Revenue Service (IRS). Accepting the seller's preferred stock can also have other adverse tax consequences.

Absent unusual circumstances, if the buyer can persuade the senior and high-yield bond lenders to accept a seller's subordinated note rather than preferred stock in the postclosing capital structure, the seller should have no objections. Alternatively, the lenders and the seller may accept preferred stock that is convertible into a note at the buyer's option once the company achieves a certain net worth or cash flow level. As a last resort, the buyer may persuade the seller six months or a year after closing, when its debt has been somewhat reduced, to convert the preferred stock into a note.

How can a seller obtain an equity kicker in the company it is selling?

Sometimes, a seller note has the same effect as an equity kicker because it serves to inflate the sales price beyond the company's real present worth, and it can be paid only if the company has good future earnings. It is also quite possible for the seller simply to retain a postclosing minority stake in the common stock of the acquired company. Alternatively, the seller can obtain participating preferred stock, in which dividend payments are determined as a percentage of earnings or as a percentage of dividend payments made to common stockholders, and in which the redemption price of the preferred stock rises with the value of the company. Some of these choices have tax significance.

COMPENSATION-RELATED INCENTIVE PLANS

What about the promise of future compensation paid to employees who stay? Is that contingent consideration?

Essentially, the answer is yes. Often, the earnout payments made by the buyer are contingent upon whether certain employees of the acquired company remain employed by the company for a specified period of time after the acquisition. One example is a stay bonus—often part of a broader employee retention plan. A *stay bonus* is essentially a long-term employee incentive plan; it sets targets for an employee (which could be as simple as staying employed by the company) and a corresponding cash or stock bonus for achieving those targets. Stay bonuses are particularly common in acquisitions of service-driven industries, such as accounting or investment management, where the value of the business is intrinsically linked to personnel.

As discussed below, the structure of any contingent consideration paid to employees can have material tax consequences. When an employee is also a shareholder of the acquired target company, an issue can arise as to whether an earnout payment that is contingent upon continued employment represents compensation for the employee-shareholder's services or consideration for the employee-shareholder's stock. The U.S. federal income tax stakes are significant. We offer some perspective below. However, it is important to consult with a tax advisor to determine how to treat the payments.

What tax issues should I keep in mind when structuring postclosing payments to employees?

Postclosing payments to employees may be taxed differently based on whether the payments are considered to be compensation or acquisition consideration. Compensation is ordinary income to the employee and subject to a marginal federal tax rate of as much as 39.6%. Acquisition consideration, in contrast, is generally taxed as capital gains, which is taxed at a maximum of 20% at the federal level (before taking into account the federal Medicare tax, which may or may not apply in a particular case). Clearly, this distinction can have material consequences to the after tax value a seller receives. In fact, the seller might be able to cut his or her tax bill in half by structuring a payment as acquisition consideration rather than as compensation.

Likewise, the classification of a payment as a compensation expense rather than acquisition consideration may have meaningful tax implications for the buyer. Compensation is a current expense and deductible by the buyer as an offset to income, lowering its taxes. Acquisition consideration, in contrast, generally must be capitalized and amortized over time (if at all). As with most tax issues, the buyer and seller will tend to be at odds with one another regarding the method of tax accounting.

How do I know whether a postclosing payment is compensation or acquisition consideration?

Evaluating whether a contingent payment made to a shareholder-employee should be classified as transaction consideration or a postdeal compensation expense depends on a number of factors. As a starting point, if the payment is tied to the retention of the employee, chances are that it's compensation. In contrast, if the payment is (1) contingent upon future performance of the business, (2) paid in proportion to the percentage ownership that the employee had of the target preacquisition, and

(3) not dependent upon the employee still working for the business, it's likely to be considered additional purchase price—and therefore acquisition consideration.[7]

A more exhaustive list of factors to consider includes the following:

- *The terms of continuing employment.* Arrangements in which the contingent payments are *not* affected by employment termination may indicate that the contingent payments are additional consideration rather than remuneration.[8] (Conversely, if the payments *are* affected by termination, this *would* be considered remuneration.)[9]

- *Duration of continuing employment.* If the period of required employment coincides with or is longer than the contingent payment period, that fact may indicate that the contingent payments are, in substance, remuneration.

- *Level of remuneration.* Situations in which employee remuneration other than contingent payments is at a reasonable level in comparison with that of other key employees in the combined entity may indicate that the contingent payments are additional consideration rather than remuneration.

- *Incremental payments to employees.* If selling shareholders who do not become employees receive lower contingent payments on a per-share basis than the selling shareholders who become employees of the combined entity, that fact may indicate that the incremental amount of contingent payments to the selling shareholders who become employees is remuneration.

- *Linkage to the valuation.* If the initial consideration transferred at the acquisition date is based on the low end of a range established in the valuation of the acquiree and the contingent formula relates to that valuation approach, that fact may suggest that the contingent payments are additional consideration. Alternatively, if the contingent payment formula is consistent with prior profit-sharing arrangements, that fact may suggest that the substance of the arrangement is to provide remuneration.

- *Formula for determining consideration.* The formula used to determine the contingent payment may be helpful in assessing the substance of the arrangement. For example, if a contingent payment is determined on the basis of a multiple of earnings, that might suggest that the obligation is contingent consideration in the business combination and that the formula is intended to establish or verify the fair value of the acquiree. In contrast, a contingent payment that is a specified percentage of earnings might suggest that the obligation to employees is a profit-sharing arrangement to remunerate employees for services rendered.

Figure 4-8 summarizes how to determine if postdeal payments are considered compensation or acquisition consideration.

Ultimately, whether a contingent earnout payment should be treated for tax purposes as compensation for the employee-shareholder's services or as consideration for the employee-shareholder's stock is to be determined under the particular facts and circumstances of each case. The parties should carefully craft the relevant provisions in the transaction documents so as to properly express their intent on this issue. As always, with careful planning and proper documentation, the parties often can increase the likelihood of the earnout payments being treated in the desired manner.

Figure 4-9 illustrates a scenario in which a contingent payment paid to employees should be characterized as a compensation expense, not as acquisition consideration.

Figure 4-8 Is It Compensation or Acquisition Consideration?

* What are the terms of continuing employment?
* What is the duration of continuing employment?
* What is the level of remuneration?
* Are employees receiving more contingent consideration than shareholders?
* What is the formula for determining consideration?

Figure 4-9 Employee Compensation

Taxation of a Prefunded (Escrowed) Compensation Agreement Under GAAP and IFRS

Facts: Company A acquires Subsidiary B from Company C for $200 million. As part of the transaction, Company A hires five employees of Subsidiary B who were deemed critical to Subsidiary B's business due to their knowledge and expertise. Also as part of the transaction, Company C agreed to fund an escrow arrangement under which these five individuals would receive a retention bonus aggregating $15 million if they remain employed by Company A for the three years following the acquisition. If any of the five individuals terminate employment, they forfeit their bonus and these amounts will revert to Company C.

Analysis: The retention arrangement represents *compensation* for postcombination services rendered to Subsidiary B, even though it is funded by Company C. Accordingly, the retention arrangement is a separate transaction from the business combination and should be reflected as expense in Company A's consolidated financial statements during the three-year employment period to the extent paid to the employees in accordance with ASC 805-10-25-20 [IFRS 3.51]. Therefore, Company A would allocate the amount paid of $200 million between prepaid compensation and consideration transferred to acquire Subsidiary B.

Note: The editors have chosen the U.S. dollar for this example; the original source did not specify a currency.
Source: PricewaterhouseCoopers, *A Global Guide to Accounting for Business Combinations and Noncontrolling Interests: Application of the U.S. GAAP and IFRS Standards* (January 2013).

OTHER CONSIDERATIONS

Earlier you said to avoid using contingent consideration in a tax-free reorganization. Why is that?

In general, for the purpose of a tax-free reorganization under § 368 of the Internal Revenue Code, the continuity of interest requirement dictates that a minimum percentage of a consideration package *by value* must be in the form of the acquiring corporation's stock (generally assumed to be about 40%). In addition, if the value of the acquiring corporation's stock is measured as of the closing date, the possibility of price fluctuations between signing and closing can make the tax treatment of a transaction uncertain.

In order to address this issue, the applicable regulations define the circumstances under which the acquiring corporation's stock will be valued as of the last business day before the day on which a deal is signed (referred to as the "signing-date rule"). As a result, pursuant to the signing-date rule, a transaction may still qualify as tax-free even if the relative value of the acquiring corporation's stock declines between signing and closing.

Regulations applicable only to contracts with fixed consideration provide a safe harbor for consideration placed in escrow to secure the target's performance of customary covenants. These rules also allow for contingent consideration so long as the non contingent consideration meets the continuity of interest test and the contingency does not prevent (to any extent) the target's shareholders from being subject to the economic benefits and burdens of ownership of the acquiring corporation's stock after the last business day before the first date the contract becomes a binding contract.[10]

Why is it difficult to use contingent consideration in bankruptcies?

Certainly, it would be an attractive alternative—for a previously bankrupt business might have unusually low earnings visibility upon which to base a valuation. However, using contingent consideration for, say, an asset sale under § 363 of the U.S. Bankruptcy Code would likely be impossible because the section's definition of "cash collateral" is cash, negotiable instruments, documents of title, securities, deposit accounts, or other cash equivalents, and it is made clear that the cash collateral must be "free and clear."[11]

CONCLUSION

In this chapter, we learned how to use contingent consideration to bridge expectations between a buyer and seller—particularly when operating conditions are uncertain. For those who find more comfort in certainty, you're in luck: our next chapter describes how to create value through tax structure. For nothing in this world can be said to be certain, except death and taxes.

CHAPTER 5

Unlocking Value Using Tax Structure

The hardest thing in the world to understand is the income tax.

—Albert Einstein

INTRODUCTION

The best things in life are free, but sooner or later the government will find a way to tax them. However, as the investment bank Morgan Stanley once pointed out in an advertisement, "You must pay your taxes, but there's no law that says you gotta leave a tip." So the goal for law-abiding (but sensible) dealmakers is to pay only what is due and no more. How to achieve this goal varies widely by situation. This variety, in turn, greatly affects the valuation of businesses—both before and after an acquisition.

Readers will either love or hate this chapter on "Unlocking Value Using Tax Structure," which is both the longest and driest chapter in this book. We are proud that this book, like others in *The Art of M&A* series, tackles tax law questions head-on, whereas many M&A survey texts prefer to stick to a holding pattern at 50,000 feet. If your eyes start to glaze over at the thought of tax law, wake up! We know the subject can be dull at times. However, buyers and sellers have good reason to pay attention to tax and related accounting issues; as such factors can impact the valuation and financial modeling of a company in seemingly countless ways. Issues to consider include the following:

- Which types of legal entities are constituents to the transaction? Whether the buyer or seller is a C corporation or some form of pass-through entity can have a material impact on valuation.
- What is the contemplated structure of the transaction? Is there an opportunity to increase the "size of the pie" with a tax-advantaged structure?

- How is management being compensated in the deal? Different structures of management participation may create vastly different tax results.

- How will the target be taxed postacquisition? Is the buyer preserving the favorable tax attributes of the seller? Are there opportunities to create new tax shields as part of the deal?

- Are there any unintended tax consequences from the transaction, perhaps from the perspective of state tax laws or future disposition of the newly acquired operations?

You will also find that this chapter is a bit more conceptual than others—despite the fact that we have tried to include numerical examples where possible. There's a reason for this. Tax, perhaps more so than any other aspect of M&A, hinges upon the facts and circumstances of a particular situation. Accordingly, we have attempted to present the basic tools needed to refine your valuation and/or transaction model. For those looking for an even deeper dive into M&A tax, we refer you to *The Art of M&A Structuring: Techniques for Mitigating Financial, Tax, and Legal Risk.*

This chapter addresses several key themes. First, we discuss general tax issues impacting valuation. Second, we examine choice of legal entity and how that impacts valuation. Third, we look at basic M&A transaction structures. Finally, we consider the tax implications of those various transaction structures.

GENERAL TAX ISSUES IMPACTING VALUATION

How can tax issues affect company valuation in general?

From the purchaser's point of view, the principal goal of tax planning is to minimize, on a present value basis, the total tax costs of not only acquiring but also operating and even selling the acquired corporation or its assets. As discussed in Section I of this book, the root of all company valuation is cash flow. The analyst is tasked with determining how much cash flow a particular business will be able to generate over time. The amount of tax a company must pay on its income impacts these cash flows and, therefore, the company's valuation. In this way, taxes, in effect, are a cost of doing business—just like payroll and raw materials. Accordingly, the postacquisition tax profile of the business—whether operated as a stand-alone or merged into other operations of the acquirer—can have a material impact on how much the acquirer is willing to pay for the deal, particularly if the target's tax rate is expected to change after the deal. In addition, effective tax planning provides various safeguards to protect the parties from the risks of potential changes in circumstances or tax law.

Just as taxes may impact the acquirer's M&A valuation, so too can they influence the seller's perspective. From the seller's point of view, the primary objective of tax strategy is to maximize, on a present value basis, the aftertax proceeds from the sale of the acquired corporation or its assets. This tax planning includes, among other things, deciding how to structure the transaction, developing techniques to provide tax benefits to a potential buyer at little or no tax cost to the seller, and structuring the receipt of tax-deferred consideration from the buyer. After all, most would-be sellers are going to be focused on the transaction proceeds they would be taking home *after* the government takes its cut. In fact, the purchaser should attempt to minimize the tax costs of the transaction to the seller in order to gain advantage as a bidder. For instance, which deal would you rather take: an offer to purchase your business for $100 million, which would be taxed at 40% due to an inefficient tax structure, or an offer for $80 million, which would be taxed at 20% as a result of some effective tax planning? Clearly, offer #2, as illustrated in Figure 5-1, puts more aftertax dollars in the seller's pockets and is thus a more attractive deal, all else equal. As a result, tax matters to nearly any constituent of a transaction.

How does transaction structure influence valuation?

In the United States and many other jurisdictions, the taxes to be paid will depend partly on the structure used to accomplish the change of

Figure 5-1 Tax Matters

	Offer #1	Offer #2
Valuation	$100 million	$80 million
Tax rate	40%	20%
After tax proceeds	$60 million	$64 million

control: Did the acquirer purchase assets from the company, or did the buyer acquire the stock of the target? Also, the amount of tax payable will depend partly on the accounting principles applied when recording the acquisition.

Importantly, these tax and accounting matters tend to be a zero-sum game: More often than not, the most advantageous tax plan for the buyer is the least advantageous plan for the seller. For example, the tax benefit of a high tax basis in the assets of the acquired corporation may be available to the purchaser only at a significant tax cost to the seller, such as double-taxation of the transaction. But buyers rarely, if ever, pursue tax benefits at the seller's expense, because the immediate and prospective tax costs of a transaction are likely to affect the price. Generally, the parties will structure the transaction to minimize their aggregate, combined tax costs and allocate the tax burden between them through an adjustment in price.

What is tax basis?

A taxpayer's basis in an asset, also known as its *tax basis,* is the value at which the taxpayer carries the asset on its tax balance sheet. An asset's basis is initially its historical cost to the taxpayer. This *initial basis* is sub-sequently increased by capital expenditures and decreased by deprecia-tion, amortization, and other charges, becoming the taxpayer's *adjusted basis* in the asset. Upon the sale or exchange of the asset, gain or loss for tax purposes is measured by the difference between the amount realized for the asset and its adjusted basis.

Example. Assume that Seller Corporation owns the assets listed in Figure 5-2. The first column (Assets) identifies assets. The second col-umn (Adjusted Basis) lists the original cost of each asset adjusted to reflect depreciation that has occurred for the asset. (Note that some assets, such as working capital and land, are not depreciated.) The third column (Estimated Fair Market Value), gives the value of the asset in today's mar-kets. The fourth column (Potential Gain) then calculates the potential gain if Seller Corporation were to sell any of the assets. This is calculated by comparing the estimated fair market value of each asset to its adjusted basis. The fifth and last column (Taxes) shows the tax due assuming a 40% rate of taxation.

Figure 5-2 Assets, Adjusted Basis, FMV, Potential Gain, and Taxes ($000s)

Asset	Adjusted Basis	Estimated Fair Mkt Value	Potential Gain	Taxes at 40%
Working capital	$25,000	$25,000	$0	$0
Land	50,000	100,000	50,000	20,000
Commercial building	12,750	30,000	17,250	6,900
Truck equipment	1,200	4,000	2,800	1,120
Packaging equipment	3,429	10,000	6,571	2,629
Total assets	**$92,379**	**$169,000**	**$76,621**	**$30,649**

How can a seller reduce tax costs?

The simplest way to reduce the seller's tax bill is to postpone the recognition of gain. This may be accomplished in a tax-free or partially tax-free acquisition or via the installation sale route. These subjects are discussed in more detail later in this chapter. In deals that are immediately taxable, the seller should analyze whether the proposed transaction subjects it to more than one level of taxation.

What is the current tax rate on corporate income in the United States and globally?

The highest statutory tax rate for the United States is 40%, which is high compared to many other countries; worldwide, the current average is 23.68%.[1] However, the calculation of tax can be complex and is a moving target due to changing regulations globally. Moreover, the effective tax rate can differ from the maximum statutory rate. This is due to exemptions and other factors, including, for example, the use of some of the structural and transactional techniques discussed in this chapter. Accordingly, a recent study found that major U.S. multinationals were paying an effective tax rate of around 13% on average.[2]

Which tax issues typically arise in an acquisition or divestiture?

There is no definitive checklist of tax issues that may arise in every acquisition or divestiture. The specific tax considerations for a transaction depend on the facts and circumstances of the particular deal. Certain tax terms and issues, however, many of which are interrelated, are far more common than others:

- A primary issue is the *basic structure of the transaction*: whether the transfer is devised as a stock acquisition or an asset acquisition (both of which are defined later in this chapter) and whether the transaction can be structured as a tax-free reorganization or if the transfer will be immediately taxable. The optimal structure is generally the one that maximizes the aggregate tax benefits and minimizes the aggregate tax costs of the transaction to the acquired corporation, the seller, and the buyer.

- Another initial question to be resolved in many acquisitions is the *choice of entity*: whether the operating entity will be a C corporation, an S corporation, a limited liability company (LLC), a general or limited partnership, or a trust. We discuss these various legal entities, and the tax impact to valuation, later in this chapter.

- The tax implications of the *financing (cash, debt, and/or equity)* must also be analyzed.

- The issue of *management participation and compensation* should also be addressed. Top-level managers of the company being acquired may be invited to purchase stock, or they may be granted stock options, stock appreciation rights, bonuses, or some other form of incentive compensation. Chapter 4 illustrates circumstances in which management's participation in the deal is taxed as transaction consideration versus compensation. The difference, from a tax standpoint, can be considerable.

- In addition, tax advisors (particularly for the purchaser) should examine the *tax effects* that the proposed structure will have on the postacquisition operations of the company. For example, consideration should generally be given to net operating losses (NOLs), credit carrybacks and carryforwards, amortization of intangible assets (other than goodwill), the alternative minimum tax, planned asset dispositions, elections of taxable year and accounting methods, integration of the company's accounting

> methods into the buyer's existing operations, foreign tax credits, and the interrelationships among the differing tax systems of the countries in which the combining companies do business. We touch on tax attributes later in this chapter.

- Tax advisors should also give attention to other matters, including the *effects of state tax laws*, the tax consequences of future *distributions* of the acquired company's earnings, and the ultimate *disposition* of the acquired company or its assets.

These issues should be analyzed with an eye on pending and recent M&A-related tax legislation, keeping retroactivity in mind.

Which structural issues are usually the most important?

The two structural issues parties should consider as early on as possible are (1) the choice of entity, and (2) whether the buyer should structure the deal to obtain a cost basis or carryover basis in the assets of the acquired corporation. As discussed in more detail later in this chapter, an acquirer typically can obtain either a cost basis or a carryover basis in the target's assets regardless of whether the deal is a stock or asset acquisition. As a result, the acquirer should initially address its tax objectives and preferred legal structure as separate and distinct issues.

Earlier you said that a target's tax rate might change after the acquisition. Why?

There are a variety of factors that may influence how the target's tax profile might change following an acquisition. Two common reasons for this are the target's business entity changing as a result of the deal and the target otherwise losing a favorable tax attribute, such as an NOL carryforward, as a result of the transaction. For instance, an S corporation (which, as discussed below, is a pass-through entity for tax purposes) has tax advantages that a C corporation does not enjoy.[3] However, to qualify as an S corporation, the business must meet a long list of specialized qualifications. If an S corporation is merged into a C corporation, it will, in all likelihood, lose its favorable tax status due to the merger. Accordingly, the acquirer will have to tax-affect the S corporation's earnings stream to reflect the target's tax profile postacquisition, a process called *tax-effect accounting* (using the noun form and spelling for the term). Otherwise, the acquirer may overstate the value of the S corporation.

Another common reason for a target's tax rate to change after an acquisition is when it will be folded into the buyer's operations, which have a different geographic footprint in higher- (or lower)-taxing jurisdictions. These types of transactions have attracted heightened political attention in recent years, as so-called "tax inversions."

What is tax inversion, and can you provide an example?

Tax inversion describes any tactic that results in a company changing its parent company domicile to a lower-tax country in order to pay less U.S. tax. In the M&A context, it is most typically a cross-border merger in which the lower-taxed entity becomes the parent and the higher-taxed entity becomes the subsidiary, thus potentially reducing taxes for the subsidiary entity.

One example is the $11 billion merger between Burger King and Tim Hortons in 2014. Putting aside the strategic logic of the transaction, there was also an apparent tax benefit from the deal. This was a merger between a company in the United States (Burger King), which has a 35% federal tax rate (or 40% adding state and local) and a company in Canada (Tim Hortons), which has a 26.5% tax rate.[4] More importantly, however, by moving its headquarters to Canada after the deal, Burger King could access offshore profits that were previously subject to U.S. federal taxation upon repatriation, even though they had already been taxed in the local country in which they were generated. The United States is one of the few countries to impose this double taxation on offshore profits.

What are the potential tax consequences of inversion via M&A for Burger King and other inverters?

As a very general rule, when headquarters are located in a low-tax country, the effective tax levied on the company's earnings can be lower, depending on the specific tax rules of the country in question.

If we were to take Burger King at its word, the merger with Tim Hortons was strategic, not motivated by tax savings. In the press release announcing the deal, Alex Behring, executive chairman of Burger King and managing partner of its then majority owner, 3G Capital, said:

> By bringing together our two iconic companies under common ownership, we are creating a global QSR powerhouse. [QSR, the new company's ticker symbol on the New York Stock Exchange and the Toronto Stock Exchange, stands for "quick-service restaurants."] Our combined size, international footprint, and industry-leading growth trajectory will deliver superb value and opportunity for both Burger King and Tim Hortons shareholders, our dedicated employees, strong franchisees, and partners.[5]

That said, it does seem likely that the entity known as Burger King (along with Tim Hortons, now a part of Restaurant Brands International) will lower its tax payments in 2015 and the foreseeable future due to the change in headquarters.

Complaints about several attempted tax inversions via M&A in 2014 led to new tax rules reducing the advantages of this tactic. Passed by the U.S. Treasury in September 2014, the new rules require that former owners of a U.S. entity own less than 80% of a new combined entity. Now if there is an 80% overlap in ownership (by vote or value) of the inverted entity before and after the transaction, the new foreign parent is treated as U.S. owned. The new rules also prevent inverted companies from:[6]

- Accessing a foreign subsidiary's earnings while deferring U.S. tax through the use of loans (known as "hopscotch" loans);
- Restructuring a foreign subsidiary in order to have tax-free access to the subsidiary's earnings; and
- Transferring cash or property from a controlled foreign corporation (CFC) to the new parent to completely avoid U.S. tax.

What does it mean to "tax-affect" the estimated future earnings of a company in a valuation?

An acquirer would *tax-affect* a target's earnings, and therefore its valuation, in order to adjust the target's cash flows to make an "apples-to-apples" comparison with companies in a different tax category.

Example. Two companies, Centaurus Corp. and Scorpius Corp., both have pretax income of $10 million. However, Centaurus Corp. is taxed as a so-called C corporation, which as described later in this chapter, is subject to taxation at both the company level and the individual shareholder level. Scorpius Corp., in contrast, is an S corporation, which is only subject to taxation at the shareholder level—and not the company level. As stand-alone companies, then, Centaurus's $10 million of pretax income is only worth $4.8 million after tax to its shareholders, whereas Scorpius's identi-cal pretax income is worth $6.0 million. However, if Centaurus were to acquire Scorpius, it would violate the S corporation tax rules and Scorpius would be subject to Centaurus's tax rates going forward. As a result, if Centaurus were considering the potential acquisition of Scorpius, it should tax-affect the target's pretax income to evaluate its earnings stream on a comparable basis (Figure 5-3).

Should I always tax-affect the target's earnings?

No. It depends, in large part, on the facts and circumstances of the particu-lar case. If both the acquirer and the target are pass-through entities, and assuming the transaction does not change that status for either party, then there really would be no reason to tax-affect the target's cash flows.

Also, there are certain situations in which an appraiser might not tax-affect earnings when the intended use of the valuation is for some purposes other than an acquisition or investment. For instance, there is a long history of academic and legal debate about whether to tax-affect the earnings of a pass-through entity, such as an LLC or S corporation, when

Figure 5-3 Example of Tax-Affected Earnings ($000s)

		Centaurus		Scorpius		
				Actual		**Tax-Affected**
Pre tax income			$10,000		$10,000	$10,000
(−) Corporate-level income tax	40%	(4,000)	0%	−	40%	(4,000)
(=) Net income available to shareholders		6,000		10,000		6,000
(−) Personal income tax	20%	(1,200)	40%	(4,000)	20%	(1,200)
(=) Net proceeds to shareholders		**$4,800**		**$6,000**		**$4,800**

Note: Assumes dividends are "qualified" and subject to a maximum tax rate of 20%

the valuation is being used for a divorce settlement or trust and estate work. *Gross v. Commissioner* was one of the earliest cases in which the United States Tax Court rejected the concept of tax-affecting the earnings of S corporations.[7] In more recent years, however, there have been other cases, such as *Delaware Open Radiology Assocs. v. Kessler* (2006)[8] and *Bernier v. Bernier* (2007, 2012),[9] that do allow for this approach.[10]

Ultimately, the rules in tax court are extremely technical. Consult with tax counsel before making a decision. Similarly, the rules for whether to tax-affect earnings in a divorce settlement vary from state to state. Ask local counsel to research whether there's any legal precedent in the particular jurisdiction before drawing any independent conclusions of your own. It may be that the courts in your state have already decided the issue for you.

What roles do state and local taxes play in structuring mergers, acquisitions, and buyouts?

State and local taxes generally play a secondary role in planning M&A transactions. First, most state income tax systems are based largely on the federal system, particularly in terms of what is taxable, to whom, when, and in what amount. Second, when the company being acquired operates in a number of states, it can be inordinately difficult to assess the interaction of the various state tax systems. This is not to say that tax planners should ignore a transaction's state tax consequences. Although a detailed discussion of state income tax consequences deserves a book of its own, several extremely important state tax issues will be mentioned throughout the following discussion.

First and foremost, there are income taxes. These vary from state to state and may affect companies located outside the state.[11] Beyond income taxes, there are numerous taxes imposed by states and localities that may affect an acquisition. Although these rarely amount to structural prohibitions or incentives, they often increase costs. For example, when real estate is being transferred, there will often be unavoidable real property gain, transfer, or deed recordation taxes. Perhaps the most notorious of the real property gain and transfer taxes worth mentioning specifically is that imposed by New York State upon certain sales of real estate and controlling interests in entities holding real estate. (New York State's real estate transfer tax was repealed on July 13, 1996, but is illustrative of potential pitfalls.) New York State's "Tax on Gains Derived from Certain Real Property Transfers," formerly referred to as "gains tax," imposed a tax of 10% on gains derived from transfers of real property where the property was located in the state and the consideration for the transfer was $1 million or more. This tax, which applied to transfers of controlling interests as well as acquisitions, was different and separate from other federal, state, or local income taxes that may have arisen from the real property transfer.

Purchases of assets may not be exempt from a state's sales tax. Many states offer exemptions, but this should not be taken for granted. Check it out.

Certain types of state and local taxes not directly associated with an acquisition can be significantly affected by an acquisition or by the particular structure of the acquisition. For example, a state's real property and personal property taxes are based on an assessment of the value of the property owned by a taxpayer. Often, a transfer of property ownership will trigger a reassessment of the value of the property.

Can you provide some specific examples of acquirer-related expenses in an acquisition and explain whether they are typically deductible?

The points below briefly touch upon some examples. This discussion of fees includes not only investment banking expenses, but also legal, accounting, tax, and consulting fees. It is important to keep in mind that the facts and circumstances of each specific situation may lead to different conclusions.

- An acquirer generally may immediately deduct the fees related to an *unsuccessful acquisition attempt* under § 165 of the Internal Revenue Code ("the Code").
- The acquirer may typically immediately deduct *due diligence–related fees* if the acquirer and target are in the same line of business. If the parties are in different lines of business, the

acquirer must capitalize and amortize due diligence fees over a 60-month period, as provided in § 195 of the Code.

- Fees that the acquirer incurs upon obtaining *debt financing* for the deal must be capitalized and amortized over the term of the debt.

- Advisory fees related to securing *equity financing* generally may not be deducted or amortized.

- If the acquisition is structured as an *asset purchase for tax purposes*, the fees are allocated among the assets and increase the acquirer's basis in such assets. To the extent such assets are depreciable or amortizable, the fees generate a tax shield over the life of the assets.

- If the acquisition is structured as a *stock purchase for tax purposes*, the fees are neither deductible nor amortizable. Instead, the fees increase the acquirer's basis in the stock acquired. This higher basis would be factored into any future tax liability upon a sale or taxable liquidation of the target by the acquirer.

- An acquisition structured as a *tax-free reorganization* is generally treated the same as an acquisition structured as a stock purchase.

What are some specific examples of target-related expenses in an acquisition, and are they typically deductible?

A handful of examples are described below. As with acquirer-related expenses, the facts and circumstances of each specific situation are ultimately determinative.

- A target generally may immediately deduct the fees related to an *unsuccessful sale attempt* under § 165 of the Code.

- If the acquisition is structured as an *asset purchase for tax purposes*, the transaction is a taxable event for the target. As a result, there is little practical distinction between whether

the expenses are immediately deductible, increase the basis
of the assets sold, or effectively lower the purchase price. In
any event, the fees lower the target's corporate-level gain on
the sale.

- If the acquisition is structured as a *stock purchase for tax
  purposes*, the target generally may deduct expenses up to the
  point that the target makes a final decision to move forward
  with the transaction (e.g., by corporate resolution). From that
  point forward, the target generally must capitalize fees.

- As in the case of acquirer-related expenses, an acquisition
  structured as a *tax-free reorganization* is generally treated
  the same as a stock purchase.

Does the IRS play a direct role in business acquisitions?

Generally speaking, no. Unlike certain transactions regulated by federal
agencies such as the Federal Communications Commission and the Federal Trade Commission, advance approval from the IRS is not required
before consummating an acquisition, divestiture, or reorganization. Ordi-
narily, the IRS will not have occasion to review a transaction unless and
until an agent audits the tax return of one of the participants.

An important and often useful exception to this rule is that the parties to a transaction can often obtain a private letter ruling issued by the
National Office of the IRS. Such a ruling states the agency's position
with respect to the issue raised and is generally binding upon the IRS.
Requesting such a ruling is serious business and should never be under-
taken without expert legal help.

What are loss carryovers and carrybacks?

If a corporate taxpayer has an excess of tax deductions over its taxable
income in a given year, this excess becomes an NOL for that taxpayer.
Section 172 of the Code allows that taxpayer to use its NOL to offset taxable income in subsequent years (a *carryover* or *carryforward*) or to offset
taxable income in earlier years (a *carryback*). For most taxpayers, an NOL

may be carried back for up to two taxable years and may be carried forward for up to 20 years.

Under other provisions of the Code, certain tax losses or tax credits that are unusable in a given year may be carried forward or carried back to other tax years. Examples of such deductions or credits are capital losses, excess foreign tax credits, and investment credits. Generally, Code provisions for a company's ability to utilize NOL carryovers also apply to these other items. For the purposes of simplicity, all these items tend to be grouped together with loss carryovers. This is a practice that we will follow in the discussion here.

Generally speaking, each state has its own NOL carryback and carryforward rules, which may not necessarily match the federal rules. Therefore, an acquired corporation may have different amounts of available federal and state NOLs.

What role do loss carryovers play in mergers and acquisitions?

As stated earlier, a potential advantage to carryover basis acquisitions—both taxable stock purchases and tax-free reorganizations—is the carryover of the seller's tax basis and favorable tax attributes to the buyer. To the extent that a buyer can purchase a corporation and retain favorable NOL carryovers, it can increase the aftertax cash flow generated by the activities of the acquired corporation and, to some extent, utilize those losses to offset tax liability generated by the buyer's own operations.

Over the course of many years, Congress and the IRS have imposed various limitations on the use of loss carryovers by persons other than those who owned the entity at the time the loss was generated. For example, after a substantial ownership change, an acquiring corporation can deduct only the NOLs of the acquired corporation up to a certain limit, called a "Section 382 limitation," and must meet a "continuity of business enterprise" requirement. *Continuity of business enterprise* means the continuation of a significant business of the acquired corporation or the continued use of a significant portion of the corporation's business assets. These rules have achieved a level of complexity that is extreme even by the standard of tax law.

What happens when corporations having loss carryovers acquire other corporations that generate taxable gains?

The Code covers this in § 384, which imposes limitations upon a loss corporation's ability to offset its losses against taxable gains recognized by subsidiaries it acquires and with which it files a consolidated tax return. These limitations also apply where the loss corporation acquires the gain assets from another corporation in a tax-free reorganization or liquidation that results in a carryover of basis. Loss carryovers of the acquiring corporation include unrealized built-in losses.

CHOICE OF LEGAL ENTITY

How does the target's legal entity impact valuation and M&A modeling?

The legal structure of the target often will influence the tax structure of the deal—that is, whether an acquirer has the option of structuring either an asset deal or a stock deal (both of which we describe in greater detail later in this chapter).

What are some of the most common types of legal entities available to a business?

Though an exhaustive discussion is outside the scope of this chapter, a business may generally take a number of legal forms: (1) a C corporation, (2) an S corporation, (3) a partnership, either general or limited, or (4) an LLC. Choosing the appropriate legal form depends on the unique circumstances of the constituent parties and is important for tax, liability, financing, and other purposes.

What are the primary differences among the four types of business entities?

A regular, or C, corporation is a separate taxpaying entity. Therefore, the corporation pays taxes on its earnings, and shareholders pay taxes on their dividends. Partnerships, S corporations, and LLCs, in contrast, are known as pass-through entities and generally are not separate taxpaying entities.

Because S corporations, partnerships, and LLCs are typically exempt from federal taxation (instead passing the tax liability with respect to earnings directly through to their owners), these entities are commonly referred to as pass-through entities. The earnings of pass-through entities are taxed directly at the partner or shareholder level, whether or not distributed or otherwise made available to such persons. Moreover, pass-through entities may generally distribute their earnings to the equity owners free of tax.

What are pass-through entities?

Pass-through entities are structures that permit one level—rather than two levels—of taxation. There are four types of pass-through entities: (1) partnerships, both general and limited, (2) LLCs, (3) S corporations, and (4) C corporations that file consolidated income tax returns with their corporate parents. The tax treatment of each is subject to certain nuances:

- The earnings of a C corporation are subject to double taxation, but the consolidated return provisions (generally) permit the earnings of subsidiary members of the consolidated return group to be taxed only to the ultimate parent.
- The earnings of an S corporation, with certain exceptions, are subject to taxation only at the shareholder level.
- The earnings of a partnership are also subject to a single tax, but only to the extent that such earnings are allocated to noncorporate partners (unless the partner is an S corporation).
- Partnership earnings that are allocated to corporate partners are subject to double taxation, just as though the income were earned directly by the corporations.

What is a C corporation?

The Code defines a *C corporation* as any corporation that is not an S corporation. The term "C corporation" as used in this chapter, however, excludes corporations granted special tax status under the Code, such as life insurance corporations, regulated investment companies (mutual funds), or corporations qualifying as real estate investment trusts (REITs).

What is an S corporation?

An *S corporation* is simply a regular corporation that meets certain requirements and elects to be taxed under Subchapter S of the Code. Originally called a "small business corporation," the S corporation designation was designed to permit small, closely held businesses to be conducted in corporate form, while continuing to be taxed generally as if operated as a partnership or an aggregation of individuals. As it happens, the eligibility requirements under Subchapter S, keyed to the criterion of simplicity, impose no limitation on the actual size of the business enterprise.

Briefly, an S corporation may not (1) have more than 100 shareholders, (2) other than estates and a very limited class of trust, have as a shareholder any person who is not an individual (i.e., a corporation cannot be a shareholder of an S corporation), (3) have a nonresident alien as a shareholder, (4) have more than one class of stock, (5) be a member of an affiliated group with other corporations, or (6) be a bank, thrift institution, insurance company, or certain other types of business entity.

It should be noted that not all states recognize the S corporation. In those that do not, the corporation pays state income taxes as if it were a C corporation. For those states that do recognize S corporations, both resident and nonresident shareholders of the state in which the corporation does business must file returns and pay taxes to that state. In such cases, a shareholder's state of residence will usually (but not always) provide a credit against its own tax.

What is a partnership for tax purposes?

Except under rare circumstances, a *partnership for tax purposes* must be a bona fide general or limited partnership under applicable state law. With certain exceptions, LLCs and S corporations are treated as partnerships for tax purposes, meaning that they have many of the tax benefits available under current tax law.

Can you provide an illustration of how the target's choice of entity might influence a deal?

Assume an acquirer approaches a conglomerate about buying out of its many divisions. The buyer offers a purchase price of $100 million for assets that have an adjusted tax basis of $40 million in the hands of the seller. Further assume a 40% corporate tax rate, a 20% tax rate on qualified dividends, and a 20% tax rate on long-term capital gains.[12]

First, let's look at what the aftertax proceeds would be to the target's shareholders if the target were a C corporation. As such, the target would have to pay taxes on the sale of the assets,[13] and the shareholders would have to pay taxes on the distribution of proceeds. In this case, the aftertax proceeds to the shareholders would be only around $61 million from a $100 million sale, as illustrated in Figure 5-4. The C corporation would pay $24 of tax for each $100 of realized value: ($100 realized value − $40 tax basis)(40% tax rate). This would leave $76 out of each $100 to be divided among shareholders as dividends. On top of the $24 (per $100) of corporate tax, the shareholders would pay an additional $15 (per $100) of personal tax on the dividends (assuming the dividends are qualified). Accordingly, the shareholders would clear around $0.61 on the dollar from the sale.

Now, let's consider what the aftertax proceeds would be to the target's owners if the target were a pass-through entity, such as an LLC or S corporation. Because an LLC is a pass-through entity, the target itself does not pay any taxes on the sale proceeds; the transaction is taxed only at the

Figure 5-4 Tax Implications of Partial Divestiture: C Corporation ($ in millions)

Purchase price	$100.00
Less: Basis, assets	(40.00)
Taxable gain	60.00
Corporate taxes at 40%	(24.00)
Dividends	76.00[1]
Less: Tax on dividends at 20%	(15.20)[2]
Shareholders' after tax proceeds	$60.80

[1]Purchase price of $100 less corporate taxes of $24
[2]Assumes distribution is a qualified dividend

Figure 5-5 Tax Implications of Partial Divestiture: Pass-Through Entity ($ in millions)

Purchase price	$100.00
Less: Basis, assets	(40.00)
Taxable gain	60.00
Corporate taxes	-
Dividends	100.0
Less: Long-term capital gains tax at 20%	12.00[1,2]
Shareholders' after tax proceeds	$88.00

[1]Assumes assets sold are capital assets and therefore qualify for long-term capital gains rates
[2]Tax is calculated as 20% of taxable gain of $60

owner's level. Accordingly, the owners in aggregate would pay $12 of tax: ($100 realized value – $40 tax basis)(assuming a 20% tax rate on long-term capital gains and/or alternative minimum tax). So while the shareholders of the C corporation shared nearly 40% of their sale proceeds with the government, that rate was only 12% for the owners of the LLC (Figure 5-5).

Accordingly, where the target is a C corporation, chances are that an asset purchase will be prohibitively expensive, whereas a pass-through entity, such as an LLC or S corporation, would likely face a lower tax burden, all else equal. Importantly, there are tax structures available (discussed later in this chapter) that can narrow the gap. But clearly these types of issues, left unattended, can have a materially adverse effect on the deal.

BASIC M&A STRUCTURES

When one company acquires another, what are the various forms that the transaction can take?

Three general forms may be used for the acquisition of a business:

- A purchase of the assets of the business (referred to by a variety of names, including *asset deal, asset transaction, asset purchase, asset acquisition,* and *asset sale*);
- A purchase of the stock of the target owning the assets (referred to as a *stock deal* or similar variations as with an asset deal); and
- A statutory merger of the buyer (or an affiliate) with the target.

As a general rule, asset deals and stock deals are taxable transactions. (The subsequent issue, as described later, is whether the transaction will be subject to one or two levels of taxation.) Statutory mergers may qualify as tax-free reorganizations, provided certain criteria are met.

Importantly, these forms of transaction are legal structures for the deal. These legal structures may, or may not, reflect how the tax authorities look at the deal. As confusing as this might sound, a "stock deal for legal purposes" may actually be an "asset deal for tax purposes" if, for instance, the parties can use § 338 of the Code. Accordingly, legal structure does not always translate automatically to the tax structure of the deal. We'll delve into this later.

As described later in this chapter, asset deals for tax purposes are also referred to as cost (or stepped-up) basis transactions, while stock deals for tax purposes are known as carryover basis transactions. This distinction can have a material impact on the aftertax cash flows that the acquirer harvests from the target postacquisition.

The key to avoiding confusion is to think of legal structure as separate and distinct from tax structure. An asset deal for *legal purposes* creates certain mechanical rights and obligations—yes, the buyer can pick and choose which assets and liabilities it assumes, but if any of the assets are subject to nonassignability provisions, the buyer must seek consent from a third party. Separately, an asset deal for *tax reasons* allows the buyer to benefit from a stepped-up basis in the assets, although the seller may face two levels of taxation.

If you are already becoming frustrated with these seemingly contradictory terms, take a deep breath. Many M&A professionals are similarly confused with these nuances. Some readers might be familiar with the old saying, "In the land of the blind, the one-eyed man is king." M&A is replete with technical nuances. If you take the time to understand them, you can create real value.

What happens in an asset transaction for legal purposes?

In an asset transaction for legal purposes, the target transfers all the assets used in the business that is the subject of the sale. These include real estate, equipment, and inventory, as well as "intangible" assets such as contract rights, leases, patents, and trademarks. These may be all or only some of the assets owned by the selling company. The target executes the specific kinds of documents needed to transfer the specific assets, such as deeds, bills of sale, and assignments.

When is an asset transaction necessary or desirable?

Many times, the choice of an asset transaction is dictated by the fact that the sale involves only part of the business owned by the selling corporation. Asset sales are generally the only choice in the sale of a product line that has not been run as a subsidiary corporation with its own set of books and records. Also, as a legal matter, the buyer in an asset sale generally assumes only the liabilities that it specifically agrees to assume. This ability to pick and choose among liabilities generally protects the buyer from undisclosed liabilities of the seller. Exceptions do apply, however.

In other cases, an asset deal is not necessary but is chosen because of its special tax advantages. Often, the tax basis of assets is materially lower than their selling price. In these cases, the buyer generally can realize significant tax savings from structuring the transaction as an asset deal, stepping up the assets' old low basis to the newly high basis of the acquirer's purchase price. (Chapter 6 illustrates the impact of a stepped-up basis and its carryover impact to depreciation and amortization in the context of a purchase price allocation.) Conversely, if the seller's tax basis is higher than what the acquirer is paying—if the assets are being sold at a loss— the buyer is generally better off inheriting the tax history of the business by doing a stock transaction, and thus keeping the old high basis. This is because the higher the acquirer's basis is postacquisition, the lower the taxes it will pay in the future.

What are the disadvantages of an asset sale?

For the purposes of M&A valuation and financial modeling, the biggest disadvantage of an asset sale is the potentially high tax cost. That is, an asset acquisition is frequently subject to double taxation: the seller is taxed as a corporation, and then the seller's shareholders are taxed upon distribution of the sale proceeds.[14] In order to address this double-taxation issue, some transactions can be structured under § 338 of the Code so as to trigger just one level of taxation.[15]

What is § 338 of the Code?

Section 338 of the Code applies to taxable acquisitions. The provision enables an acquirer to treat a purchase of stock as a purchase of assets for tax purposes. This election can be attractive to the acquirer because the buyer obtains a stepped-up basis in the target's assets. This step-up, in turn, provides the acquirer with a higher depreciable tax base in the assets and generates higher tax deductions in future years. We discuss § 338 of the Code extensively in the Principles of Taxable Acquisitions section, below.

Can you provide a diagram of an asset transaction?

Figure 5-6 illustrates an asset transaction. In each diagram throughout this book, SH represents a shareholder, a square represents a corporation, and a circle represents corporate assets. Vertical and diagonal lines indicate the ownership of stock or assets, and arrows represent the flow of cash, assets, stock, and so on.

Figure 5-6 Asset Transaction

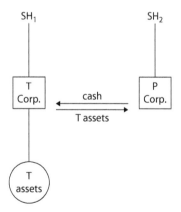

1. SH_1 owns 100% of the stock of T; SH_2 owns 100% of the stock of P
2. P purchases all assets of T in exchange for cash

What happens in a stock transaction?

The seller transfers its shares in the target to the buyer in exchange for an agreed-upon payment. Usually the transfer involves all company shares. Although the buyer occasionally will buy less than all of the stock in a public company (through a tender offer), this rarely occurs in purchases of private corporations—typically only when some previous stockholder who will be active as a manager of the postacquisition company retains a stock interest.

When is a stock transaction appropriate?

A stock transaction is appropriate whenever the tax costs or other problems of doing an asset transaction make the asset transaction undesirable. Asset transfers simply produce too onerous a tax cost in many transactions. Apart from tax considerations, a stock deal may be necessary if the transfer of assets would require unobtainable or costly third-party consents or where the size of the company makes an asset deal too inconvenient, time consuming, or costly.

Sellers frequently prefer stock deals because buyers will assume all corporate liabilities. This often is not as big an advantage as it appears initially, however, because the buyer will usually seek to be indemnified against any undisclosed liabilities.

What would a diagram of a stock transaction look like?

Figure 5-7 illustrates a stock transaction.

TAX IMPLICATIONS OF M&A STRUCTURES

How are the above M&A structures handled from a tax perspective?

The rest of this chapter is focused on answering this question. However, Figure 5-8 distills the next 10,000-plus words into one chart. In a nutshell, the most common tax treatments to buyers and sellers are as follows:

- A cash purchase of stock is typically taxable to the seller. The acquirer inherits a carryover basis, unless the transaction qualifies under § 338 or 338(h)(10) for a stepped-up basis.

Figure 5-7 Stock Transaction

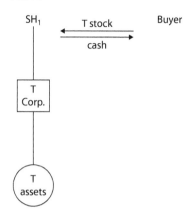

1. SH$_1$ owns 100% of the stock of T
2. Buyer purchases 100% of the stock
   of T in exchange for cash

- A stock-for-stock exchange is not taxable to the seller, assuming the transaction qualifies as a Type B reorganization. The acquirer, however, still inherits a carryover basis.

Figure 5-8 M&A Transaction Structures and Corresponding Tax Implications

M&A Transaction	Taxable to Seller?	Acquirer's Basis in Assets
Stock acquisition		
Cash purchase of stock	Yes	Carryover basis, unless transaction qualifies under § 338 or 338(h)(10), in which case the acquirer receives a stepped-up basis
Stock-for-stock exchange	No, assuming transaction qualifies as a Type B reorganization	Carryover basis
Asset acquisition		
Cash purchase of assets	Yes	Stepped-up basis
Stock-for-assets exchange	No, assuming transaction qualifies as a Type C reorganization	Carryover basis
Statutory merger		
Target merges into acquirer's, with target shareholders receiving stock of the acquirer	No, assuming transaction qualifies as a Type A reorganization. Even if overall transaction qualifies, nonstock portion (i.e., boot) is taxable	Carryover basis

- A cash purchase of assets is nearly always taxable to the seller. The buyer, in this case, gets a stepped-up basis.
- A stock-for-assets exchange, in contrast, would not be taxable to the seller—provided the transaction qualifies as a Type C reorganization. Like other tax-deferred deals, the acquirer steps into the tax basis of the seller.
- Lastly, a statutory merger is not taxable to the selling shareholders, assuming the deal qualifies as a Type A reorganization. However, the nonstick portion (known as "boot" in tax law nomenclature) is taxable even if the overall transaction qualifies. The buyer in a statutory merger accepts a carryover basis.

How is basis treated in an asset acquisition for tax purposes compared to a stock acquisition for tax purposes?

The basis a purchaser takes in the assets acquired is the primary distinction between an *asset acquisition* and a *stock acquisition* for tax purposes. When a purchaser directly acquires the assets of a corporation, and the acquired corporation is subject to tax on the sale or exchange of the assets, the basis of the assets to the purchaser is their cost. This is called *cost* or *stepped-up basis*.

The benefit of this stepped-up basis is that the buyer can write up the tax basis of the assets and depreciate them over time—potentially creating an annual tax benefit, assuming that the price the buyer pays for the assets is higher than the adjusted basis of those assets on the seller's balance sheet.

Example. Recall the example of Seller Corporation in Figure 5-2. Figure 5-9 illustrates the value of the depreciation tax shield if Acquirer Corp. were to purchase each asset at fair market value. Whereas Seller Corp. takes $3.5 million of annual depreciation expense against these assets, Acquirer Corp. could deduct $4.0 million annually against its taxable income from the stepped-up basis. This shields an incremental $500,000 of taxable income, for a net economic value of roughly $200,000, assuming a 40% tax rate.

In contrast, when a purchaser instead acquires the stock of a corporation, the basis of the assets in the possession of the corporation is generally not affected. This is called *carryover basis* because the basis of an asset in the acquired corporation "carries over" on the change of stock ownership.

Figure 5-9 Annual Tax Benefit from a Stepped-Up Basis ($000s)

Current Basis Assets	Cost	Adjusted Basis	Useful Life (in years)	Salvage Value	Annual Depreciation	Tax Shield at 40%
Working capital	$25,000	$25,000	N/A	N/A	N/A	N/A
Land	50,000	50,000	N/A	N/A	N/A	N/A
Commercial building	15,000	12,750	30	1,500	450[1]	180
Truck equipment	12,000	1,200	5	1,200	2,160[1]	864
Packaging equipment	8,000	3,429	7	1,600	914[1]	366
Total assets	**$110,000**	**$92,379**	**N/A**	**$4,300**	**$3,524**	**($1,410)**

Stepped-up Basis Assets	Estimated FMV[2]	New Basis	Useful Life (in years)	Salvage Value	Annual Depreciation	Tax Shield at 40%
Working capital	$25,000	$25,000	N/A	N/A	N/A	N/A
Land	100,000	100,000	N/A	N/A	N/A	N/A
Commercial building	30,000	30,000	30[3]	1,500	950[1]	380
Truck equipment	4,000	4,000	2[3]	1,200	1,400[1]	560
Packaging equipment	10,000	10,000	5[3]	1,600	1,680[1]	672
Total Assets	**$169,000**	**$169,000**	**N/A**	**$4,300**	**$4,030**	**($1,612)**

Annual Tax Benefit	
Value of new tax shield	$1,612
Value of current tax shield	(1,410)
Annual savings	**($202)**
Percent savings	*14%*

[1]Assumes straight-line depreciation over IRS's suggested useful life
[2]FMV: Fair market value
[3]Based on the condition of each asset versus IRS's suggested useful life

With the exception of a stock acquisition governed by the provisions of § 338 of the Code, the acquisition of all or part of the stock of a corporation does not alter the bases of the assets owned by the corporation. (In a § 338 transaction, which is an indirect asset acquisition, the acquisition's cost basis in each asset is generally its fair market value.) And with the exception of an asset acquisition governed by the Code's tax-free reorganization provisions, the acquisition of the assets of a corporation will produce a cost basis to the purchaser.

Which types of transactions are carryover basis, or stock, transactions?

As a general rule, a carryover basis, or stock, transaction includes any transaction in which the stock or assets of a corporation are acquired by the purchaser, and the bases of the assets are not increased or decreased upon change of ownership. There are several types of stock or carryover basis transactions. The direct purchase of the acquired corporation's stock in exchange for cash and debt is the most straightforward stock acquisition. Another transaction that is treated as a sale of stock for tax purposes is the merger of the acquiring corporation into the acquired corporation—a *reverse merger*—in which the shareholders of the acquired corporation relinquish their shares in exchange for cash or debt in a fully taxable transaction. Another common stock transaction is the acquisition of the stock or assets of a corporation in a transaction free of tax to its exchanging shareholders.

Which types of transactions are cost basis, or asset, transactions?

Broadly speaking, a cost basis, or asset, transaction includes any transaction in which the preacquisition gains and losses inherent in the assets acquired are triggered and recognized by the acquired corporation. There are several types of cost basis transactions. The direct purchase of the assets from the acquired corporation in exchange for cash or indebtedness is the quintessential asset acquisition. Another common asset transaction is the statutory merger of the acquired corporation into an acquiring corporation—a *forward cash merger*—in which the shareholders of the acquired corporation exchange their shares for cash or other property in a fully taxable transaction. In certain circumstances, a corporation may acquire the stock of another corporation and elect under § 338 of the Code to treat the stock acquisition, for tax purposes, as an asset acquisition.

Who benefits from a cost, or stepped-up, basis?

Generally, the buyer. High tax basis in an asset is always more beneficial to its owner than low basis. The higher the basis, the greater the depreciation or amortization deductions (if allowable) and the less the gain (or the greater the loss) on the subsequent disposition of the asset. An increase in these deductions and losses will reduce the tax liabilities of the purchaser or the acquired corporation during the holding period of the assets, thereby increasing aftertax cash flow. For the same reasons, a high basis in the acquired corporation's assets will enhance their value to a potential carryover basis purchaser.

The purchase of an acquisition target should generally be structured to maximize the basis of the assets of the acquired corporation. If a purchaser's prospective cost basis of the assets of the acquired corporation exceeds its prospective carryover basis, an asset acquisition or step-up transaction is generally more beneficial to the purchaser than a stock acquisition. If a purchaser's prospective carryover basis exceeds its prospective cost basis in the assets of the acquired corporation, a stock acquisition is generally more beneficial to the purchaser than an asset, or cost basis, acquisition.

The primary exceptions to this rule occur in a situation in which (1) the purchaser would acquire beneficial tax attributes—NOLs, tax credits, or accounting methods—in a carryover basis transaction that would be lost in a step-up transaction, and (2) the value of such tax attributes to the purchaser exceeds the value of the stepped-up basis in the acquired corporation's assets that it would have obtained in a cost basis transaction.

Will a purchaser's cost basis in an asset generally be greater than its carryover basis?

Yes. Where an asset has appreciated in value, or where the economic depreciation of an asset is less than the depreciation or amortization deductions allowed for tax purposes, a purchaser's prospective cost basis in the asset will exceed its prospective carryover basis. The depreciation and amortization deductions allowed for tax purposes for most types of property are designed to exceed the actual economic depreciation of the property. As a result, the fair market value of most assets, which represents the prospective cost basis of the asset to a purchaser, generally exceeds the adjusted tax basis. The aggregate difference between the purchaser's prospective cost and carryover bases of the acquired corporation's assets is often substantial.

What are the tax consequences of a cost basis, or asset, acquisition for the acquired corporation?

The general rule is that the basis of an asset in the possession of an acquired corporation may not be stepped up to cost or fair market value without the recognition of taxable gain to the corporation. In a cost basis transaction, the acquired corporation will generally be subject to an immediate tax on an amount equal to the aggregate step-up in the bases of the assets. In addition, the sale or exchange of an asset may trigger the recapture of investment or business tax credits previously taken by the acquired corporation on the acquisition of the asset.

What are the tax consequences of a cost basis, or asset, acquisition for the shareholders of the acquired corporation?

The shareholders of the acquired corporation will be subject to tax upon the receipt of the asset sales proceeds (net of the corporate-level tax) from the acquired corporation, whether the proceeds are distributed in the form of a dividend, in redemption of the shareholder's acquired corporation stock, or in complete liquidation of the acquired corporation. If the asset sales proceeds are retained by the acquired corporation, then the value of those proceeds is indirectly taxed to the shareholders upon the sale or exchange of the stock of the acquired corporation.

Under what circumstances will an acquired corporation and its shareholders be subject to double tax on a cost basis, or asset, acquisition?

The acquired corporation and its shareholders will typically be subject to double tax where (1) the acquired corporation sells, or is deemed for tax purposes to sell, its assets to the purchaser in a taxable transaction; (2) the shareholders of the acquired corporation will ultimately receive the proceeds of the sale, either directly or indirectly through the sale of their stock in the acquired corporation; and (3) the proceeds received by the shareholders of the acquired corporation will be taxable to them. The cost basis transaction in these circumstances causes the proceeds of the sale to be taxed twice, first to the acquired corporation and again to its shareholders. There are several significant exceptions to this general rule.

The most common exception occurs where the acquired company is a C corporation: The proceeds from the sale of the acquired corporation's stock by a corporate shareholder will likely be taxed again upon their ultimate distribution to noncorporation shareholders.

Example. Let's revisit Seller Corp. from Figures 5-2 and 5-9. Assume that Acquirer Corp. is prepared to pay $169 million for the business, regardless of whether the deal is structured as an asset deal for tax purposes or a stock deal for tax purposes.[16] The shareholders in Seller Corp. have $20 million in basis in their stock, which they have held for more than one year. Assume a 40% corporate tax rate and a 20% long-term capital gains tax rate.

If the sellers were to choose the asset deal, Seller Corp. first pays $30.6 million of corporate tax on the $76.6 million of gains—leaving $138.3 million to be dividended out to shareholders. Seller Corp. distributes this cash and then completely liquidates. Because the transaction is a liquidation, the shareholders can net their $20 million in stock basis against the $138.3 million dividend and pay long-term capital gains tax of $23.7 million on the difference. Ultimately, these two levels of taxation yield $94.7 million of aftertax proceeds to the shareholders—or roughly $0.56 on the dollar from the original $169 million deal price.

Contrast this $0.56 on the dollar for an asset deal to the $0.71 on the dollar the shareholders would receive under a stock deal. Here, the match is simpler. The sellers receive $169 million for their shares; they have $20 million of basis in their stock; so they pay $29.8 million in long-term capital gains tax. This leaves them with $119.2 million after tax—$24.5 million, or 26%, more than they would have received under the asset sale. Figure 5-10 illustrates the tax implications to sellers of an asset sale versus a stock sale.

On balance, which structure is preferable: an asset or stock acquisition?

Generally, a stock acquisition is preferable to an asset acquisition because of the adverse tax consequences of an asset acquisition to the seller. The immediate tax cost to the acquired corporation and its shareholders on the basis step-up amount of asset acquisition is generally greater than the present value of the tax benefits to the purchaser.

Figure 5-10 Tax Impact on Sellers of an Asset Sale versus a Stock Sale ($000s)

	Asset Deal	Stock Deal
Sale proceeds from asset sale	$169,000	$0
Tax basis in assets	(92,379)	–
Corporate-level gain	76,621	–
Corporate-level tax	30,649	–
Sale proceeds from asset sale	169,000	–
Less: Corporate-level tax	(30,649)	–
Dividend to shareholders	138,351	–
Sale proceeds from stock sale	–	$169,000
Tax basis in stock	(20,000)	(20,000)
Shareholder-level gain	118,351	149,000
Less: Shareholder-level tax	(23,670)	(29,800)
After tax proceeds to shareholders	**$94,681**	**$119,200**
Difference ($)		*$24,519*
Difference (%)		*26%*
Levels of taxation	Two	One

Under what circumstances is a cost basis, or asset, acquisition justifiable for tax purposes?

An asset, or cost basis, acquisition is generally advisable for tax purposes in situations where the double-tax burden to the seller can be partially or wholly avoided and in situations where double tax is inevitable regardless of structure. For instance, the seller may be able to avoid the double-tax burden where it has tax losses from other corporate activities that can off-set the taxable gains that arise from the sale of assets. Alternatively, where the sale price of the assets is less than the seller's tax basis in those assets, the seller may actually generate a tax benefit from structuring the deal as an asset sale rather than as a stock sale.

From a tax standpoint, under what circumstances are carryover basis transactions more beneficial to a purchaser than cost basis transactions?

There are two situations where a carryover basis, or stock, transaction may be more beneficial to the purchaser than a cost basis, or asset, acquisition. The first is where the carryover basis of the acquired corporation's assets to the purchaser exceeds their cost basis. This excess represents potential tax benefits to the purchaser—noncash depreciation deductions or taxable losses—without a corresponding economic loss. That is, the tax deductions or losses from owning the assets may exceed the price paid for such assets. The second situation occurs where the acquired corporation possesses valuable tax attributes—NOL carryovers, business tax credit carryovers, or accounting methods, for example—that would inure to the benefit of the purchaser. Situations where carryover basis transactions are preferable to the purchaser over cost basis transactions, however, are more the exception than the rule.

PRINCIPLES OF TAXABLE ACQUISITIONS

What are the two principal methods of structuring taxable acquisitions?

As discussed previously, taxable acquisitions may generally be structured in one of two ways: either as the purchase of a target's assets (a cost basis, or step-up, transaction) or as the purchase of the target's stock (a carryover basis transaction). There are a number of variations on these two methods, including a § 338 transaction and its related § 338(h)(10) structure.

What are the tax consequences to the acquirer in a taxable asset acquisition?

In a taxable asset acquisition, the acquirer typically purchases assets directly from the target in exchange for cash, stock, debt, or any other form of security or property. The acquirer may also assume certain liabilities of the target, such as a mortgage on property or a lease on equipment, which may or may not be directly related to the assets the acquirer is buying. Alternatively, a taxable asset acquisition may be structured as a reverse cash merger, in which the acquirer forms a transitory subsidiary that merges into the target and target shareholders receive cash (and/or notes) from the acquirer.

From a tax perspective, the treatment of the acquirer is relatively straightforward: the purchase is usually not a taxable event for the acquirer unless the acquirer has used property as part or all of the consideration. This chapter generally does not delve into asset exchanges.

Under § 1012 of the Code, the acquirer takes a cost basis in the assets acquired. The acquirer's cost basis is typically the sum of (1) the consideration paid for the assets (i.e., cash, notes, etc.), (2) the dollar value of the target's liabilities assumed by the acquirer in connection with the transaction, and (3) the acquirer's transaction expenses. For a brief discussion of how the purchase price is allocated among the assets acquired, see the section below entitled Structuring Installment Sales.

What is the principal benefit to the acquirer of an asset acquisition over a stock acquisition?

As briefly noted above, the step-up in basis is the primary tax benefit to an acquirer for structuring an asset deal instead of a stock deal. The acquirer writes up the purchased assets to their fair market value. In many cases, the allocation of purchase price to specific assets will also create new intangible assets on the acquirer's balance sheet that did not exist on the seller's. The most common example is goodwill, which is deductible over a 15-year period under § 179 of the Code. Other examples include non-compete agreements, the value of patents or other intellectual property, and the economic value of the seller's at-will workforce. (In many cases, the acquirer can amortize the value ascribed to these assets in less than the 15-year period prescribed for goodwill.)

As noted above, an asset purchase enables the acquirer to write up the purchased assets to their fair market value. As a result, the assets will typically have a higher tax basis in the hands of the acquirer than they did in the hands of the seller. This, in turn, means that the assets usually generate higher tax deductions (i.e., depreciation, amortization, etc.) for the acquirer than they did for the target. Accordingly, an asset transaction—where available or otherwise tax efficient for the target—in many cases can generate a substantially better tax shield for the acquirer than a stock transaction.

What are the tax consequences to the target in a taxable asset acquisition?

The transaction is a taxable event to the target, which recognizes gain or loss on the assets sold. In effect, the target is taxed as if it had sold each

asset separately. While a thorough discussion of the taxation of asset dis-
posals is outside the scope of this book, we note a few important considerations. First, the target generally recognizes in its amount realized the
dollar value of liabilities assumed by the acquirer. Second, under certain
circumstances, these rules reclassify capital gain as ordinary income, and
certain assets, such as inventory or depreciable property, may be subject to
recapture provisions of the Code. This may increase the tax consequences
from the deal for the target. Third, the deal is a taxable event regardless of
whether the disposal is followed by a liquidation of the target. However,
if the target is liquidated, the target may trigger § 336(d)(2), which disal-
lows precontribution built-in losses on property previously contributed by
shareholders to the target in a § 351 transaction or as a contribution of
capital. Generally, this section of the Code applies only if the property had
been contributed as part of a tax-avoidance plan.

What is the principal detriment to the target of an asset acquisition over a stock acquisition?

From a tax perspective, the primary disadvantage to the target of an asset
sale is that the transaction may be subject to two levels of taxation: one
upon the sale of the assets to the acquirer and a second upon the liquidation
of the target and distribution of proceeds to the shareholders. The scenarios
in which this double-taxation may arise are discussed in more detail below.

What are the tax consequences to the target's shareholders in a taxable asset acquisition?

As noted above, the sale is a taxable event to the shareholders if the target is a pass-through entity. If the target is a C corporation, the tax consequences to the target's shareholders generally depend on whether the
target liquidates following the asset sale.

- *If the target does not liquidate*, the sale is not a taxable event
  for the shareholders. However, in certain circumstances, a target
  that sells a substantial amount of assets and retains only cash or
  securities could be considered a personal holding company or an
  investment company. In the case of a personal holding company,

the target shareholders may be subject to substantial penalties if the IRS determines the target has not paid out sufficient dividends. In the case of an investment company, the target may be subject to federal regulation.

- *If the target liquidates*, the tax consequences are further differentiated by whether the target is an 80%-plus-owned subsidiary of another corporation. If the target is not, the distribution is a taxable liquidation and the target's shareholders recognize capital gain or loss on their stock under § 331(a) of the Code. To the extent the asset acquisition is structured as an installment sale (including a transaction with seller takeback financing), the target shareholders are typically able to defer a portion of their capital gain or loss. Installment sales are discussed in more detail below. If the target is an 80%-plus-owned subsidiary of another corporation, the distribution is a tax-free liquidation to the target's parent under § 332 of the Code, but a taxable distribution to minority shareholders.

A key takeaway in evaluating a potential asset sale is that the transaction may involve double taxation: the target is taxed upon the sale of the assets, and the target's shareholders are taxed upon any distribution of proceeds and/or liquidation of the target, unless one of the exemptions described above applies.

What are the tax consequences to the acquirer in a taxable stock acquisition?

In a straightforward taxable stock acquisition, the acquirer purchases the stock of the target from the target's shareholders, and the acquirer takes a cost basis in its newly acquired stock. More importantly, however, the acquirer takes a carryover basis in the assets purchased. As a result, these assets must be depreciated or amortized using the same methods, useful lives, and so on as the target had in effect at the time of the transaction. In addition, a stock acquisition does not create tax-deductible goodwill as an asset acquisition does. From a tax perspective, these are the biggest drawbacks to the acquirer of a stock purchase over an asset acquisition.

What are the tax consequences to the target in a taxable stock acquisition?

The tax consequences to the target of a simple taxable stock acquisition are relatively straightforward. The transaction is generally not taxable to the target, and the tax attributes of the target's assets do not change. However, many taxable stock acquisitions are structured as § 338 or 338(h) (10) transactions. Where permitted, these structures permit a stock sale to be taxed as an asset sale. Both § 338 and 338(h)(10) transactions are discussed in more detail below.

What are the tax consequences to the target's shareholders in a taxable stock acquisition?

The tax consequences to the target's shareholders from a "plain vanilla" taxable stock acquisition are equally straightforward. The transaction is a taxable event, and the shareholders are subject to capital gains or losses based on the difference between the amount realized from the transaction and their respective tax bases in the target's stock. As noted above, some stock acquisitions are structured as § 338 or 338(h)(10) transactions. The tax consequences to the target's shareholders can be difficult under these structures and are described in the discussion that follows.

Can the acquirer ever obtain a stepped-up basis in a taxable stock acquisition?

Yes, the acquirer may obtain a stepped-up basis if the acquirer meets the requirements of a qualified stock purchase under § 338 or the criteria of § 338(h)(10) and the purchaser makes the requisite elections.

Under § 338, the acquirer purchases the stock of the target for legal purposes but is treated as if it had acquired the assets of the target for tax purposes. From a mechanical perspective, this is achieved in five steps:

1. The acquirer purchases the stock of the target via a qualified stock purchase, as defined below;
2. The target sells all of its assets at fair market value to a hypothetical intermediary corporation;

3. This hypothetical intermediary corporation takes an aggregate basis in the target's assets equal to the consideration that the acquirer pays for the target's stock;

4. The acquirer purchases the stock of this hypothetical intermediary corporation; and

5. The acquirer makes an irrevocable § 338 election no later than the fifteenth day of the ninth month beginning after the month in which the acquisition date (as defined below) occurs.[17]

Figure 5-11 illustrates the mechanics of a § 338 transaction and summarizes the tax consequences for each constituent corporation.

A § 338(h)(10) transaction is similar to a § 338 transaction but is applicable where the target is a subsidiary of another corporation. The § 338(h)(10) structure allows the parent to avoid double taxation upon the target's deemed asset sale and subsequent liquidation. Figure 5-12 illustrates the mechanics of a § 338(h)(10) transaction and summarizes the tax consequences for each party to the acquisition.

What is a qualified stock purchase?

In order to make a § 338 election (and thus obtain asset acquisition treatment for a stock acquisition), the acquirer must make what's known as a *qualified stock purchase*. This requires that a corporation acquire at least 80% of a target's stock from a seller unrelated to the corporation (i.e., a party that is not an affiliate of the corporation) within a 12-month acquisition period. The first date on which these purchases are made is known as the *acquisition date*. A number of additional considerations further clarify the definition of a qualified stock purchase:

- First, only a corporate acquirer can qualify, not an individual.
- Second, the transaction must provide the corporate acquirer with a cost basis, not a carryover or transferred basis. This generally requires that the seller be unrelated to the acquirer and that the acquirer pay in cash or debt. The transaction cannot be structured as a tax-free reorganization, as discussed in more detail below.

- Third, any stock ownership prior to the acquisition date does not count toward the 80% requirement. As a result, an acquirer who has owned 20% or more of another corporation for more than 12 months cannot qualify.

What are the tax consequences for the target in a § 338 acquisition?

In a § 338 transaction, the acquisition is legally structured as a purchase of stock by the acquirer but is taxed as a purchase of assets. The target is taxed as if it had sold 100% of its assets at fair market value to a hypothetical intermediary corporation, the stock of which is sold to the acquirer. The target is treated as if it had sold *all* its assets in the transaction, even if the acquirer purchased *less than 100%* of the target's stock. Because the acquirer is technically buying the target's stock, the acquirer bears the legal burden of paying the target's tax obligation. However, this shifting of tax obligation is usually factored into the final purchase price.

Example. For instance, assume there are 100 shares issued and outstanding of the target (T), none of which is owned by the acquirer (A). T has assets with a fair market value of $1,000 and an adjusted basis of $750. T has no liabilities prior to the asset sale. Assume further that T shareholders, who own 90 shares of T (90%), agree to sell their stock to A for $810 in a transaction that qualifies under § 338. Although A is purchasing only 90% of T's stock, T is taxed as if it had sold 100% of its assets. Accordingly, T has a taxable gain of $250 (total assets' fair market value of $1,000 less assets' aggregate basis of $750). If we assume for the sake of simplicity that T's corporate tax rate is 40%, A will ultimately be responsible for paying the $100 tax ($250 × 40%) due by T.

What are the tax consequences to the hypothetical intermediary corporation in a § 338 transaction?

The hypothetical intermediary corporation exists only to allow for a stepped-up basis in the target's assets before the intermediary turns around and theoretically sells the stock to the acquirer. According to § 338(b)(1) of the Code, the intermediary takes an aggregate basis in the target's stock equal to (1) the grossed-up basis of the acquirer's recently purchased stock in the target (i.e., since the acquisition date, as defined in the qualified stock purchase rules described above), plus (2) the basis of the acquirer's nonrecently purchased stock (i.e., prior to the acquisition date), plus (3) the liabilities of the target that the acquirer has assumed (including the tax liability from the transaction, as described above).

Where the acquirer buys 100% of the target's stock, the intermediary's basis in the assets is straightforward and is equal to the acquirer's purchase price plus any liabilities the acquirer assumes. The basis calculation is more complex where the acquirer purchases less than 100% of the target's stock in the § 338 transaction. In this scenario, the intermediary's basis is equal to (1) the liabilities of the target that the acquirer assumes, plus (2) the result of the following calculation:

$$\text{Purchase price} \times \frac{100\% - \text{Percentage of target stock the acquirer previously owned}}{\text{Percentage of stock the acquirer purchased in the § 338 transaction}}$$

Example. Building on the fact pattern from the preceding question, T sells 100% of its assets to the hypothetical intermediary corporation (I). A is purchasing less than 100% of the stock of T, but I takes an aggregate basis of $1,000 in T's assets. This basis is the sum of (1) the $100 tax liability A assumes from T, plus (2) $900, which is the product of $810 × (100% – 0%)/(90%).

What basis does the acquirer take in the target stock?

The acquirer takes a cost basis in the target's stock, that is, the consideration paid out of pocket plus any liabilities assumed. The tax basis of each individual asset is written up to its fair market value, and the excess is allocated to goodwill.

Example. In the fact pattern above, A acquired 90% of T's stock. A's basis in these shares is equal to the $810 paid plus the $100 tax liability assumed, or $910. Figure 5-11 illustrates the execution of a § 338 transaction.

Figure 5-11 Section 338 Transaction Structure

Tax Consequences to Acquirer	Tax Consequences to Intermediary Corp.	Tax Consequences to Target
• Acquirer makes election within 12 months	• Intermediary gets a "grossed-up" basis	• Amount realized: FMV of all target's assets
• Acquirer takes a cost basis in target's stock	• Where the acquirer buys 100% of the target's stock, the intermediary's basis in	• **Adjusted basis:** Target's basis in each asset
• Acquirer obtains a depreciation tax shield from the "grossed-up" basis in the target's assets	the assets simply equals the acquirer's purchase price + liabilities transferred from the target to the purchaser (*including* the target's tax liability from the sale)	• ⊠ Is gain/(loss) at corporate level
• Acquirer is obligated to pay target's gain on sale of assets. This is usually factored into the final purchase price	• Where the acquirer buys less than 100% (but 80% or more) of the target's stock, the purchase price in the above formula is adjusted as follows:	

$$\text{Purchase price} \times \frac{100\% - \text{Percentage of target stock previously owned by acquirer}}{\text{Percentage of stock acquired in the § 338 transaction}}$$

[1]FMV: Fair market value.

Who pays the taxes due by the target in a § 338 transaction?

The acquirer pays the taxes due by the target, as it is a liability inherited by the acquirer. However, the acquirer's basis is increased by the amount of this tax liability, and the acquisition price is usually adjusted to account for the shifting of tax burden.

What is a § 338(h)(10) transaction, and how is it related to § 338?

A § 338(h)(10) transaction is a specific type of § 338 acquisition that involves the sale of a subsidiary by a corporate parent. Under § 338(h)(10) of the Code, a corporate parent may sell the stock of the subsidiary target to an acquirer in a transaction that is a stock sale for legal purposes but is deemed an asset sale for tax purposes. A typical asset sale results in two levels of taxation (one at the target level upon the sale of the assets and a second level upon liquidation), whereas a typical stock sale results in only one level of taxation (at the shareholder level). However, in a § 338(h)(10)

Figure 5-12 Section 338(h)(10) Transaction Structure

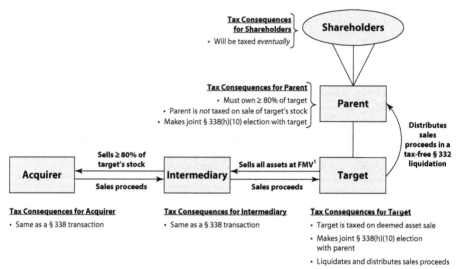

¹FMV: Fair market value

transaction, the target is taxed upon the sale of its assets, but the parent is not taxed upon the sale of its stock. In addition, the acquirer will obtain a stepped-up basis in the assets of the target, similar to a § 338 transaction.

The Code permits the § 338(h)(10) transaction structure because the parties could achieve the same result if the subsidiary target sold its assets in a straightforward asset sale and then liquidated tax-free under § 332 of the Code. (Tax-free liquidations of a subsidiary under § 332 are discussed in more detail later in this chapter.) Figure 5-12 illustrates the execution of a § 338(h)(10) transaction structure.

STRUCTURING INSTALLMENT SALES

What are installment sales, and how can they help in structuring a merger, acquisition, or buyout?

An *installment sale* is a disposition of property (by a person who is not a "dealer" in such property) in which at least one payment is to be received after the close of the taxable year in which the sale occurs. Basically, an installment sale is a sale or exchange for a promissory note or other debt instrument from the buyer. In the case of an installment sale, the gain on the sale is recognized, pro rata, whenever principal payments on the note are received, or if earlier, upon a disposition of the installment obligation. For example, if A sells property to B for a note with a principal amount of $100 and A's basis in the property was $60, A realizes a gain of $40. Since the ratio of the gain recognized ($40) to the total amount realized ($100) is 40%, this percentage of each principal payment received by A will be treated as taxable gain. The other $60 will be treated as a nontaxable return of capital.

Installment sale treatment is available only with respect to a debt obligation of the buyer itself, as opposed to a related third-party issuer. An obligation of the buyer will not qualify if it is payable on demand or, generally, if it is in registered form and/or designed to be publicly traded. Note, however, that an installment obligation may be guaranteed by a third party and may even be secured by a standby letter of credit. In contrast, installment obligations secured by cash or cash equivalents, such as certificates of deposit or U.S. Treasury instruments, do not qualify.

Which kinds of transactions are eligible for installment sale treatment?

The installment method is generally available for sales of any property other than installment obligations held by a seller and other than inventory and property sold by dealers in the subject property. Subject to certain exceptions, installment treatment is generally available to a shareholder who sells his or her stock or to a corporation or other entity that sells its assets. Installment treatment is not available for sales of stock or securities that are traded on an established securities market.

How are purchase price allocations made for tax purposes?

Although businesses are usually bought and sold on a lump-sum basis, for tax purposes each payment in an installment sale transaction is broken down into a purchase and sale of the individual assets, both tangible and intangible. There is no specific requirement under the tax laws that a buyer and seller allocate the lump-sum purchase price in the same manner.

Because each party is inclined to take a position most favorable to itself, and because the IRS has an interest in maintaining consistent principles in this domain, the IRS has litigated reallocation issues fairly often over the years. At the same time, the courts and, to a lesser extent, the IRS, have tended to defer to allocations of purchase price agreed upon in writing between a buyer and seller in arm's-length transactions.

Are there any rules governing the allocation of purchase price?

Yes. If the seller transfers assets constituting a business and determines its basis as the consideration (e.g., purchase price) paid for the assets, then this transfer is considered a § 1060(c) "applicable asset" acquisition. Both buyer and seller in such a transaction must use the "residual method" to allocate the purchase price received in determining the buyer's basis or the seller's gain or loss. This method, which is also used for a stock purchase, requires that the price of the assets acquired be reduced by cash and cash-like items; the balance must be allocated to tangible assets, followed by intangibles, and finally by goodwill and going-concern value. IRS regulations state that both buyer and seller are bound by the allocations set forth in the acquisition agreement.

What about amortization of intangibles following an acquisition?

Section 197 of the Code sets a uniform standard of 15 years for amortization of intangibles at a rate of 100%. Exceptions to the 15-year rule include the following:

- Land
- Financial interests
- Certain computer software
- Certain interests or rights acquired separately
- Interests under leases and debt instruments
- Sports franchises

- Mortgage services
- Transaction costs

These are treated with either longer periods (e.g., land) or shorter periods (e.g., computer software). All other forms of goodwill and other intangibles are amortized at 15 years (either with certain restrictions meant to discourage purchase of intangible-rich companies for tax reasons). In general, § 197 benefits acquirers of companies that have intangibles with a long life that normally would have to be amortized over a longer period. Businesses tend to like to write off intangibles as quickly as possible, as this creates cash in hand from tax savings and rids the company of a drag of profits.

PRINCIPLES OF TAX-FREE TRANSACTIONS

What are the tax consequences of a typical tax-free reorganization?

As an example of the classic tax-free acquisition, Al Smith (Smith) owns all the stock of Mom and Pop Grocery, Inc. (Grocery), which is acquired by Supermarkets, Inc. (Supermarkets). In the transaction, Smith surrenders to Supermarkets all his stock in Grocery solely in exchange for voting stock of Supermarkets. This is a fully tax-free reorganization known as a "B reorganization," in which Smith recognizes no immediate gain or loss.

The corollaries to tax-free treatment here as elsewhere are carryover and a substituted basis and holding period. In other words, Smith obtains a basis in his Supermarkets stock equal to his basis in the Grocery stock surrendered (substituted basis) and continues his old holding period in the stock. Similarly, Supermarkets takes a basis in the Grocery stock acquired equal to Smith's basis (carryover basis) and also picks up Smith's holding period.

What are the advantages of tax-free transactions to sellers and buyers?

By participating in a tax-free transaction, the seller is provided the opportunity to exchange stock in the acquired corporation for stock of the buyer without the immediate recognition of gain. Because the seller will have a basis in the buyer's stock that is the same as the seller's old basis in the acquired corporation's stock (also known as a *substituted basis*), tax is deferred only until the acquired corporation's stock is ultimately sold. Where the acquired corporation is closely held and the buyer is publicly held, the seller may obtain greatly enhanced liquidity without a current tax.

Additionally, although death and taxes are both said to be inevitable, a seller participating in a tax-free transaction may utilize the former to avoid the latter. Under a long-standing but controversial rule in the Code, an individual's estate and beneficiaries may take a new, fair market value basis in the decedent's properties at his or her death. Thus, a seller may avoid the payment of any tax on the buyer's stock received in exchange for the old acquired corporation stock by holding this new stock until the seller's death.

For the buyer, there are two principal advantages to a tax-free acquisition. First, if the buyer can use its stock in the transaction, it may not incur significant debt. Where equity financing in general is attractive from a buyer's point of view, it will often make sense to do so in a business acquisition. Second, although subject to certain limitations, the acquired corporation's tax attributes (including net operating loss carryovers) will remain usable after the acquisition.

Which kinds of transactions may qualify for tax-free treatment?

Every transaction involving an exchange of property is taxable unless otherwise specified in the Code. Thus, corporate acquisitions are generally taxable to the seller of stock or assets. However, several types of acquisition transactions may be tax-free to the seller, but only to the extent that the seller receives stock in the acquiring corporation (or in certain corporations closely affiliated with the acquiring corporation).

In general, tax-free acquisitions fall into three categories: statutory mergers, exchanges of stock for stock, and exchanges of assets for stock. Except for § 351 transactions (which are beyond the scope of this book), all available tax-free acquisition transactions are provided under § 368 of the Code. In all, considering the various permutations of its provisions, § 368 ultimately sets forth more than a dozen different varieties of acquisition reorganizations. The most commonly used forms of reorganizations are the Types A, B, C, and D reorganizations. (Others are Type F and G reorganizations and various hybrids.)

What is the rationale behind the tax authorities' permitting transactions in the form of tax-free reorganizations?

Transactions that qualify under § 368 of the Code for tax-free (or tax-deferred, to be more precise) reorganization—either in part or in whole—are considered a shuffling of assets, or in more technical terms a mere readjustment of a continuing business enterprise that results in a continuity of investment.

What are the main categories of tax-free reorganizations?

Generally, there are four types of tax-free reorganizations: (1) *acquisitive transactions*, in which one business enterprise effectively acquires or otherwise combines with a second business enterprise; (2) *divisive transactions*, which can include a spin-off, split-off, split-up, and other form of divestiture-related transaction; (3) *nondivisive, nonacquisitive transactions* (rarely sought after by taxpayers; the provisions historically were used by the IRS to attack liquidation-reincorporation strategies in which the corporate taxpayer sought to generate tax losses or a step-up in the basis of its assets); and (4) *bankruptcy transactions*. This chapter includes a discussion of acquisitive tax-free reorganizations and a limited discussion of recapitalizations (nondivisive, nonacquisitive transactions).

STRUCTURING TAX-FREE REORGANIZATIONS

Where in the Code can I find the requirements for qualifying a transaction under the tax-free reorganization rules?

The key tax-free reorganizations mentioned above—Types A through C—are contained within § 368 and the IRS's regulations promulgated thereunder.

How does a transaction qualify as tax-free under § 368?

To qualify as tax-free reorganizations under § 368, all acquisitive reorganizations must meet three nonstatutory requirements. First, the reorganization must have a *business purpose*. That is, a transaction must be motivated by a legitimate business purpose other than tax avoidance. This requirement arises most frequently in the context of divisive reorganizations, which are beyond the scope of this book. The second requirement, probably the most burdensome, is the *continuity of proprietary interest* requirement. Third, the acquiring corporation must satisfy the *continuity of business enterprise* requirement. The second and third requirements are discussed in more detail below.

What is continuity of proprietary interest?

Continuity of proprietary interest is a legal doctrine that frequently arises in applying the Code's tax-free reorganization rules to a specific transaction. The general reasoning behind the continuity of interest doctrine is that a reorganization is the amalgamation of two corporate enterprises. Accordingly, the equity owners of both enterprises must continue to be owners following the transaction. The continuity of interest requirement is intended to prevent transactions resembling sales from being accorded tax-free treatment. Stock typically maintains a shareholder's continuity of proprietary interest in a business, while debt and cash do not.

What is continuity of business enterprise?

Continuity of business enterprise is a second legal doctrine that frequently arises in applying the Code's tax-free reorganization rules to a specific transaction. Generally, the doctrine requires that the acquirer either (1) continue the acquired corporation's "historic business" or (2) use a "significant portion" of the acquired corporation's "historic business assets" in a business. The term "significant portion" takes a relative meaning, that is, the portion of assets that are considered significant are relative to their importance in the operation of the target's business. However, all other facts and circumstances, such as the net fair market value of those assets, are also considered. If the acquired corporation has more than one line of business, the acquirer is only required to continue one of the target's lines, although the transaction is still subject to the "significant portion" requirement. Alternatively, the Code generally permits the acquirer to use the target's assets in *any* business—not just the acquired corporation's historic business.

What are some examples of the continuity of business enterprise requirement?

Regulation § 1.368–2 of the Code provides a handful of examples. In one example, the acquirer (A) manufactures computers, and the target (T) manufactures components for computers. T sells all its output to A. On January 1, 2016, A decides to buy imported components only. On March 1, 2016, T merges into A. A continues buying imported components but retains T's equipment as a backup source of supply. The use of the equipment as a backup constitutes use of a significant portion of T's historic business assets, thus establishing continuity of business enterprise. A is not required to physically continue T's business in this illustration.

In a second example, the target (T) is a manufacturer of boys' and men's trousers. On January 1, 2015, as part of a plan of reorganization, T sells all of its assets to a third party for cash and purchases a highly diversified portfolio of stock and bonds. As part of the plan, T operates an investment business until July 1, 2018. On that date, the plan of reorganization culminates in a transfer by T of all its assets to an acquirer (A), a regulated investment company, solely in exchange for A voting stock. The continuity of business interest requirement is not met. T's investment activity is not its historic business, and the stocks and bonds are not T's historic business assets.

What is a Type A reorganization?

A *Type A reorganization* (named after its alphabetic place in § 368) is very simply "a statutory merger or consolidation." This type of reorganization has other, more complex names, such as *reorganization not solely for voting stock*, as distinct from a *B reorganization*, which *is* solely for voting stock (see below). It is also referred to as a *tax-free forward merger*, as opposed to the taxable forward merger and taxable reverse merger forms discussed earlier (there is no tax-free reverse merger). To qualify for a Type A reorganization, the most important consideration is whether the shareholders of the selling corporation (the target, or T) maintain continuity of proprietary interest by owning stock in the acquiring corporation (the acquirer, or A). In order to satisfy the IRS's advance ruling requirements, the parties generally should structure the transaction so that the acquirer pays at least 50% of the transaction consideration in the form of A stock—which can be either voting or nonvoting stock and may be common or preferred shares. The rest of the consideration (up to 50%) can be in the form of cash, debt, or property (commonly referred to as "boot").

If the acquirer is a subsidiary of another corporation, may it use its parent's stock as transaction consideration in a Type A reorganization?

Yes. In the event the acquirer is a controlled subsidiary of another corporation (the acquirer's parent or, in tax parlance, a "controlling corporation"), target shareholders can receive parent stock for their shares if (1) no acquirer (i.e., subsidiary) stock is used in the transaction, and (2) the transaction would otherwise have qualified as a Type A reorganization if acquirer stock had been used instead of parent stock. This alternative is particularly attractive if the parent is publicly traded but the acquirer subsidiary is not. In addition, if the parent is a holding company of other subsidiaries, the parent company stock may offer more diversification to the sellers.

How long must the target shareholders hold their new shares under a Type A reorganization?

The Code generally permits the target's shareholders to sell or otherwise dispose of their shares after the transaction, although the IRS may collapse all the transactions (i.e., view all steps of a transaction as a single, integrated transaction) in applying the continuity of interest test. In particular, the IRS must consider whether a subsequent disposal of shares is part of the overall "plan," for example, whether, prior to the transaction, the target's shareholders entered into a binding agreement to sell their shares postacquisition. In situations in which the IRS finds the subsequent disposal to be part of the overall transaction plan, the agency will treat the reorganization and disposal as one integrated transaction and will apply the continuity of interest test to the integrated transaction. This process is also known as the *step transaction doctrine* and is a fact-based test not subject to mechanical application of the Code. (It is important to note here, however, that the lack of a binding commitment may not be sufficient to overcome this test.)

Does the step transaction doctrine always work against the taxpayer's interest?

No. The step transaction doctrine can also work in the taxpayer's favor. This was highlighted in a 2001 revenue ruling (2001-46) in which the IRS collapsed a two-step reorganization involving a reverse triangular merger (which, as described below, has a 20% boot limitation) into a Type A reorganization (which, as noted above, has a more relaxed 50% limitation). In the ruling, the IRS addressed the situation where, in the first step, an acquirer (A) formed a new merger subsidiary (S) and merged S into a target corporation (T), which was the surviving corporation. (This structure is generally known as a *reverse triangular merger*.) The T shareholders exchanged all of their stock for a mix of consideration involving 70% A voting stock and 30% cash. In the second step, T was merged into A as part of the same overall plan. An advantage of this structure, which is illustrated in Figure 5-13, is that A does not need to obtain shareholder approval for the transaction. But if T merged into A directly (and without the interim transaction with S), A's shareholders may have a right to approve the transaction.

If the two steps were viewed individually, the first step would fail to qualify as a tax-free reverse triangular merger because, based on the requirements described in more detail later in this chapter, the fact that 30% of S's consideration to T shareholders was in the form of cash meant S acquired only 70%—not the requisite 80%—control of T in a single transaction using A voting stock. In that scenario, the first step of the

Figure 5-13 Integrated Transaction Illustration

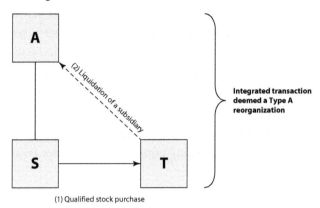

(1) Qualified stock purchase

transaction would be treated as a qualified stock purchase under § 338, and the second step would be treated as a § 332 liquidation. The implication to the constituent corporations could be that the acquisition is treated as a taxable event.

However, in Revenue Ruling 2001-46, the IRS determined that the step transaction doctrine should apply in the above situation. As a result, the Service collapsed the qualified stock purchase and subsequent merger into a statutory merger of T into A, rather than a qualified stock purchase followed by a liquidation. This permitted the transaction to qualify as a Type A reorganization, which permits up to 50% boot.

What is a creeping transaction?

A *creeping transaction* (sometimes also referred to as *creeping control*) is generally defined as two or more purchases by the acquirer of target stock as part of the same overall plan (i.e., to which the step transaction doctrine applies). Without the creeping transaction doctrine, the parties to a Type A reorganization could easily circumvent the spirit of the Code's reorganization rules. For example, the acquirer could structure a two-step transaction in which step one involved a taxable purchase of an otherwise prohibited percentage of target stock, say 75%, and step two involved a statutory merger that would otherwise qualify under the Type A reorganization rules. Where the two-step transaction is effected as part of the same overall plan, the IRS will evaluate the continuity of propriety interest requirement as if the transactions all occurred at the same time. In cases in which multiple transactions are not part of the same overall plan, however, the IRS will treat the prior purchases as "old and cold" (in tax parlance) and apply the continuity of propriety interest test to only the relevant transaction(s). As with the step transaction doctrine, the IRS makes a fact-based determination in evaluating a potential creeping transaction.

What is a "dropdown," and does it preclude a transaction from qualifying under the Type A rules?

In a *dropdown*, the acquirer transfers all or part of the recently acquired assets of the target to a subsidiary that the acquirer controls. The Code permits a dropdown in a transaction that otherwise qualifies as a Type A reorganization.

Must all target shareholders in a Type A reorganization receive the same mix of consideration?

No. The tax rules define whether the target's shareholders as a group—not individually—maintain a continuity of propriety interest. As a result, the acquirer may pay some target shareholders in cash or debt, but others in stock, so long as the minimum percentage is met overall. This point adds a degree of flexibility to the potential transaction structure and can allow the acquirer to meet the objectives of differing shareholder classes. It should be noted, however, that shareholders receiving cash or other forms of boot will be taxed on a prorata portion of their shares. The taxation of boot consideration is discussed later in this chapter.

May the acquirer sell a portion of the target's historic operating assets following a Type A reorganization?

Generally, yes. According to Revenue Ruling 2001-25 and Revenue Ruling 88-48, a transaction will still qualify as a Type A reorganization notwithstanding the sale of a portion of the target's assets after the merger and as part of a plan that includes the merger, where the proceeds from the sale continue to be held by the surviving corporation.

Does federal tax law ever permit the acquirer to pay less than 50% of the transaction consideration in stock and still have the transaction qualify as a Type A reorganization?

In some older tax case law, courts have permitted acquirers to pay less than 50% of the transaction consideration in stock. In a 1938 Supreme Court decision, for example, the court permitted Type A treatment to a transaction that involved 38% of the consideration paid in preferred stock. But as noted above, this lower threshold generally would not qualify for the IRS's advance ruling purposes and could potentially result in a lengthier and costlier transaction process. It is highly unadvisable to push the 50% threshold limit without the advice of competent tax legal counsel. If the transaction is found not to qualify as a Type A reorganization, all the transaction consideration will be taxable to the target's shareholders. This can create a tax-inefficient scenario for the sellers, and the acquirer would lose the target's tax characteristics (NOLs, high "earnings and profits," etc.).

How is nonstock consideration taxed in a Type A reorganization?

To the extent that the T shareholders receive boot—that is, consideration other than stock, such as cash or debt—such shareholders must recognize realized gain on the nonstock consideration. The prorata portion of the transaction that involves boot is generally treated as a taxable asset acquisition, as discussed above.

What is a Type B reorganization?

A *Type B reorganization* is a stock-for-stock exchange in which one company buys the stock of another company using only ("solely") its own stock. Under a Type B reorganization, the target becomes a subsidiary of the acquirer, which must "control" the target immediately after the transaction. Under § 368(a)(1)(B) of the Code, the term "control" is defined as ownership of 80% or more of the target's voting power and 80% or more of each class of the target's voting stock. Figure 5-14 provides an illustration.

Figure 5-14 Type B Reorganization

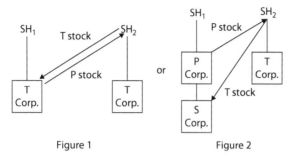

Figure 1   Figure 2

"B" Reorganization (Figure 1)
1. SH$_1$ owns 100% of the stock of P; SH$_2$ owns 100% of the stock of T
2. SH$_2$ transfers all the stock of T to P
3. In exchange for its stock of T, SH$_2$ receives shares of the stock of P

Triangular "B" Reorganization (Figure 2)
1. In a triangular "B" reorganization, P owns 100% of the stock of S
2. SH$_2$ transfers all the stock of T to S
3. In exchange for its stock of T, SH$_2$ receives shares of the stock of P

Must the acquirer purchase 80% of the target's voting power and stock in one transaction?

No. The Type B reorganization rules do not require a purchase of 80% or more of the target's voting power and stock all at once, but rather require only that the acquirer control the target immediately following the deal. If the acquirer uses only voting stock as the transaction consideration, the acquirer may purchase target stock in one or more tranches (i.e., a creeping transaction, as discussed above within the context of Type A reorganizations). But if more than one purchase is made, only the transaction that pushes the acquirer over the control threshold (80%) can qualify for tax-deferred treatment under the Type B reorganization rules. In the event the acquirer made one or more previous purchases of target stock using transaction consideration other than voting stock (e.g., cash, debt, or nonvoting stock), these previous purchases will disqualify the creeping transaction from Type B reorganization treatment unless the prior purchases are deemed "old and cold" (see above). There is no bright-line "old and cold" test, but Regulation § 1.368–2(c) includes examples that suggest purchases separated by 12 months or less would probably not qualify, whereas transactions separated by several years probably would.

What kind of stock may the acquirer use in a Type B reorganization?

The acquirer may use only voting stock in a Type B reorganization, and generally even the smallest amount of nonvoting stock will disqualify Type B treatment altogether. The voting rights associated with these shares are not restricted to just extraordinary corporate events, such as a merger, but extend unconditionally to votes on routine corporate matters.

Can the target or the target's selling shareholders receive cash under any circumstances in a Type B reorganization?

Yes, in some instances. There are three principal scenarios in which the Code permits the target or the target's shareholders to receive cash in a Type B reorganization: (1) the redemption of fractional shares by the acquirer; (2) payment of the target's transaction expenses (but not the target shareholders' transaction expenses), such as accounting, legal, and other reorganization costs; and (3) buyouts of dissenting minority shareholders who object to the transaction. Under this third exception, only the target or other target shareholders may purchase the dissenting shareholders' stock. The acquirer may not purchase such stock, nor may the acquirer indirectly provide the funds for these purchases. To the extent that the T shareholders receive boot, such shareholders must recognize realized gain on the nonstock consideration. The prorata portion of the transaction that involves boot is generally treated as a taxable stock acquisition, as discussed above.

What about earnouts, holdbacks, and other forms of contingent consideration? Are they permitted under a Type B reorganization?

Generally speaking, the Code permits contingent consideration in Type B reorganizations assuming, of course, that the contingent consideration is paid only in voting stock. In an *earnout*, the selling shareholders are entitled to additional consideration if the target meets certain financial milestones postclosing. (Chapter 4 discusses earnouts in more detail.) In a *holdback*, the selling shareholders are entitled to additional consideration assuming a certain representation made at the time of closing is later confirmed to be accurate.

Does the step transaction doctrine apply to a Type B reorganization?

Yes. Accordingly, if the acquirer redeems a selling shareholder's shares for cash postreorganization, the redemption may disqualify the entire transaction from Type B treatment if the acquirer agreed to redeem the target shareholder's shares as part of the broader transaction.

Are dropdowns permitted in a Type B reorganization?

Assuming the transaction otherwise qualifies as a Type B reorganization, the acquirer is permitted to transfer the target's assets to a controlled subsidiary after the reorganization.

If the acquirer is a subsidiary of another corporation, may it use its parent's stock as transaction consideration in a Type B reorganization?

Yes. Similar to a Type A reorganization, the acquirer may exchange the voting stock of a controlling corporation (i.e., the acquirer's parent) for target stock, assuming that (1) no acquirer stock is used in the transaction, and (2) the transaction would otherwise have qualified as a Type B reorganization if acquirer stock had been used instead of parent stock.

What is a Type C reorganization?

A *Type C reorganization* is a transaction in which one company buys "substantially all" of the assets of another company using its own voting stock, and the target corporation subsequently liquidates. The IRS defines "substantially all" as either (1) 90% of the target's net assets (i.e., assets less liabilities—the book value of the assets acquired), or (2) 70% of the target's gross assets (measured at fair market value). In some situations, courts have approved Type C reorganizations that involved

Figure 5-15 Type C Reorganization

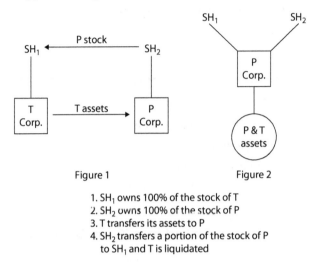

Figure 1   Figure 2

1. SH$_1$ owns 100% of the stock of T
2. SH$_2$ owns 100% of the stock of P
3. T transfers its assets to P
4. SH$_2$ transfers a portion of the stock of P
   to SH$_1$ and T is liquidated

asset percentages below these thresholds, particularly where the target retains liquid assets, such as cash, in order to pay creditors. However, if the target redeems stock held by dissenting shareholders for assets, the IRS will count such assets toward the "substantially all" test described above (assuming the redemptions are part of the overall reorganization). A Type C reorganization is also sometimes referred to as a *practical merger* because, although the transaction consideration flows into the target (and not directly to the target's shareholders), the Code requires the target to liquidate following the reorganization and distribute the acquirer stock and the target's remaining assets and liabilities to the target's shareholders. Figure 5-15 provides an illustration.

Must the target corporation always liquidate following a Type C reorganization?

In rare cases, the IRS has waived this requirement. These have generally been limited to rare situations in which (1) the selling company's shareholders all intend to reincorporate the target's remaining assets, and (2) the new corporation's shares would be held in exactly the same ownership percentages as the target, but (3) it is generally impractical for the target's shareholders to do so. However, even in these cases, the IRS will tax the target corporation and its shareholders as if the target had liquidated the remaining assets and the shareholders had subsequently contributed them to form a new corporation. So, from a practical perspective, there is probably little difference.

Can the target receive any consideration other than voting stock of the acquirer under any circumstances in a Type C reorganization?

While the acquirer generally must use voting stock to compensate the target, there are a number of exceptions (sometimes referred to as *boot relaxation rules*) in which the acquirer may use consideration other than voting stock. First, the acquirer can assume liabilities of the target without violating the "solely for voting stock" requirement. Second, the acquirer can use stock of its parent as transaction consideration (see below). Third and finally, the acquirer may use cash or other non-voting-stock consideration if the transaction involves assets with at least 80% of the fair market value of the target's total assets. In the case of this third exception, the dollar value of any liabilities assumed by the acquiring corporation, and the dollar value of any liability to which any asset acquired by the acquiring corporation is subject, shall be treated as cash paid to the target corporation.

Regulation § 1.368–2(d)(2) provides an example of the third exception. Assume, for instance, that Corporation T has assets with a fair market value of $100,000 and liabilities of $10,000. In exchange for these assets, Corporation A transfers $82,000 worth of its own voting stock, assumes the $10,000 in liabilities, and pays $8,000 in cash to Corporation T, which subsequently liquidates. The transaction qualifies as a Type C reorganization even though Corporation A pays cash for a portion of Corporation T's assets (either directly or indirectly by assuming liabilities). The dollar value of Corporation T's liabilities plus the deemed cash involved ($18,000 combined) is less than 20% of the fair market value of its assets ($100,000).

On the other hand, if the assets of Corporation T worth $100,000 were subject to $50,000 in liabilities, an acquisition of all the assets, subject to the liabilities, for any consideration other than solely voting stock of Corporation A would not qualify as a Type C reorganization; the liabilities of Corporation T ($50,000) are in excess of 20% of the fair market value of its assets ($100,000). However, if Corporation A were interested in acquiring all of Corporation T's assets, the parties might consider a Type A reorganization instead.

To the extent that the T shareholders receive boot, such shareholders must recognize realized gain on the nonstock consideration. The prorata portion of the transaction that involves boot is generally treated as a taxable asset acquisition, as discussed above.

Can creeping acquisitions arise in a Type C reorganization?

Yes, though the area is not well settled from a legal perspective. While a Type C reorganization is by definition a stock-for-assets exchange, a creeping acquisition can occur in two scenarios. First, a creeping acquisition may arise where the acquirer purchases more than 20% of the target's assets for non-voting-stock consideration and subsequently acquires some or all of the remaining assets solely for voting stock. In this case, the best advice is to follow the step transaction doctrine—if both the first and second transactions were part of the same overall plan, the IRS would probably disqualify the second transaction for Type C reorganization treatment.

Second, a creeping acquisition may arise in certain historical transactions where the acquirer already owns more than 20% or more of the target's stock, acquires all of the target's assets solely for voting stock, and the target subsequently liquidates and distributes the acquirer stock to the target's shareholders. In the only adjudicated example of note, the federal Court of Appeals for the Second Circuit held in a 1958 case that this transaction structure violates the Type C reorganization rules because the acquirer purchased more than 20% of the target's assets in the liquidation of the target in exchange for the target stock the acquirer previously owned. However, the IRS subsequently promulgated Regulation § 1.368–2(d)(4)(i), which states that the prior acquisition of a target corporation's stock by an acquiring corporation generally will not by itself prevent the "solely for voting stock" requirement in a Type C reorganization from being satisfied for transactions occurring after December 31, 1999. Even under this exception, however, the step doctrine still applies.

This creeping acquisition problem likely would not arise where the acquirer previously owned less than 20% of the target's stock because the boot relation rules discussed above would create an exemption. Nor would this problem likely arise where the acquirer previously owned more than 80% of the target, as the transaction would probably qualify as a tax-free liquidation of a subsidiary under §§ 332 and 337 of the Code.

Are dropdowns permitted in a Type C reorganization?

Assuming the transaction otherwise qualifies as a Type C reorganization, the acquirer is permitted to transfer the target's assets to a controlled subsidiary after the reorganization.

If the acquirer is a subsidiary of another corporation, may it use its parent's stock as transaction consideration in a Type C reorganization?

Yes. Similar to Type A and Type B reorganizations, the acquirer may exchange the voting stock of a controlling corporation (i.e., its parent) for target stock, assuming that (1) no acquirer stock is used in the transaction, and (2) the transaction would otherwise have qualified as a Type C reorganization if acquirer stock had been used instead of parent stock.

What is a Type D reorganization?

A *Type D reorganization* is a transaction in which a company transfers its assets down into a subsidiary. This kind of transaction would disqualify a company from meeting the requirements of § 355 (spin-offs), although there are still some complicated loopholes here. Type D reorganizations are generally outside the scope of this book and are not discussed in substantially more detail.

What is a forward triangular merger, and when might an acquirer consider using this structure?

A *forward*, or *direct, triangular merger* (also known as a *forward*, or *direct, subsidiary merger*) is a form of tax-free reorganization. The structure generally involves the acquirer (A) creating a new, wholly owned acquisi-tion subsidiary (S) into which A contributes A stock tax-free under § 351 of the Code. The target (T) is then merged into S under state law (and dis-solves), with the former T shareholders receiving A stock in exchange for their T stock. S is the surviving corporation after the reorganization and remains a wholly owned subsidiary of A.

An acquirer might structure a forward triangular merger if it wishes to keep the target corporation's liabilities segregated in a separate subsid-iary, as even using a dropdown structure as discussed above can poten-tially open up the acquirer to legal liability beyond the target's book value. In addition, A's shareholders are not required to vote on the deal, since A is technically not a party to the deal. Since A is the only shareholder of S, the structure can streamline the shareholder approval process and cut down on considerable time and expense—particularly if A is a widely held corporation.

What are the requirements to qualify for a forward triangular merger?

A forward triangular merger functions like a hybrid of Type A and Type C reorganizations (acquiring 90% of net assets or 70% of gross assets), so it may not come as a surprise that the requirements are similar. In order to qualify for tax-free treatment, the transaction must meet the following requirements:

- S must acquire substantially all of the assets of T, with "substantially all" being defined in the context of a Type C reorganization, as described above.
- The reorganization would have qualified as a Type A reorganization but for the fact that T is merged into S instead of its controlling corporation A.
- S may not use its own stock, only that of A, as consideration in the transaction. Consistent with the Type A reorganization requirements, S may generally use its own debt securities, cash, or other property for up to 50% of the consideration. To the extent that the T shareholders receive boot (consideration other

than stock, including cash or debt), such shareholders must recognize realized gain on the nonstock consideration. The prorata portion of the transaction that involves boot is generally treated as a taxable asset acquisition, as discussed above.

CONCLUSION

This chapter has helped dealmakers "render unto Caesar" as the old imperative goes, without rendering too much. We've discussed general tax issues and legal entity choice, and reviewed basic M&A transaction structures, considering their tax implications. In the next chapter, the reader will finally get the payoff for the hard work of mastering this technical material: the challenge and satisfaction of building a transaction model.

CHAPTER 6

Building a Transaction Model

On two occasions I have been asked, 'Pray, Mr. Babbage, if you put into the machine wrong figures, will the right answers come out?' ... I am not able rightly to apprehend the kind of confusion of ideas that could provoke such a question.

> —*Charles Babbage,* Passages from the Life of a Philosopher, *1864*

Garbage in, garbage out.

> —*Attributed to George Fuechsel, IBM, late 1950s*

INTRODUCTION

At long last, we arrive at the final phase of M&A valuation and financial modeling—building a transaction model. To get here, we had to clear away the clutter of competing M&A valuation approaches by identifying the two that are most essential: comparable companies/transactions and DCF analysis. Dominant on Wall Street, these approaches can be complementary. One is solidly based on a known past (what valuations have peer companies received in the marketplace?), the other on a predictable future (what kind of free cash flow can this deal generate?). But value is one thing and payment is another. So we considered two real-world game-changers: contingent payments (paying for the deal more slowly) and taxes (structuring the deal to pay less if legally possible). In this process, we were preparing you, the reader, to build a sturdy M&A valuation model that can stand the test of time. Are you ready?

The discussion that follows walks through the process of building a transaction model, drawing upon all the depth of knowledge that you have accumulated so far in this text, and includes:

- Building a flexible assumptions tab
- Creating a Sources & Uses table
- Establishing expected synergies and cost savings
- Preparing a purchase price allocation
- Constructing a proforma income statement and balance sheet
- Producing a proforma cash flow reconciliation
- Conducting an accretion/dilution analysis
- Performing various sensitivity analyses

One final point—readers who wish to download electronic copies of the model discussed in this chapter, as well as other useful M&A content, should visit www.ARTofMA.com.

ASSUMPTIONS TAB

What is an assumptions tab?

An *assumptions tab* is one of the most important aspects of a flexible transaction model, as it summarizes all of the key inputs that drive the analysis. There are four key reasons to include a flexible and thoughtful assumptions tab in your model. First and foremost, it shows other decisionmakers your inputs. Often, you create a transaction model in order to secure financing, board approval, or counterparty support for your deal. That means that someone else is going to review your analysis. How can they truly understand how you derived your output (e.g., forecasts) unless you show them the inputs?

Second, you need the ability to efficiently change the assumptions behind your analysis. Build the assumptions tab in such a way that allows you to quickly change the numbers, updating the results throughout the entire model immediately. For example, your projections for an acquisition target might be driven by top-line growth of 8%, targeted margins of 20%, and a cost of debt of 8%. However, your audience might want to see how a downside economic scenario might impact your expected returns. A flexible assumptions tab enables the user to stress-test the model; change any of the above inputs in just one cell and it will automatically flow through to the rest of the statements.

Third, a well-constructed assumptions tab will help demonstrate your understanding of the business. Another party—perhaps a key investor—is going to review your assumptions and make a judgment about you and the amount of due diligence you have conducted leading up to the potential acquisition. If your assumptions are data driven and logical, you will likely instill confidence in your audience. Moreover, an elegant assumptions tab will allow you to react to countless "what-if" questions that your audience will inevitably throw your way.

Finally, an assumptions tab forces the analyst to put any inputs that are hard wired into the model in one location, thereby minimizing the chance for errors. *Hard wiring* (also known as *hard coding*) refers to entering a specific number, rather than formula, into a spreadsheet—a small nuance to financial modeling that can cause major problems if left unchecked. Even the most thoughtful analysis and conclusion about a potential transaction can be derailed by simple mistakes that often involve hard coding data throughout the output, thus disabling many of the quantitative analysis and sensitivity scenarios. There is an old saying on the Street—"garbage in, garbage out."

What are the key assumptions that should drive the transaction model?

An effective transaction model is flexible enough to allow you to exercise your growing expertise and creativity around deal terms and structure. More importantly, a thoughtful transaction model will enable all parties to consider a wide range of possible scenarios and to ultimately answer the question: Is this a fair deal? The assumptions tab will reflect all of the salient deal points: How much of the target is the buyer purchasing? What are the sources of funds? Can we toggle back and forth between a stock and asset deal to determine an optimal structure? What are the expected financial benefits from the combined company in terms of cost savings or increased revenue? What is the maximum price the buyer can pay before the deal will dilute EPS? What are the transaction fees? Each of these questions can be distilled down to an input cell on the assumptions tab.

The assumptions presented below are simply suggestions; the specific transaction you are contemplating may call for other assumptions. In any case, most or all of the deal assumptions should be grouped into a single tab of your model so that anyone can see, at a glance, what assumptions you are making.

What best practices should I keep in mind when creating the assumptions tab?

First and foremost, Figure 6-1 is merely a starting point. When developing your assumptions tab, it is critical to keep in mind that no two deals are the same. Beware of using "plug and chug" template models that are all-inclusive (overwhelming the reader with unwieldy detail), too "streamlined" (ignoring valuable structuring alternatives), or simply irrelevant (perhaps one designed to analyze a transaction in a completely different industry).

Second, as previously mentioned, avoid hard coding values within, or in place of, formulas. For example, when calculating interest expense, do not type into Excel, =80*.06, to calculate what 6% interest is on an $80 million bond. Instead, enter 80 and .06 into two separate cells on the assumptions tab, and then draw on those inputs to calculate the answer in the body of the analysis (or output). Not only will this provide you with more flexibility to change variables independently, it mitigates the risk of inadvertently leaving a stale number in a random cell—potentially disrupting the entire model and, more importantly, derailing the deal.

Third, some of the model outputs—such as IRRs and payback periods—may be referenced back to this tab, making it easy for the user to see the bottom-line impact of even modest changes to a deal's structure and terms. For instance, what happens to IRRs if top-line growth slows from 8% to 4%? Linking some of the financial returns back to your assumptions tab will save you time as you explore different transaction scenarios.

Last but not least, any cells that contain model inputs—for instance, the target's valuation or the percentage of consideration that will be paid in cash—should be in blue font, whereas any cells that contain a formula

Figure 6-1 Selected Transaction Assumptions

Valuation
Transaction size
Percentage acquired
Implied valuation
Implied multiple(s)

Financial
Revenue growth rates
Fee concessions
Expense assumptions
Capacity constraints (of PPE or human talent)

Structure
Mix of consideration (cash, equity, debt, assumed liabilities)
Amount paid at close
Asset or stock deal
Tax elections

Sources of Acquisition Currency
Cash
Debt financing (amount, term, and pricing)
Equity financing (issued in exchange vs. raised externally)
Seller financing (amount, term, and pricing)
Contingent consideration

Transaction Fees
M&A advisory fees
Legal fees
Financing fees
Other transaction fees (e.g. accounting, etc.)

Synergies and Cost Savings
Source
Amount
Timing

Purchase Price Allocation
Step-up of target's fixed assets
Depreciation period (years)
Amount of excess purchase price to allocate to intangibles
Amortization period (years)

Other
Tax rate

or other output should be in black text. It's a simple tip, yet an invaluable one. The user of the model needs to understand what data drives the analysis, so that it can be "tweaked." Blue font in an Excel spreadsheet with a white background leaps from the computer screen but looks like regular font when printed out on a black and white printer.

One final point that may save your deal and your sanity one day—before you hand off your model, *always* print it out in its entirety and hand check as many of the calculations as possible. You are likely to find mistakes in print that you miss on screen. Just as importantly, you may discover that you completely forgot to format the print area (a personal pet peeve!).

Appendix 6A to this chapter contains a sample assumptions tab that drives the full transaction model that we discuss later in this chapter.

SOURCES & USES TABLE

What is a Sources & Uses table?

Creating a Sources & Uses table is an important component of building a transaction model, as it provides a high-level overview of the deal. A *Sources & Uses table* summarizes how the acquirer's funds will be used in a deal. How much is the buyer paying in cash versus stock? Is the buyer borrowing money and, if so, how much and from whom? How much of this cash is going to the selling shareholders versus paying down debt or covering transaction costs?

In the plainest form, the sources illustrate where the money is coming from and the uses summarizes where it is going. This table, which may appear either on the assumptions tab or as a standalone tab of the model, must balance—that is, the sources of capital must equal the uses of capital. Importantly, this table should be linked to the assumptions section of the transaction model so that the buyer can consider various transaction structures and financing alternatives. Although the table sounds simple, there are situations in which the table flagged a capital shortfall well before it "blew up" a deal.

(Too) many years ago, a business school professor of two of this book's authors suggested that his students think about a Sources & Uses table in the context of buying a house. A buyer and seller agree to financial terms for the purchase and sale of a home. Who are the various parties to be paid at close, how much does each get, and where is the buyer getting the money? Let's start with the "uses" side of the table—assume a purchase price of $500,000; the seller has a mortgage of $350,000 on the home, while the broker is due a commission of 6% (or $30,000) from the

Figure 6-2 Sources & Uses Table for the Purchase of a $500,000 Home

Sources	Amount	% of Total	Uses	Amount	% of Total
Bank Mortgage	$400,000	80%	Pay Down Mortgage	$350,000	80%
Cash on Hand	100,000	20%	Broker's Commission	30,000	6%
			Net Cash to Seller	120,000	24%
Total Sources	**$500,000**	**100%**	**Total Uses**	**$500,000**	**100%**

seller at closing. The buyer has $100,000 of cash in the bank, and needs to borrow the balance from a bank. Figure 6-2 contains a Sources & Uses table for this hypothetical home purchase.

The sources of capital in this transaction include the buyer's $100,000 of cash on hand and a $400,000 bank mortgage, for a total of $500,000. This cash is first used to pay down the seller's existing mortgage of $350,000. Next, the broker is due a $30,000 commission at closing. The net cash to the seller of $120,000 is the *plug*, or difference between the purchase price less the identified liabilities that makes the Sources & Uses table balance. At its most fundamental level, a Sources & Uses table in a corporate acquisition works the same way.

What sources and uses are common in an M&A transaction?

The list of potential sources of capital can be quite long, but common examples include the following:

- The buyer's cash on hand
- New bank or mezzanine debt
- Assumption of target's existing debt
- Seller financing
- Assumption of minority interest
- Earnouts or other forms of contingent consideration
- Rollover of equity from selected sellers
- Equity of the buyer

The potential uses of capital are far more wide-ranging, and ultimately depend upon the target's capitalization as well as transaction structure. For instance, is the seller required to pay down the target's debt at close or has the buyer agreed to assume these obligations? Also, are the sellers allowed to dividend out excess working capital at close or does it all stay in the business? Common uses of capital in a corporate acquisition include the following:

- Working capital adjustment
- Refinanced debt
- Assumed debt
- Escrow account to cover representations and warranties
- Capitalized financing fees
- Transaction costs
- Rollover of existing equity
- Estimated tax payments (if appropriate)

Appendix 6B to this chapter contains a sample Sources & Uses table that reflects the full transaction model that we discuss later in this chapter.

MODELING SYNERGIES AND COST SAVINGS

Can a transaction model capture anticipated deal synergies?

Yes. In fact, this is one of the purposes of modeling. After all, synergy is a form of value creation, or ways in which management increases the worth of shareholders' investment in a business. Value creation, itself, can refer to a wide variety of scenarios:

- Manufacturing gains from converting raw materials into finished goods, and subsequently selling them at a higher price;
- Scale economies from increasing output rates, thereby spreading fixed costs over a larger number of units;
- Cost savings from headcount reductions of duplicative roles; and

- Production efficiencies by redesigning workflow into a series of repeatable tasks, and exchanging lower-cost workers for higher-skilled labor.

Synergy is often used as an overarching term that refers to value creation in the M&A context—particularly in the case of a strategic buyer. The term refers to the extra value that an acquirer can achieve by combining with another business: hence the cliché: "When does $1 + 1 = 3$ in M&A? One word: synergy!" In Chapter 1 we mentioned vertical synergy being possible through economies of scale, and horizontal synergy accruing from increase in market share. In Chapter 2 we described transactions seeking cost and revenue synergies. In this chapter we will show how the financial effects of these and other forms of synergy can be captured in a transaction model.

Is synergy only possible in the M&A context?

The undertone of the term synergy is that the value-add is generally only possible if two businesses were to combine, and that neither could fully achieve them without the other. In fact, if either company could generate comparable value creation by going it alone, what would be the point of the added risk and complexity of a business combination?

Now, it's entirely possible that the target is simply undermanaged; that a more skilled management team could step into the existing business and increase profits vis-à-vis a more thoughtful business plan and/or improved execution. New management might have the ability to sell the company's product into new markets, relocate production to lower-cost regions, recapitalize the balance sheet to a more efficient structure, and so on. This is not a hypothetical situation: in fact, there are countless private equity firms and other financial sponsors, with billions of managed assets, implementing this strategy.

The authors would argue that improvements to a standalone business's operations or capital structure are not synergies in the classic sense of the word, but rather profit improvements. But from a modeling standpoint, there are clearly strong parallels between synergies in the M&A context and revenue increases, cost-outs, and balance sheet restructurings of standalone businesses. As such, most of this chapter is relevant beyond strategic M&A transactions.

What are the various types of synergies that can be reflected in a transaction model?

Broadly speaking, synergies fall into one of two categories: revenue synergies and cost synergies. *Revenue synergies* refer to the opportunity of two combined businesses to generate more revenue than either firm would independently. Very often, this involves selling more products or services or raising prices due to a business combination. Commonly referenced examples include the following:

- Marketing and selling complementary products
- Cross-selling into a new customer base
- Sharing distribution channels
- Accessing new markets (e.g., through the target's existing expertise)
- Eliminating competition in the marketplace

The other major type of synergy is *cost synergies*, which are also referred to as *cost savings*. These are expense reductions due to operating improvements implemented after the transaction. Potential sources of cost synergies include:

- Eliminating redundant headcount
- Shutting down surplus facilities
- Reducing overhead (e.g., consolidating functions such as accounting, IT, and marketing)
- Increasing purchasing power (i.e., enhancing bargaining power with suppliers due to greater combined size)

This book generally uses the term cost savings rather than cost synergies, because it is the term that the authors are more accustomed to encountering over the years. However, the terms are generally interchangeable.

How do I go about identifying potential synergies in a transaction?

There are a variety of ways in which synergies might appear in a transaction, the vast majority of which are heavily dependent upon the specific companies involved. Many times, synergies are a byproduct of a thoughtful due diligence process. Areas to consider include the following:

- Leveraging the enhanced purchasing power of the combined organization, thereby driving down purchasing costs;
- Scaling back general and administrative expenses in areas such as human resources, accounting, finance, and so on;
- Trimming sales and marketing expenses, particularly if a single salesforce can manage the offerings of both the buyer and the seller;
- Consolidating excess infrastructure, such as warehouses, R&D facilities, distribution centers, etc.; and
- Eliminating redundancies among management levels.

How difficult is it to realize synergies?

In practice, synergies are "easier said than done." While cost synergies are difficult to achieve, revenue synergies are even harder. This is often because it can be difficult to predict, with accuracy, how cleanly the respective companies' salesforces will integrate or whether there might be any channel conflict that follows. Chapter 2 in this book contains an excellent example of failed revenue synergies in the merger of the manufacturer of aluminum wheels for heavy-duty trucks and the manufacturer of brake kits for the same kinds of trucks. On paper, the deal appeared to pose terrific cross-selling opportunities. However, in practice, the sales channels turned out to be entirely different.

The discussion in Chapter 2 also highlights the little-discussed possibility of revenue *attrition* from an acquisition. This was the case when two LTL companies, Roadway Corporation and Yellow Corp., merged in the early 2000s. Rather than creating revenue synergies, the combination actually led to revenue losses as some shippers who used both Roadway and Yellow for LTL trucking elected to resource some of the business to a third trucking company postmerger for risk management purposes.

How do I factor synergies and cost savings into my transaction model?

Synergies and cost savings have a direct impact on the transaction model. Recall the cliché we mentioned earlier, "When does 1 + 1 = 3? Synergies!" Like many clichés, there is an element of truth to this statement.

The process of creating a proforma income statement generally involves combining the standalone financials of both a buyer and a target, and then adjusting these subtotals with the expected synergies and cost savings. So really, the formula above should be restated: rather than, "1 + 1 = 3," it should read, "1 + 1 + synergies = 3."

In terms where the proforma income statement should reflect the synergies and cost savings, revenue synergies typically will fold into consolidated sales, vendor savings will offset the consolidated cost of sales line, and other overhead savings will supplement consolidated SG&A expenses.

We illustrate an example later in this chapter. Please also see Appendix 6C for a sample synergies and cost savings schedule and Appendix 6E for a sample proforma income statement.

PURCHASE PRICE ALLOCATION

What is a purchase price allocation?

A *purchase price allocation* (PPA) involves allocating the total purchase price to a target's individual assets and liabilities. This analysis is required under U.S. GAAP if the transaction involves a change of control.[1] A separate PPA analysis may be required for tax purposes,[2] although the discussion that follows focuses on the impact of a PPA on the combined companies' GAAP financials.

What exactly happens in a PPA analysis?

In a PPA analysis, a buyer allocates the transaction consideration it paid to acquire the target—including cash and stock, as well as liabilities assumed—across all of the target's identifiable assets and liabilities, valuing each item at fair value as of the acquisition date. This analysis includes a valuation of the target's entire balance sheet, including both tangible and intangible assets. To the extent the purchase price is greater than the fair value of the target's identifiable assets and liabilities (which is frequently the case), such excess is allocated to goodwill. For the purposes of an accounting-based PPA analysis, *fair value* is defined as "the price that would be received to sell an asset or paid to transfer a liability in an orderly transaction between market participants at the measurement date."[3]

Figure 6-3 contains a graphical representation of how three components—fair value of tangible assets, fair value of intangible assets, and goodwill—build up to the definition of purchase price in a PPA.

Some tangible assets and liabilities—such as cash, accounts receivable, and accounts payable—are usually straightforward to value in a PPA; these are readily identifiable and there rarely is a material change to the carrying value on the target's balance sheet.[4] Other tangible assets—such as inventory and fixed assets—require a little more work. The buyer may need to adjust the carrying values based on independent appraisals; but here again, this part of the process is fairly intuitive.

Identifying and valuing all of the target's intangible assets can be more challenging. *In many cases, the M&A transaction will actually create new assets and liabilities that did not previously exist on the target's balance sheet.* Consider Microsoft's acquisition of 800 patents from America

Figure 6-3 Allocating Purchase Price Across a Target's Various Assets and Liabilities

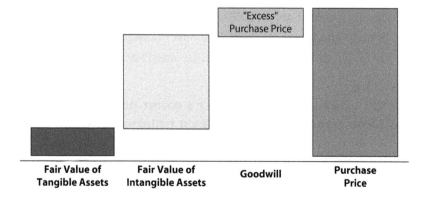

Online (AOL) in 2012. Much of the $1 billion that Microsoft paid were for assets that did not appear anywhere in AOL's financial statements; many investors had no clue that these assets existed, let alone that they represented more than a billion dollars in value.[5] These patents did not appear on AOL's balance sheet because AOL had developed them internally, and only a small portion of the resources invested into creating them could be capitalized under U.S. GAAP. The accounting rules are different for an acquirer of a patent, such as Microsoft in the case of AOL. Under U.S. GAAP, Microsoft capitalized the value of AOL's patents and amortized the expense of the purchase over the remaining lifetime of the patents.

Are situations like AOL, which had substantial hidden value on its balance sheet, rare?

It is actually quite common that a target has substantial intangible assets not reflected on its balance sheet. Rarely will there be a line item on a target's balance sheet that reads "internally developed software" or "customer lists," but these are in fact assets of the target in many transactions. A PPA analysis requires the buyer to methodically pour through the target's business for identifiable intangible assets such as these. The buyer must then determine whether each such asset has an identifiable remaining useful life (e.g., a patent or copyright) or if it has an indefinite life (e.g., a trademark). Each of these assets must be modeled differently.

Once the acquirer has accounted for all identifiable assets—both tangible and intangible—there will probably still be "excess" purchase price; that is, the deal value will be greater than the value of each individual asset, a concept that most readers will recognize as the target's goodwill. Accordingly, the final step in a PPA analysis is to allocate any excess purchase price to purchased goodwill. The buyer does not assign a useful life to goodwill, but rather tests the amount (at least) annually for impairment.

How do I determine whether I must create a new intangible asset on the target's balance sheet?

An acquirer should recognize an intangible asset (apart from goodwill) if it arises from contractual or legal rights, or if it is considered *separable*—i.e.,

Figure 6-4 Intangible Assets Commonly Valued in a Purchase
Price Allocation

Marketing-Related Intangibles	Customer-Related Intangibles
· Trademarks	· Customer lists
· Trade names	· Customer contracts
· Product (brand) lines	· Customer relationships
· Non compete agreements	
Contract-Related Intangibles	**Employment Contracts**
· Licensing agreements	· Technology-related intangibles
· Service contracts	· In-process research and development
· Lease agreements	· Patents
· Franchise agreements	· Software
· Operating rights	· Proprietary technology
· Broadcasting rights	· Trade secrets
· Use rights	

meaning that it is capable of being separated from the target and transferred, whether individually or in combination with a related asset or liability. Figure 6-4 summarizes some intangible assets that are commonly valued in a PPA.

How do I calculate the acquirer's purchase price?

The acquirer's purchase price is calculated as the value of the assets transferred by the acquirer (i.e., including cash), plus the liabilities assumed by the acquirer from the former owners and any equity issued by the acquirer. Transaction costs—such as direct payments to investment bankers, consultants, attorneys, appraisers, accountants, etc.—are treated as period expenses. As such, they are not capitalized as part of calculating the purchase price and should not be allocated to the target's assets and liabilities.

Can you illustrate a representative PPA analysis?

Consider the following example. Inland Technologies (Inland) is an upstart biotechnology firm that is in later-stage trials of a highly promising new drug. The company is all-but assured to conclude favorable Phase III trials upon closing a critical round of venture financing that is just about to close. Industry competitor, Argon Pharmaceuticals (Argon), faces a weak pipeline of new drugs and, with a slipping stock price, feels compelled to make a major statement to the financial markets. Argon agrees to acquire Inland for total purchase price of $250 million.

Inland has a simple balance sheet. The company has: (1) $5 million of cash in the bank; (2) $10 million of net property, plant & equipment (PP&E) on its balance sheet, although the appraised value is $12 million; and (3) an internally-created portfolio of patents that do not appear on Inland's balance sheet, but which are worth $125 million. The company has no liabilities.

Figure 6-5 illustrates the write-up of the balance sheet value of Inland's PP&E and the creation of two new balance sheet line items—a patent portfolio and purchased goodwill.

Accordingly, Argon would allocate its $250 million purchase price across Inland's assets as follows: (1) $5 million to cash; (2) $12 million to Inland's PP&E, which would be amortized over its useful economic life; (3) $125 million to a new asset, patent portfolio, which would be amortized over its remaining patent life; and (4) $108 million to goodwill, which would be tested annually for impairment.

Figure 6-6 bridges Inland's balance sheet value of $15 million to Argon's total purchase price of $250 million.

Figure 6-5 Example of Goodwill Calculation ($ in millions)

Inland's Assets	Book Value	Write-Up	Fair Value
Cash on hand	$5	$0	$5
Property, plant & equipment, net	10	2	12
Patent portfolio	–	125	125
Total value	15	127	142

Purchase Price Allocation		
Purchase price		$250
Less: Book value of net assets		(15)
Excess purchase price		235
Less: Write-up of net assets		
Property, plant & equipment, net	$2	
Patent portfolio	125	(127)
Goodwill		**$108**

Figure 6-6 Bridge from Book Value to Total Purchase Price (Not to Scale)

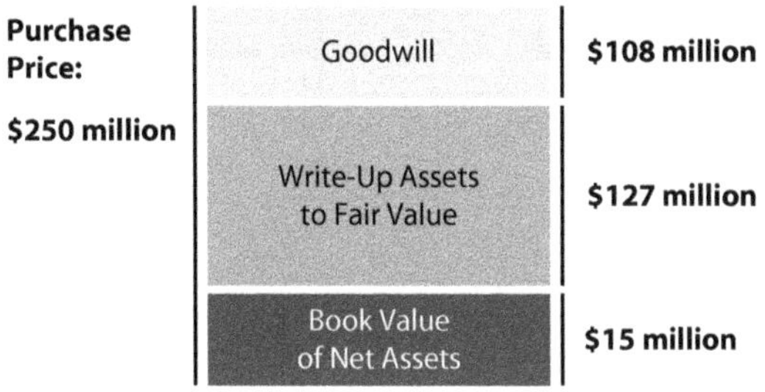

What if the purchase price is less than the fair value of the target's assets? How is that handled?

In the event the fair value of all identifiable assets is larger than the purchase price, the transaction is deemed a *bargain purchase* for accounting purposes. Although rare, a buyer in a bargain purchase must still write up the value of the target's tangible and identifiable intangible assets to fair value; but rather than having "negative goodwill," the buyer must recognize the difference between the target's identifiable net assets and the purchase price as a gain to current earnings. This gain has the effect of increasing goodwill from a would-be negative value to zero.

Let's revisit the Inland sale above, making a few tweaks to the assumptions. As mentioned previously, Inland is all-but assured to conclude favorable Phase III trials but is low on cash and needs to close a critical round of venture financing. Just as the deal is about sign, scandal hits the management team, causing irreparable damage to the company's brand—although the value of its technology remains intact. With no other alternative except to file bankruptcy, Inland sells to Argon at a distressed valuation of $100 million.

Figure 6-7 illustrates how Argon's low-ball price of $100 million is allocated across Inland's assets, and how the transaction generates a one-time earnings gain of $42 million.

Accordingly, Argon would allocate its $100 million purchase price across Inland's assets as follows: (1) $5 million to cash; (2) $12 million to Inland's PP&E, which will be amortized over its useful economic life; (3) $83 million to a new asset, patent portfolio, which will be amortized

Figure 6-7 Example of a Bargain Purchase ($ in millions)

Inland's Assets	Book Value	Write-Up	Fair Value
Cash on hand	$5	$0	$5
Property, plant & equipment, net	10	2	12
Patent portfolio	–	125	125
Total value	15	127	142

Purchase Price Allocation		
Purchase price		$100
Less: Book value of net assets		(15)
Excess purchase price		85
Less: Write-up of net assets		
Property, plant & equipment, net	$2	
Patent portfolio	125	(127)
Goodwill (Bargain Purchase)		**$42**

over its remaining patent life; and (4) $0 to goodwill. Argon reports a gain of $42 million in current earnings.

Figure 6-8 bridges Inland's balance sheet value of $15 million to Argon's total purchase price of $100 million (including the $42 million gain).

What is the effect of a PPA to our transaction model?

The biggest impact that a PPA has to the transactional model is that the accounting adjustments are likely to change the target's depreciation and amortization expense. As noted above, a PPA has the effect of either

Figure 6-8 Bridge from Book Value to Total Purchase Price (Bargain Purchase)

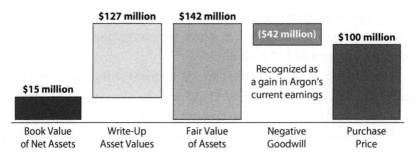

writing up, or writing down, the carrying value of many of the target's assets and liabilities. Often, the PPA creates new line items—such as a carrying value for the target's customer lists—on the acquirer's balance sheet that the target did not previously report on its balance sheet. Based on these new carrying values, the acquirer will recalculate the appropriate amount of depreciation and amortization.

Precisely how much new depreciation and amortization is created depends on a number of variables. However, the fundamentals of U.S. GAAP clearly still apply:

- Tangible assets are depreciated, as appropriate, over their useful economic lives;
- Intangibles with finite lives are amortized over their useful lives; and
- Intangibles with indefinite lives (like goodwill) are not amortized, but rather are tested for impairment.

More often than not, the PPA will result in a higher depreciation and amortization expense once the business is in the hands of the acquirer than what the target reported before the deal. It is important that the acquirer understand the target's postdeal expense structure—even for noncash line items such as depreciation and amortization—so that all parties can accurately forecast both GAAP-based earnings, as well as cash flows, after closing.

This understanding is particularly important when the acquirer is publicly traded: this is because the PPA can result in some unexpected earnings "quirks" that must be properly flagged for public investors, based on personal experience. Consider the acquisition of a manufacturing company. During the PPA, the value of the target's inventory is written up to fair value. This is a seemingly meaningless nuance but it can have dramatic effects on a company's financials. Consider, for instance, a target with 40% gross margins. Inventories valued at $60 (i.e., at cost) are actually worth $100 after processing. The acquirer therefore must write up the value of the inventory to $100, yet this leaves no booked profits when the inventory is later sold for that amount. Indeed, we have witnessed multiple acquirers—to the dismay of research analysts—announce acquisitions and then book little profit until the buyer turns the target's inventory postclosing. In such cases, we have seen the gross profit margin, as reported for book purposes, of an acquired manufacturing business compress overnight from 40% to 5% (or lower)—merely due to some accounting "fiction" until the buyer cycles through that acquired inventory. This has created unnecessary confusion on more than one earnings call!

So the target's depreciation and amortization expense is likely to increase as a result of a PPA?

More often than not, the answer is yes. Figures 6-9 and 6-10 expand upon the earlier illustration of Argon Pharmaceuticals' $250 million acquisition of Inland Technologies.

First, we calculate the proforma depreciation expense. Prior to the acquisition, Inland's annual depreciation expense was $2.0 million on property, plant, and equipment of $10.0 million. As noted in Figure 6-7, Argon writes up the value of this PP&E to $12.0 million as part of the deal. If we were to assume straight-line depreciation of this

Figure 6-9: Calculation of Proforma Depreciation Expense

Proforma Depreciation Expense ($000s)		
Current Depreciation Expense		$2.0
Write-Up of PP&E, net	$2.0	
Depreciation Period (yrs)	5.0	
Incremental Depreciation Expense		0.4
Proforma Depreciation Expense		**$2.4**

Figure 6-10 Calculation of Proforma Amortization Expense

Proforma Amortization Expense ($000s)		
Current Amortization Expense		$0.0
Write-Up of Patent Portfolio	$125.0	
Avg. Remaining Life (yrs)	12.0	
Incremental Amortization Expense		10.4
Proforma Amortization Expense		**$10.4**

$2.0 million write-up over five years, the incremental depreciation expense would be $400,000 annually. Combined with the preacquisition depreciation expense of $2.0 million, the proforma depreciation expense would be $2.4 million.

Next, we determine the proforma amortization expense following the write-up of Inland's patent portfolio. Prior to the acquisition, Inland did not have any amortization expense related to its patents because they were internally developed. As noted in Figure 6-5, Argon writes up the value of this patent portfolio to $125.0 million as part of the deal. If we were to assume straight-line depreciation of this amount over the remaining life of those patents (which, for sake of illustration, we have assumed is 12.0 years), the incremental amortization expense would be $10.4 million annually. Inland did not have any amortization expense prior to the acquisition, so this is also the company's proforma amortization.

Must I conduct a PPA even in a stock deal?

From a financial reporting standpoint, yes—whether the acquirer is buying the stock or assets of the target has no impact on whether a PPA is necessary. In either case, an acquirer must complete a PPA under U.S. GAAP provided that there is a change of control.

Federal income tax requirements are different. From a tax reporting perspective, a buyer must complete a PPA for either (1) an asset purchase, or (2) a stock purchase for which a § 338 election is made. As discussed in Chapter 5 of this book, an acquirer that makes a § 338 election accounts for a stock purchase as if it were an asset purchase.

What about contingent consideration? How is that treated in a PPA?

All contingent consideration is included in business combination accounting and is measured at fair value as of the date of the acquisition. Accordingly, contingent consideration—as well as contingent liabilities, for that matter—should be included in a PPA for financial reporting purposes.

(Although this chapter is focused primarily on PPAs for book purposes, it is worth noting that a tax-focused PPA generally does not include contingent consideration and liabilities.)

As described in Chapter 4, contingent consideration is an obligation of the acquirer to transfer additional transaction consideration to the target's former owners if certain future events occur or conditions are met. Such an obligation should be recorded as a liability on the buyer's books. By the same token, contingent consideration may also involve the seller refunding a portion of the purchase price if specified conditions are not met. The acquirer should record this right as an asset on its balance sheet.

As also discussed in Chapter 5, be sure not to confuse contingent consideration with compensation expense. That is, if the seller is required to perform certain services over the contingency period in order to earn the amount, or must still be employed by the combined entity at the conclusion of that period, the contingent payment is likely to be considered compensation rather than transaction consideration. Future payments such as these should be accounted for as an expense in future periods and therefore not be included in the purchase price valuation.

When during the deal process should I start thinking about a PPA?

The sooner, the better. A PPA might seem like a mere accounting afterthought to some, but the buyer's PPA can influence how much of the transaction consideration is taxed to the seller as capital gains versus ordinary income. As a result, the analysis can actually have a significant impact on the seller's aftertax proceeds.

In fact, the buyer and seller typically have competing incentives when it comes to the purchase price allocation.[6] The buyer wants more purchase price allocated to assets that can be recovered more quickly: inventory, accounts receivable, and equipment, for example. The seller wants more purchase price allocated to assets that will result in capital gain: goodwill being the most typical example. As a result, the PPA discussion should come up as part of the conversation around valuation and transaction structure.

PROFORMA INCOME STATEMENT
AND BALANCE SHEET

Doesn't it seem late in the modeling process to just now start building a proforma income statement and balance sheet?

One might say that building a transaction model is like baking a cake: it's built one layer at a time and the end product doesn't fully come together until the end.

Like layers in a cake, each step in the preceding discussion—building a flexible assumptions tab, creating a Sources & Uses table, establishing expected synergies and cost savings, and preparing a purchase price allocation—is required before we can start thinking about what the combined entities' proforma financial statements will look like. Each of these steps influences a wide range of variables: The assumptions tab reflects which growth scenario is discounted into the model; the Sources & Uses table summarizes capitalization; the expected synergies and cost savings affect margins; and the PPA impacts depreciation and amortization on both the income statement and cash flow reconciliation, as well as the carrying value of assets on the proforma balance sheet. Moreover, a transaction model is holistic; the entire model is interconnected—update an assumption on one tab and it will change the output on another.

The good news is that the transaction model starts to gain momentum once we have established a starting point for the preceding steps. Now that we have a framework of assumptions in place, we can proceed to constructing a proforma income statement, balance sheet, and cash flow reconciliation.

At its most fundamental core, constructing a proforma income statement comes down to adding together everything on the buyer and seller's income statements (i.e., from revenue down to net income) and, as appropriate, adjusting the combined line items to reflect synergies and cost savings, the new depreciation and amortization schedule, and the acquirer's updated capitalization. The analyst may also need to normalize the income statement for certain items that distort the picture of the business's true operating performance. Key examples would include transaction-related expenses, such as advisory or financing fees. This helps to ensure that the transaction model can provide an accurate basis for forward-looking analysis.

This is starting to feel a little overwhelming! Can you walk me through an example?

Sure. Let's walk through the build-up of all the components so far that lead to the proforma income statement and balance sheet. Assume Buyer agrees to acquire Target effective December 31, 2015. Below are some of the key deal terms:

- Valuation: $185 million for 100% of the equity
- Implied valuation: 8.6x for the Target, 10.0x for the Buyer
- Mix of consideration: 45% cash, 55% stock
- Buyer will issue new debt to fund a portion of the cash component
- Selling shareholders to deliver the Target unencumbered (i.e., pay down debt)
- Synergies/cost savings: Revenue, raw materials purchases, and SG&A

Build a Flexible Assumptions Tab

The assumption tab in Figure 6-11 summarizes all of the key drivers of the transaction structure. For simplicity sake, we only use one growth scenario. Accordingly, Figure 6-11 contains all the data points necessary to build out and drive a proforma income statement and balance sheet.

Create a Sources & Uses table

Figure 6-12 contains a Sources & Uses table based on these assumptions. Of the total $185 million purchase price, 55% (or $101.8 million) will be in Buyer stock and 45% (or $83.3 million) will be in cash. Of the $83.3 million in cash to be paid to the Target, $35 million will be used to redeem existing debt and $48.3 million will be distributed to the selling shareholders. The buyer finances this $83.3 million of cash from three sources: $25 million from a new bank line of credit, $50 million by issuing new subordinated debt, and the balance from cash on hand.

Figure 6-11 Assumptions Tab

Valuation		Deal Structure		
Transaction size	$185,000	(A)sset or (S)tock purchase?		S
% acquired	100.0%	338(h)(10) election (Y/N)?		N
Implied valuation	$185,000	**Transaction Fees**		
Target's Forward EBITDA ($)	$21,530	M&A advisory fees (%)		1.5%
Implied EBITDA Multiple (x)	8.6x	Other transaction fees (%)		1.0%

Consideration		Acquisition Debt		
Amount in cash ($)	$83,250	Facility	Bank Line	Sub Debt
Percentage of total mix	45.5%	Size of facility ($)	$25,000	$50,000
		Duration (yrs)	5.0	7.0
Amount in assumed liabilities ($)	$0	Interest rate (%)	6.5%	10.0%
Percentage of total mix	0.0%	Financing fees (%)	1.0%	3.0%
		Repayment schedule:		
Amount in Buyer stock ($)	$101,750	Year 1	$5,000	$0
Percentage of total mix	55.0%	Year 2	$5,000	$0
Price per share	$25.00	Year 3	$5,000	$0
# shares issued	4,070	Year 4	$5,000	$0
		Year 5	$5,000	$0

Synergies and Cost Savings			
Source	Revenue	Vendor	SG&A
Include (Y/N)?	Y	Y	Y
Amount:			
Year 1	2.0%	0.5%	1.0%
Year 2	4.0%	1.0%	3.0%
Year 3	6.0%	1.5%	3.0%
Year 4	6.0%	2.0%	3.0%
Year 5	6.0%	2.5%	3.0%

Purchase Price Allocation		
Assets:	Fair Value	Years
Cash and Equivalents	$0	
Accounts Receivable	$0	
Inventory	$0	
Other Current Assets	$0	
PP&E, net	$2,500	5
Customer Lists	$40,000	5
Liabilities:	Fair Value	Years
Accounts Payable	$0	
Accrued Expenses	$0	

Growth Assumptions		
Annual Changes in	Buyer	Seller
Revenue	2.5%	5.0%
Gross margins (bps)	10	20
SG&A	2.0%	3.5%
Dep'n & Amortization Expense	2.0%	7.0%
Tax rate	30.0%	N/A

Figure 6-12 Sources & Uses Table

Sources ($000s)	Amount	% of Total	Uses ($000s)	Amount	% of Total
Issue new stock	$101,750	53.2%	Buyer stock to sellers	$101,750	53.2%
Draw down on bank line	25,000	13.1%	Refinance Target's debt	35,000	18.3%
Issue subordinated debt	50,000	26.1%	Cash to Sellers	48,250	25.2%
Cash on hand	14,625	7.6%	Advisory fees	2,775	1.5%
			Financing fees	1,750	0.9%
			Other transaction fees	1,850	1.0%
Total Sources	**$191,375**	**100.0%**	**Total Uses**	**$191,375**	**100.0%**

$185 million of transaction consideration
($83.3 million in cash)

The deal requires $6.4 million in total transaction fees: (1) M&A advisory fees of $2.8 million (1.5% of transaction consideration); (2) financing fees of $1.75 million (1% for the bank line, 3% for the subordinated debt); and (3) other transaction fees of $1.9 million (1% of transaction consideration).

Establish expected synergies and cost savings

Next, we think through the various opportunities for synergies and cost savings. In this particular transaction, the Buyer and Target are in highly complementary business lines. As a result, the parties see three areas for potential savings:

- **Revenue synergies** from cross-selling into each others' respective distribution channels. In fact, this was a key driver of the transaction and is expected to yield the biggest financial benefit from the combination. Over time, the parties conservatively believe that this cross-selling will increase combined sales by roughly 6%, or roughly $62 million annually, by the 2018e timeframe. The benefits are expected to phase in over three years at equal amounts.
- **Vendor savings** from buying more raw materials in bulk. Over time, the Buyer and Seller believe they will save roughly 2.5% of their cost of sales, or approximately $18.5 million annually. However, some of these vendor agreements are under long-term supply agreements. As a result, the parties have assumed that this benefit phases in ratably over five years.

- **Cost savings** from eliminating redundant administrative functions in selected cases. This is probably the least important driver of the deal, as both the Buyer and the Target have strong corporate cultures and are not inclined to tamper with either's success. However, the parties believe a reasonable target is 3% of SG&A, or roughly $4.0 million. These are in areas that should not be particularly disruptive to the business, so the benefits should come earlier. Approximately one-third of this amount is expected in Year 1 of the deal, with the full amount benefiting the income statement by Year 2.

Figure 6-13 summarizes these expectations.

Prepare a purchase price allocation

The final step before we can compile a proforma income statement is to conduct a PPA analysis, which will drive the proforma depreciation and amortization expense. First, we calculate the total purchase price under the definition used for PPA. As mentioned previously, the Buyer is using $185 million of total cash and stock to effect the transaction. However, we can also arrive at this number by starting with the total transaction uses of $191.4 million in Figure 6-12, and subtracting selected items: $2.8 million for M&A advisory fees; $1.75 million for financing fees; and $1.85 million for other transaction-related costs. This implies a purchase price of $185 million.

Figure 6-13 Expected Synergies and Cost Savings

Synergies & Cost Savings ($000s)	Year 1	Year 2	Year 3	Year 4	Year 5
Revenue Syneries (Cross-Selling)					
Percentage of Sales	2.0%	4.0%	6.0%	6.0%	6.0%
Dollar Benefit	$19,749	$40,691	$62,884	$64,795	$66,771
Vendor Savings					
Percentage of Cost of Sales	0.5%	1.0%	1.5%	2.0%	2.5%
Dollar Benefit	$3,254	$6,721	$10,413	$14,342	$18,521
SG&A Cost Savings (Admin)					
Percentage of SG&A Expense	1.0%	3.0%	3.0%	3.0%	3.0%
Dollar Benefit	$1,237	$3,800	$3,890	$3,983	$4,077

Figure 6-14 Calculation of Purchase Price for PPA Analysis

Purchase Price Allocation ($000s)	
Total Purchase Price:	
Total Transaction Uses	$191,375
Advisory fees	(2,775)
Financing fees	(1,750)
Other transaction fees	(1,850)
Total Purchase Price	**$185,000**

Next, we compare this $185 million purchase price to the book value of the Target's net assets. The Target's full balance sheet is in Appendix 6G later in this chapter, but in summary includes $107.6 million in assets and $82.0 million in liabilities, implying $25.7 million in book value. Subtract this amount from the $185 million purchase price, and the buyer has $159.3 million of excess purchase price to allocate across the Target's assets and liabilities. After commissioning an appraisal by outside experts, the Buyer has determined that the Target's PP&E should be written up by $2.5 million to fair value and that the Target's customer list is worth $40 million. These amounts are subtracted from the $159.3 million of excess purchase price, creating $116.8 million of goodwill on the pro-forma balance sheet. This analysis is illustrated in Figure 6-15.

In the final step of the PPA, we calculate the incremental depreciation and amortization expense that the Target will show on its proforma

Figure 6-15 Write-Up of Tangible and Intangible Assets to Fair Value

Purchase Price Allocation ($000s)	
Total Purchase Price:	$185,000
Less: Book Value of Target's Net Assets	
Target's assets	107,614
Target's liabilities	81,950
Book Value of Net Assets	25,664
Excess Purchase Price	**$159,336**
Less: Write-Up of PP&E, net	(2,500)
Less: Write-Up of Identifiable Intangible Assets	(40,000)
Total Goodwill Created	**$116,836**

Figure 6-16 Incremental Depreciation & Amortization Expense

Incremental Depreciation Expense ($000s)	
Write-Up of PP&E, net	$2,500
Depreciation Period (yrs)	5.0
Incremental Depreciation Expense	**$500**

Incremental Amortization Expense ($000s)	
Write-Up of Customer Lists	$40,000
Amortization Period (yrs)	5.0
Incremental Depreciation Expense	**$8,000**

income statement as a result of the sale. As illustrated in Figure 6-16, the Target's PP&E increases by $2.5 million to fair value, while its customer lists are worth $40 million. If we assume that each of these amounts are expensed over five years, the Target will report incremental depreciation and amortization expense of $500,000 and $8 million, respectively. This is illustrated in Figure 6-16.

Construct a proforma income statement and balance sheet

Against this backdrop, we now turn our attention to creating the proforma income statement. The good news is that most of the heavy lifting is complete; building the income statement from here is primarily a function of assembling the above pieces. First, we compile the combined companies' proforma revenue. This starts by simply combining the standalone revenue for each of the Buyer and the Seller, and then layering in revenue synergies illustrated in Figure 6-13.

Then we move methodically down the income statement. The process of forecasting proforma gross profit is the same as revenue—start with the cost of sales for each of the Buyer and Seller and layer in the vendor savings summarized in Figure 6-13. One aspect of the combined financials starts to come out here—Figure 6-17 shows proforma gross margins expanding more than 400 basis points in the five-year period from 2015a to 2020e, even despite mid-single-digit revenue growth. This is a good illustration of the financial benefits of the proposed combination.

Figure 6-17 Proforma Revenue

Proforma Income Statement ($000s)	Actual Results		Projected Results				
Fiscal Year Ending December 31:	2014a	2015a	2016e	2017e	2018e	2019e	2020e
Revenue							
Buyer's Revenue	$741,360	$763,601	$782,691	$802,258	$822,315	$842,872	$863,944
Target's Revenue	180,572	195,018	204,769	215,007	225,757	237,045	248,898
Subtotal	921,932	958,619	987,459	1,017,265	1,048,072	1,079,918	1,112,842
Revenue Synergies (Attrition)	–	–	19,749	40,691	62,884	64,795	66,771
% of subtotal	N/A	N/A	2.0%	4.0%	6.0%	6.0%	6.0%
Total Revenue, proforma	**$921,932**	**$958,619**	**$1,007,209**	**$1,057,956**	**$1,110,956**	**$1,144,713**	**$1,179,612**
% growth	N/A	4.0%	5.1%	5.0%	5.0%	3.0%	3.0%

Next up is EBITDA. Here again, the process begins by combining the SG&A expense from both the Buyer and Seller, as adjusted for expected cost savings, then subtracting the total from proforma gross profit. The administrative savings from the transaction are expected to be modest—starting at about $1.2 million in 2016e and ramping to about $4.1 million by 2020e. However, they are part of the substantial EBITDA margin improvement that the combined businesses expect to see over the next five years.

After calculating EBITDA, we deduct proforma depreciation and amortization expense to arrive at EBIT (Figures 6-18 and 6-19). By now the pattern is familiar—start by combining the Buyer's and Target's respective line items, and adjust the result for any deal-related factors. But while all the adjustments described above—revenue synergies, vendor savings, and SG&A savings—are all expected to benefit earnings, the

Figure 6-18 Proforma Gross Profit and Gross Margins

Proforma Income Statement ($000s)	Actual Results		Projected Results				
Fiscal Year Ending December 31:	2014a	2015a	2016e	2017e	2018e	2019e	2020e
Gross Profit							
Total Revenue, proforma	$921,932	$958,619	$1,007,209	$1,057,956	$1,110,956	$1,144,713	$1,179,612
Less: Cost of Sales							
Buyer's Cost of Sales	474,470	484,887	497,792	511,039	524,637	538,596	552,925
Target's Cost of Sales	135,429	145,288	152,962	161,040	169,544	178,495	187,917
Subtotal	609,899	630,175	650,754	672,079	694,181	717,091	740,842
Vendor Savings	–	–	3,254	6,721	10,413	14,342	18,521
% of subtotal	N/A	N/A	0.5%	1.0%	1.5%	2.0%	2.5%
Total Cost of Sales	609,899	630,175	647,500	665,358	683,768	702,749	722,321
Total Gross Profit, proforma	**$312,033**	**$328,444**	**$359,709**	**$392,598**	**$427,188**	**$441,964**	**$457,291**
% margin	33.8%	34.3%	35.7%	37.1%	38.5%	38.6%	38.8%

Figure 6-19 Proforma EBITDA and EBITDA Margins

Proforma Income Statement ($000s)	Actual Results		Projected Results				
Fiscal Year Ending December 31:	2014a	2015a	2016e	2017e	2018e	2019e	2020e
EBITDA							
Total Gross Profit, proforma	$312,033	$328,444	$359,709	$392,598	$427,188	$441,964	$457,291
Less: SG&A Expense							
Buyer's SG&A	88,963	91,632	93,465	95,334	97,241	99,185	101,169
Target's SG&A	27,086	29,253	30,277	31,337	32,433	33,568	34,743
Subtotal	116,049	120,885	123,741	126,670	129,674	132,754	135,913
Cost Savings	–	–	1,237	3,800	3,890	3,983	4,077
% of subtotal	N/A	N/A	1.0%	3.0%	3.0%	3.0%	3.0%
Total SG&A Expense	116,049	120,885	122,504	122,870	125,784	128,771	131,835
Total EBITDA, proforma	**$195,984**	**$207,559**	**$237,205**	**$269,727**	**$301,405**	**$313,192**	**$325,456**
% margin	21.3%	21.7%	23.6%	25.5%	27.1%	27.4%	27.6%

adjustment to depreciation and amortization expense are expected to be a drag on net income from the write-up of tangible and intangible assets. This higher depreciation and amortization expense understandably offsets a portion of the GAAP-based earnings benefits from the deal. However, keep in mind that these expenses are noncash, and therefore on the surface do not influence our DCF model. What's more, the combined company will likely generate some tax benefit from the stepped-up basis in these assets. So net-net, this step in the model might initially look like an earnings drag, but it can actually end up benefiting the parties.

The last two steps in the proforma income statement are to subtract proforma interest expense and taxes from EBIT (Figure 6-20). Interest expense is the more complicated of the two. In order to project proforma interest, we must map out the combined companies' debt schedule for the next five years. For the sake of simplicity, we have assumed no interest

Figure 6-20 Proforma EBIT and EBIT Margins

Proforma Income Statement ($000s)	Actual Results		Projected Results				
Fiscal Year Ending December 31:	2014a	2015a	2016e	2017e	2018e	2019e	2020e
EBIT							
Total EBITDA, proforma	$195,984	$207,559	$237,205	$269,727	$301,405	$313,192	$325,456
Less: D&A Expense							
Buyer's D&A Expense	37,068	38,180	38,944	39,722	40,517	41,327	42,154
Target's D&A Expense (historical)	9,029	9,751	10,434	11,164	11,945	12,782	13,676
Target's D&A Expense (incremental)	N/A	–	8,500	8,500	8,500	8,500	8,500
Total D&A Expense, proforma	46,097	47,931	57,877	59,386	60,962	62,609	64,330
Total EBIT, proforma	**$149,887**	**$159,628**	**$179,327**	**$210,341**	**$240,442**	**$250,584**	**$261,126**
% margin	16.3%	16.7%	17.8%	19.9%	21.6%	21.9%	22.1%

income earned on cash and equivalents. (At the time this book was written, that sum would have been a rounding error at only a few basis points.) We assume that the bank debt, which has a fixed interest rate of 6.5%, is paid off $5 million per year through 2020e. In contrast, the subordinated debt, which charges a fixed coupon of 10.0%, is interest-only for the next seven years. We then add in the amortization of financing fees, which were 1% of the bank line and 3% of the subordinated debt. Consistent with U.S. GAAP, each is capitalized and amortized over the duration of the loan, which is five years for the bank line and seven years for the subordinated debt.

Figure 6-21 illustrates the initial interest expense of $6.7 million, which gradually trends lower to $5.4 million in 2020e as a portion of the bank debt is repaid.

Tax expense is the last item that remains outstanding in our proforma income statement. Fortunately, we have assumed that the Buyer's book tax

Figure 6-21 Proforma Interest Expense

Proforma Debt Schedule ($000s)	Actual Results		Projected Results				
Fiscal Year Ending December 31:	2014a	2015a	2016e	2017e	2018e	2019e	2020e
Bank Line of Credit							
Opening Balance	N/A	N/A	$25,000	$20,000	$15,000	$10,000	$5,000
Increase (Decrease)	N/A	25,000	(5,000)	(5,000)	(5,000)	(5,000)	(5,000)
Closing Balance	N/A	25,000	20,000	15,000	10,000	5,000	–
Average Balance Outstanding	N/A	N/A	22,500	17,500	12,500	7,500	2,500
Interest Rate	N/A	N/A	6.5%	6.5%	6.5%	6.5%	6.5%
Interest Expense, Bank Debt	N/A	N/A	1,463	1,138	813	488	163
Subordinated Debt							
Opening Balance	N/A	N/A	$50,000	$50,000	$50,000	$50,000	$50,000
Increase (Decrease)	N/A	50,000	–	–	–	–	–
Closing Balance	N/A	50,000	50,000	50,000	50,000	50,000	50,000
Average Balance Outstanding	N/A	N/A	50,000	50,000	50,000	50,000	50,000
Interest Rate	N/A	N/A	10.0%	10.0%	10.0%	10.0%	10.0%
Interest Expense, Sub Debt	N/A	N/A	5,000	5,000	5,000	5,000	5,000
Amortization of Financing Fees							
Bank Debt Fees[1]	N/A	N/A	$50	$50	$50	$50	$50
Subordinated Debt Fees[2]	N/A	N/A	214	214	214	214	214
Total Financing Fees	N/A	N/A	264	264	264	264	264
Total Interest Expense and Fees							
Interest Expense, Bank Line of Credit	N/A	N/A	$1,463	$1,138	$813	$488	$163
Interest Expense, Subordinated Debt	N/A	N/A	5,000	5,000	5,000	5,000	5,000
Amortization of Financing Fees	N/A	N/A	264	264	264	264	264
Total Interest Expense and Fees	N/A	N/A	6,727	6,402	6,077	5,752	5,427

[1]Fees are 1% of $25 million borrowings, amortized over five-year term
[2]Fees are 3% of $50 million borrowings, amortized over seven-year term

Figure 6-22 Proforma Net Income

Proforma Income Statement ($000s)	Actual Results		Projected Results				
Fiscal Year Ending December 31:	2014a	2015a	2016e	2017e	2018e	2019e	2020e
Net Income							
Total EBIT, proforma	$149,887	$159,628	$179,327	$210,341	$240,442	$250,584	$261,126
Less: Interest and Tax Expense							
Interest Expense and Fees, proforma	N/A	N/A	6,727	6,402	6,077	5,752	5,427
Tax Expense, proforma	44,217	49,644	51,780	61,182	70,310	73,450	76,710
% tax rate	29.5%	31.1%	30.0%	30.0%	30.0%	30.0%	30.0
Total Net Income, proforma	**$105,670**	**$109,984**	**$120,820**	**$142,757**	**$164,056**	**$171,382**	**$178,989**
Fully-Diluted Sharecount, proforma							
Earnings per Share, proforma	N/A	N/A	80,925	80,925	80,925	80,925	80,925
	N/A	N/A	$1.49	$1.76	$2.03	$2.12	$2.21

rate of 30% is unlikely to change going forward; both companies have similar geographical footprints and the tax benefit of the depreciation and amortization shield is likely to be a bigger benefit to cash taxes rather than book taxes. Figure 6-22 rounds out the final step in our proforma income statement.

For your convenience, we have included the full proforma income statement in Appendix 6E at the end of this chapter.

How do these adjustments carry over to the proforma balance sheet?

Most of the adjustments previously discussed carry over, one way or another, to the proforma balance sheet. Figure 6-23 starts with the individual balance sheets for both the Buyer and the Target.

Based on the analyses above in Figures 6-12 (Sources and Uses) and 6-14 (Purchase Price Allocation), the items that are impacted by the acquisition are cash, PP&E, customer lists, goodwill, and the various debt lines. Of these line items, cash probably has the greatest number of moving pieces. Figure 6-24 bridges the Cash and Equivalents line from the Buyer's opening amount of $77.9 million to the proforma amount of $86.3 million. These adjustments include the following:

- Add the Target's cash of $20.9 million
- Add the new bank debt of $25 million and subordinated debt of $50 million
- Pay down the Target's existing debt of $35,000

Figure 6-23 Individual Balance Sheets for the Buyer and Target

Proforma Balance Sheet ($000s)		
Fiscal Year Ending December 31, 2015	**Buyer**	**Target**
Assets		
Current Assets		
Cash and Equivalents	$77,887	$20,867
Accounts Receivable	116,831	31,300
Inventory	93,465	25,040
Other Current Assets	38,944	10,433
Total Current Assets	**327,127**	**87,640**
PP&E, net	74,556	19,974
Customer Lists	–	–
Goodwill	–	–
Total Assets	**$401,683**	**$107,614**
Liabilities & Shareholders' Equity		
Current Liabilities		
Accounts Payable	$136,303	$36,517
Accrued Expenses	38,943	10,433
Current Portion of Long-Term Debt	–	–
Total Current Liabilities	**175,246**	**46,950**
Bank Line of Credit	–	–
Other Debt	–	35,000
Total Liabilities	**175,246**	**81,950**
Shareholders' Equity	226,437	25,664
Total Liabilities & Shareholders' Equity	**$401,683**	**$107,614**

Figure 6-24 Adjustments to Proforma Cash

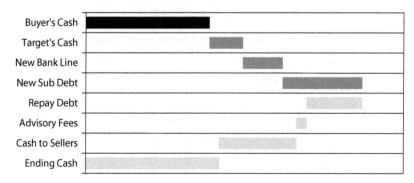

- Subtract transaction-related fees of $3.9 million
- Subtract net cash paid to the selling shareholders of $48.6 million

Figure 6-25 shows these adjustments in balance sheet form. Note that the $14.6 million of cash adjustments to the proforma balance sheet, as detailed in footnote 1 of Figure 6-25, reconciles to the cash on hand reflected in the Sources & Uses table in Figure 6-12, earlier in this chapter. The other three changes to proforma assets are a little more straightforward. Figure 6-15 illustrates:

- A write-up of the Target's PP&E by $2.5 million to fair value (see footnote 2 of Figure 6-25);
- A write-up of the Target's customer lists to $40 million, reflecting fair value (see footnote 3 of Figure 6-25); and
- The creation of $116.8 million of goodwill (see footnote 4 of Figure 6-25).

Figure 6-25 Adjustments to Proforma Assets

Proforma Balance Sheet ($000s)				
Fiscal Year Ending December 31, 2015	**Buyer**	**Target**	**Adjustments**	**Proforma**
Assets				
Current Assets				
Cash and Equivalents	$77,887	$20,867	($14,625) [1]	$84,129
Accounts Receivable	116,831	31,300	–	148,131
Inventory	93,465	25,040	–	118,505
Other Current Assets	38,944	10,433	–	49,377
Total Current Assets	327,127	87,640	(14,625)	400,142
PP&E, net	74,556	19,974	2,500 [2]	97,030
Customer Lists	–	–	40,000 [3]	40,000
Goodwill	–	–	116,836 [4]	116,836
Total Assets	**$401,683**	**$107,614**	**$144,711**	**$654,008**

[1] Adjustments to cash as follows:

New bank line of credit	$25,000
New subordinated debt	50,000
Paydown of Target's debt	(35,000)
Advisory fees	(2,775)
Financing fees	(1,750)
Other transaction fees	(1,850)
Cash paid to selling shareholders	(48,250)
Total adjustments to cash	($14,625)

[2] Write-up of Target's PP&E, net to fair value
[3] Write-up of customer lists to fair value
[4] Excess of purchase price over fair value of tangible and identifiable intangible assets

Figure 6-26 walks through a similar exercise for proforma liabilities and shareholders' equity. In total, there are three primary changes to the "right side" of the combined balance sheet:

- The buyer draws down $25 million from a new bank line of credit. Of this amount, $5 million will be repaid in 2016e and therefore appears in the current portion of long-term debt (see footnote 1 of Figure 6-26) and $20 million appears in the Bank Line of Credit entry (see footnote 2 of Figure 6-26);
- The Buyer issues $50 million of new subordinated debt (see footnote 3 of Figure 6-26);
- Securing the bank and mezzanine financing incurs $1.75 million of financing fees, which are capitalized and amortized over time (see footnote 3 of Figure 6-26); and
- The Target's existing debt of $35 million is paid off at closing (see footnote 3 of Figure 6-26).

Figure 6-26 Adjustments to Proforma Liabilities and Shareholders' Equity

Proforma Balance Sheet ($000s)				
Fiscal Year Ending December 31, 2015	Buyer	Target	Adjustments	Proforma
Liabilities & Shareholders' Equity				
Current Liabilities				
Accounts Payable	$136,303	$36,517	$0	$172,820
Accrued Expenses	38,943	10,433	–	49,376
Current Portion of Long-Term Debt	–	–	5,000 [1]	5,000
Total Current Liabilities	175,246	46,950	5,000	227,196
Bank Line of Credit	–	–	20,000 [2]	20,000
Other Debt	–	35,000	16,750 [3]	51,750
Total Liabilities	175,246	81,950	41,750	298,946
Shareholders' Equity	226,437	25,664	102,961	355,062
Total Liabilities & Shareholders' Equity	**$401,683**	**$107,614**	**$144,711**	**$654,008**

[1] Portion of bank line of credit and subordinated debt to be repaid in 2016e
[2] Reflects noncurrent portion of new bank line of credit
[3] Adjustments to Other Debt as follows:

New subordinated debt	$50,000
Capitalized financing fees	1,750
Redeem Target's debt	(35,000)
Total adjustments to Other Debt	**$16,750**

For your convenience, we have included the full proforma balance sheet in Appendix 6G at the end of this chapter.

CASH FLOW RECONCILIATION

What is a cash flow reconciliation?

A *cash flow reconciliation* complements the income statement and balance sheet; it bridges a company's net income to free cash flow based on the indirect method for reporting cash flows. This method adjusts net income for revenues, expenses, gains, and losses that appear on the income statement but do not have an effect on cash.

Why should my transaction model include this analysis?

A cash flow reconciliation is an important component of the transaction model; as described in Chapter 3 on DCF, net income is an accounting number used for reporting purposes, but free cash flow is the actual amount of cash available to investors—and therefore is a key driver of valuation models. The reconciliation is also a helpful risk-monitoring tool, as the statement is useful in determining the short-term ability of a company to cover its obligations. As such, it's often good practice to round out the proforma income statement and balance sheet with a cash flow reconciliation.

How do I construct a cash flow reconciliation?

A full cash flow statement is comprised of three parts: cash flows from operating activities, cash flows from investing activities, and cash flows from financing activities. The first section typically includes the most adjustments. To calculate cash flows from operating activities:

- Start with net income;
- Add back noncash expenses; and
- Adjust for changes in working capital.

Common noncash expenses include depreciation, amortization of financing fees, and gains/losses on the sale of equipment. Adjustments to working capital typically involve changes to accounts receivable, inventory, accounts payable, accrued expenses, prepaid expenses, and taxes payable. This arrives at cash flows provided by (or used in) operating activities.

A full cash flow reconciliation will take the analysis through cash flows from investing activities and cash flows from financing activities. Examples of cash flows from investing activities include the purchase or sale of fixed assets (e.g., land, buildings, equipment, marketable securities, and so on), payments related to corporate acquisitions, purchases and sales of investments, etc. Examples of cash flows from financing activities include payments of dividends, the issuance or repurchase of company equity, net borrowings, and so on.

Do you have a sample cash flow reconciliation that you can share?

The transaction model that we have been building out in this chapter does not include a multiyear balance sheet. This makes it difficult to construct a cash flow reconciliation for our example. However, Figure 6-27 illustrates a typical cash flow reconciliation.

ACCRETION/DILUTION ANALYSIS

What is an accretion/dilution analysis?

An *accretion/dilution analysis* is used to determine how the target's financial performance will affect the acquirer's GAAP earnings after closing—whether the acquirer's EPS will increase or decrease, given the current transaction structure. Accretion/dilution analysis is often seen as a proxy for whether or not a contemplated deal creates or destroys shareholder value. Thus it is important to estimate the accretion/dilution potential from a deal before the buyer can agree to the proposed transaction.

When is a transaction accretive? When is it dilutive?

A transaction is *accretive* if the buyer's expected future EPS increases as a result of the acquisition. For example, let's assume Buyer has EPS

Figure 6-27 Adjustments to Proforma Liabilities and Shareholders' Equity

Cash Flows from Operating Activities ($000s)	
Net income	$75,240
Adjustments:	
Depreciation and amortization	**2,544**
Changes in accounts receivable	(265)
Changes in deferred taxes	35
Changes in inventories	(2,499)
Changes in accounts payable	(560)
Changes in accrued interest	75
Loss on sale of equipment	346
Net cash flow from operating activities	**74,916**

Cash Flows from Investing Activities ($000s)	
Cash from sale of equipment	5,000
Purchase of land	(10,000)
Other cash flows from investing activities	2,544
Net cash flow from operating activities	**(2,456)**

Cash Flows from Financing Activities ($000s)	
Dividends paid	(2,500)
Sale/(purchase) of stock	15,000
Net borrowings	(1,000)
Net cash flow from financing activities	**11,500**

Effect of exchange rate changes	–
Change in cash and cash equivalents	**$83,960**

of $1.00 in the current fiscal year. It acquires Target for a mix of cash and stock, folding Target's operations into its own. Based on an attractive valuation and deal structure, Buyer's EPS is expected to improve $0.15 over the next 12 months. In this case, the acquisition is described as being 15 percent accretive to Buyer's near-term earnings. An extended period of low interest rates has made it much easier to structure accretive acquisitions throughout most of the current economic cycle, provided the deal is funded entirely from cash on hand and the target is profitable. In such situations (and provided there are not significant intangibles involved that will need to be amortized over time), the buyer generally need only backfill lost interest on cash holdings. This has not been particularly challenging given six-plus years of unusually low interest rates.

On the other hand, the transaction would be *dilutive* if the buyer's expected future EPS declines as a result of the deal. Transaction structure can influence whether a deal is accretive or dilutive. For instance, a transaction will increasingly be at risk of turning dilutive the more the mix of consideration shifts to equity from cash. This risk is compounded for publicly traded companies with low P/E ratios, particularly those looking to acquire high-growth targets. That is, a buyer with a P/E of 10x will be hard-pressed to consummate an accretive, all-stock purchase of a competitor with a P/E of 30x.

In fact, a common—albeit sometimes flawed—rule of thumb is that an acquisition is likely to be dilutive when the P/E ratio of the acquiring firm is less than that of the target firm. By the same token, the higher the P/E ratio of a company, the more likely it is that (1) the company will want to pursue an acquisition strategy, and (2) the company will want to use equity as consideration for the deal (all other things being equal, of course).

Unless there is a highly strategic, nonfinancial rationale driving a transaction, most investors dislike dilutive acquisitions. That dislike is understandable, at least in the near term—if the buyer has $1.00 of EPS as a standalone, what's the logic behind handing somcone a pile of money so that EPS can go *down*?

So all acquisitions should be accretive?

It's a practical reality that investors' initial reaction to most any acquisition announcements is to ask how accretive the deal will be. However, a dilutive acquisition might be justifiable if the buyer foresees long-term growth, or if it gains strategic advantages such as key intellectual property or technologies. These might be entirely justifiable reasons to effect a dilutive acquisition—although management would be well counseled to ensure that it understands the temperament and expectations of both its board and its shareholders.

What influences whether a transaction is accretive or dilutive?

As mentioned above, relative valuation and deal structure are two key considerations. It will be difficult for a buyer to strike an accretive acquisition of a target if the target's P/E is substantially higher than the buyer's and if stock is the preferred acquisition currency.

However, accretion/dilution analysis reflects other variables, as well. Of particular importance are the expected synergies and cost savings from the transaction—both in terms of increased revenue and decreased costs. That is, a deal could be dilutive in the near term but accretive longer term as the combined entity harvests material synergies. This is increasingly common lately in economic cycles, when prices for corporate acquisitions inch higher as more bidders enter the mix—arbitraging out the near-term benefits of some deals.

Other factors to consider are the longer-term growth rates and profitability of the buyer and seller; these also impact how accretive or dilutive the transaction is over time. It might make perfect sense for a buyer with a lower P/E to acquire a target with a higher P/E if the target is unusually profitable and is growing so quickly that it will offset the P/E premium within a couple of years.

What are the steps to conduct in an accretion/ dilution analysis?

In its purest form, an accretion/dilution analysis is a three-step process:

- **Calculate the combined companies' proforma net income from the proforma income statement.** As discussed earlier in this chapter, this income statement should include the expected synergies and cost savings, as well as the increased depreciation and amortization expense, that are expected to arise from the deal.
- **Quantify the combined companies' prorata share count.** If the acquisition is all-cash, the share count is likely to be the same as the acquirer's current share count. However, if the acquirer is issuing at least some equity to finance the deal, its share count is likely to increase.
- **Divide proforma net income by the proforma share count to arrive at proforma EPS.** If proforma EPS is higher than the acquirer's standalone EPS, the deal is accretive. If proforma EPS is lower, the deal is dilutive. In some cases, it might be

necessary to project out proforma net income for at least two to three years before the deal turns accretive. Here again, whether this is acceptable depends largely on the expected reaction of the board and investors.

How do I incorporate an accretion/dilution analysis into my transaction model?

We prepared a proforma income statement for our transaction model earlier in this chapter. As a result, the first step, calculating the combined companies' proforma net income, is already complete. The second step requires quantifying the combined companies' proforma share count. The Buyer currently has 76.9 million shares outstanding. As noted in Figure 6-12, the Buyer has agreed to issue $101.8 million of equity as part of the transaction. The Buyer's stock is currently trading at $25.00, which implies 4.1 million of new shares to be issued. This is illustrated in Figure 6-28.

The third and final step is to divide proforma net income by the proforma share count to arrive at proforma EPS, and compare that figure to the standalone EPS. The top half of Figure 6-29 summarizes the Buyer's EPS from 2016e through 2018e on a standalone basis—$1.39, $1.42, and $1.46, respectively. The bottom half illustrates the Buyer's proforma EPS—$1.55, $1.82, and $2.08, respectively.

Figure 6-29 would likely lead to a well-received press release: "Buyer acquires Target for $185 million. Transaction expected to be 10%-15% accretive to 2016e earnings, ramping to 40%-45% accretive in 2018e." In all likelihood, Buyer's stock won't still be at $25.00 after the release!

Figure 6-28 Proforma Share Count

Proforma Share Count (000s, except per-share data)	
Shares Outstanding, current	**76,855**
Value of Shares to be Issued	$101,750
Price per Share	$25.00
Number of Shares to be Issued	4,070
Shares Outstanding, proforma	**80,925**

Figure 6-29 Accretion/Dilution Analysis

Accretion/Dilution Analysis ($000, except per-share data)			
Standalone	**2016e**	**2017e**	**2018e**
Revenue	$782,691	$802,258	$822,315
Grosss Profit	284,899	291,219	297,677
EBITDA	191,434	195,885	200,437
EBIT	152,491	156,163	159,920
Net Income	106,743	109,314	111,944
Share Count	76,855	76,855	76,855
EPS	**$1.39**	**$1.42**	**$1.46**
Proforma	**2016e**	**2017e**	**2018e**
Revenue	$1,007,209	$1,057,956	$1,110,956
Grosss Profit	359,709	392,598	427,188
EBITDA	237,205	269,727	301,405
EBIT	179,327	210,341	240,442
Net Income	125,529	147,239	168,310
Share Count	80,925	80,925	80,925
EPS	**$1.55**	**$1.82**	**$2.08**
Accretion	**2016e**	**2017e**	**2018e**
EPS ($)	**$0.16**	**$0.40**	**$0.62**
EPS (%)	**11.7%**	**27.9%**	**42.8%**

SENSITIVITY ANALYSES

What is a sensitivity analysis?

A *sensitivity analysis*, also known as a *what-if analysis* or a *scenario manager*, is a tool that allows the user to see the model's output under a variety of circumstances—i.e., how the projections would respond to different "shocks." It allows the user to select specific variables in the model, change the underlying assumptions, and see the expected impact to earnings, financial returns, leverage ratios, etc.

Why is a sensitivity analysis helpful?

A sensitivity analysis allows the user to stress-test the model. Expectations can, and do, change over time; as a result, it can be instructive to see the range of possible outcomes in the event circumstances do not play out as intended at the time the deal closes.

For as much insight, expertise, and thoughtfulness that a financial model might reflect, the fact is that forward-looking assumptions may not always hold true. In fact, there's a bit of industry wisdom that says, your model will *always* be wrong—it's just a matter of which direction and by how much. Conducting sensitivity analyses enhances one's understanding of the key value drivers of a deal and flexibility to respond to new ideas that may appear at the negotiating table.

For instance, every earnings model we have ever seen assumes continued macroeconomic growth over the subsequent five years from closing. That may, in fact, turn out to be accurate, but really the odds are pretty good that some form of economic hiccup is reasonably likely in any given five-year period. It would be invaluable to know—before the fact—that a 10% downturn in sales would cause your target, whom you are thinking about levering to 6x EBITDA, would likely breach a debt covenant with only a 10% downturn in sales. A well-constructed sensitivity analysis can help predict this.

How do I incorporate a sensitivity analysis into my transaction model?

The easiest way of performing a sensitivity analysis in a transaction model is to use the data table function in Excel. Nearly any assumption discounted into the model can be analyzed: valuation, organic growth, expected synergies and cost savings, and so on. In many financial models, there is an entire tab of sensitivity analyses running what-if scenarios for a large variety of variables. For instance, how accretive is the transaction if the acquisition price were to increase by one turn of EBITDA? What happens if the cost savings do not play out as expected? What if I change the mix of consideration from 55% stock to 80%? The number of combinations is seemingly limitless.

Figure 6-30 incorporates a simple sensitivity analysis into the transaction model that we have been building throughout this chapter. Because the Buyer is publicly traded, its board is particularly focused on structuring a deal that is expected to be accretive in the first 12 months. Accordingly, the output from the model that we wish to test is the level of earnings accretion that the deal offers in 2016e.

The accretion/dilution analysis in Figure 6-29 indicates that the base-case transaction model projects Year 1 EPS accretion of 11.7%—an attractive outcome. As is the case in most any deal, price is expected to be a major discussion point when negotiations begin. The selling shareholders' view is likely to be that 8.6x is a "pretty good" price, but that the transaction would be a lot more compelling at 9.6x EBITDA—or $206.5 million. (As a reminder, the Buyer's public valuation is currently 10.0x forward EBITDA.) Understandably, the Buyer is apprehensive about overpaying for the deal and would like to understand what this increase in purchase price would mean to its expected EPS accretion.

Separately, we noted earlier that one of the biggest drivers of the transaction is the expected revenue synergies. These synergies are projected to start at 2% of revenue and increase ratably to 6% by Year 3. However, some members of the Buyer's board are beginning to question whether these forecasts are too aggressive, particularly as revenue synergies are the hardest aspect of a model to predict with accuracy. Accordingly, the Buyer's board of directors has requested a sensitivity analysis around the impact to EPS accretion at varying levels of revenue synergies in Year 1 (i.e., 2016e).

The next several figures are eye-opening. Figure 6-30 plots Year 1 revenue synergies as a percentage of sales across the horizontal axis, and the acquisition price as a multiple of EBITDA across the vertical axis. The base case assumptions are in the middle of each axis—2.0% revenue synergies and an 8.6x acquisition price. These assumptions correspond with 11.7% earnings accretion in Year 1.

Figure 6-30 Sensitivity Analysis: Impact of Revenue Synergies and EBITDA Multiple on Accretion

		Expected Revenue Synergies, Year 1				
		0.0%	1.0%	**2.0%**	3.0%	4.0%
EBITDA Multiple (x)	9.6x	−1.2%	4.9%	11.0%	17.1%	23.3%
	9.1x	−0.9%	5.2%	11.4%	17.5%	23.6%
	8.6x	−0.6%	5.5%	**11.7%**	17.8%	24.0%
	8.1x	−0.3%	5.8%	12.0%	18.2%	24.3%
	7.6x	0.0%	6.2%	12.3%	18.5%	24.7%

Figure 6-31 Sensitivity Analysis: Impact to EPS Accretion from a Higher Purchase Price

		Expected Revenue Synergies, Year 1				
		0.0%	1.0%	2.0%	3.0%	4.0%
EBITDA Multiple (x)	9.6x	−1.2%	4.9%	11.0%	17.1%	23.3%
	9.1x	−0.9%	5.2%	11.4%	17.5%	23.6%
	8.6x	−0.6%	5.5%	**11.7%**	17.8%	24.0%
	8.1x	−0.3%	5.8%	12.0%	18.2%	24.3%
	7.6x	0.0%	6.2%	12.3%	18.5%	24.7%

What happens if we were to increase the purchase price from 8.6x to 9.6x EBITDA, as the selling shareholders are likely to request? *Surprisingly, the impact to our accretion analysis is relatively modest.* This is illustrated in Figure 6-31, which shows that the Year 1 earnings accretion is still expected to be 11.0% assuming revenue synergies of 2.0% and an acquisition multiple of 9.6x. This accretion is only 70 basis points lower than in the base case scenario. While the Buyer is not yet willing to concede this point to the selling shareholders, it's a data point it can keep in its back pocket during the remainder of the negotiations.

We then turn our attention to the board's concern about whether the expected revenue synergies are too aggressive. What happens if we were to keep the acquisition price at 8.6x but lower the anticipated revenue synergies to 1.0% from 2.0%? As illustrated in Figure 6-32, *the expected earnings accretion is cut in half*—rather than the 11.7% accretion currently expected in Year 1, the earnings improvement drops to 5.5%. *This reveals a critical assumption in our transaction model*—that the top-line benefit from the combination is overwhelmingly more important than the price the Buyer must pay to close the deal. This plants a thought: What if we could link transaction value to more risk-sharing of these expected revenue synergies?

We can take the results in Figure 6-32 one step further. Let's assume the Buyer's board of directors were to ask, what's the *most* we can afford to pay for the Target if we were to assume *no* revenue synergies (for sake of conservatism)? Figure 6-33 addresses this question—the Buyer would need to lower the initial purchase price to 7.6x EBITDA (from the contemplated proposal of 8.6x EBITDA) in order for the EPS accretion to be flat assuming no revenue synergies.

Figure 6-32 Sensitivity Analysis: Impact to EPS Accretion from Lower Revenue Synergies

		Expected Revenue Synergies, Year 1				
		0.0%	1.0%	**2.0%**	3.0%	4.0%
EBITDA Multiple (x)	9.6x	−1.2%	4.9%	11.0%	17.1%	23.3%
	9.1x	−0.9%	5.2%	11.4%	17.5%	23.6%
	8.6x	−0.6%	5.5%	**11.7%**	17.8%	24.0%
	8.1x	−0.3%	5.8%	12.0%	18.2%	24.3%
	7.6x	0.0%	6.2%	12.3%	18.5%	24.7%

So what did we learn from conducting these sensitivity analyses?

The above analyses only address two variables—purchase price and expected revenue synergies—yet they bring several critical issues to the forefront that might have otherwise gone overlooked:

- In this particular transaction, expected revenue synergies are a material driver of the expected financial benefits of the transaction. This makes sense, as the top-line benefits of the deal were called out early on as a key strategic driver of the combination. However, the impact to the financial outcome is even greater than what the Buyer expected.

- Also in this particular deal, the purchase price has a relatively muted impact on earnings accretion. There are at least two reasons for this. First, the Target's valuation is 8.6x EBITDA in the base case, while the Buyer's valuation is 10.0x. There's wiggle room on price, even with the increased depreciation and

Figure 6-33 Sensitivity Analysis: Breakeven Point from Assumed Revenue Synergies

		Expected Revenue Synergies, Year 1				
		0.0%	1.0%	**2.0%**	3.0%	4.0%
EBITDA Multiple (x)	9.6x	−1.2%	4.9%	11.0%	17.1%	23.3%
	9.1x	−0.9%	5.2%	11.4%	17.5%	23.6%
	8.6x	−0.6%	5.5%	**11.7%**	17.8%	24.0%
	8.1x	−0.3%	5.8%	12.0%	18.2%	24.3%
	7.6x	0.0%	6.2%	12.3%	18.5%	24.7%

amortization from the PPA. Second, 45% of the consideration is paid in cash. Even despite the fact that the Buyer is borrowing a meaningful portion of this cash, the cost of funds are low given the current interest rate environment.

- Despite its bullish outlook for the combined companies' revenue synergies, the Buyer might want to initially propose a purchase price of 7.6x EBITDA in order to mitigate the execution risk of not realizing the full revenue synergies.

- Assuming the Target has conducted its own transaction model and likewise sees how powerful the revenue synergies might be, perhaps the parties can agree upon an earnout structure so as to increase overall valuation while addressing the Buyer's need to structure an accretive deal.

On this final point, perhaps the parties agree to an upfront valuation of $163.5 million (or 7.6x EBITDA). If the combined entity were to achieve $10 million of revenue synergies during the first calendar year (which would translate to a 1% improvement), the Buyer would pay the selling shareholders an additional $21.5 million—thereby "truing up" valuation to $185 million (or 8.6x EBITDA). This would result in 5.5% earnings accretion for the Buyer.

In contrast, if the combined entity were to achieve $20 million of revenue synergies during the first calendar year (which would translate to a 2% benefit), the Buyer would pay the selling shareholders a second payment of $21.5 million—increasing the total transaction proceeds to $206.5 million (or 9.6x EBITDA). This deal would still be 11.0% accretive to the Buyer, while meeting the Target's valuation request and mitigating the risk of striking a dilutive deal.

In a fitting note to close out this book: everyone wins!

CONCLUSION

Valuation matters, and modeling delivers it. When a deal fails, many observers are quick to find fault with the transaction's cultural or strategic fit. But sometimes these are merely symptoms; the root of the postmerger problem can be overpayment—the silent culprit that stresses cash flow and destroys corporate wealth. With the proper techniques for valuation and financial modeling, dealmakers can bypass this problem to build company value.

Our printed guidance on M&A valuation and modeling now comes to a close, but this is not the end—only the beginning. As mentioned, additional materials can be found at www.ARTofMA.com. With the help of these resources, as well as the concepts and techniques in this book, all parties to transactions will be empowered to learn the art of M&A valuation and modeling.

Best of success!

APPENDIX 6A

Sample Assumptions Tab

Assumptions Tab ($000s, except per-share data)

VALUATION				DEAL STRUCTURE			
Transaction size	$185,000			(A)sset or (S)tock purchase?			S
% acquired	100.0%			338(h)(10) election (Y/N)?			N
Implied valuation	$185,000						
				TRANSACTION FEES			
Target's forward EBITDA ($)	$21,530			M&A advisory fees (%)			1.5%
Implied EBITDA multiple (x)	8.6x			Other transaction fees (%)			1.0%

CONSIDERATION		ACQUISITION DEBT		
Amount in cash ($)	$83,250	Facility	Bank Line	Sub debt
Percentage of total mix	45.0%	Size of facility ($)	$25,000	$50,000
		Duration (yrs)	5.0	7.0
Amount in assumed liabilities ($)	$3,700	Interest rate (%)	6.5%	10.0%
Percentage of total mix	2.0%	Financing fees (%)	1.0%	3.0%
		Repayment schedule:		
Amount in Buyer stock ($)	$101,750	Year 1	$5,000	$0
Percentage of total mix	55.0%	Year 2	$5,000	$0
Price per share	$25.00	Year 3	$5,000	$0
# shares issued	4,070	Year 4	$5,000	$0
		Year 5	$5,000	$0

SYNERGIES AND COST SAVINGS

Source	Revenue	Vendor	SG&A
Include (Y/N)?	Y	Y	Y
Amount:			
Year 1	2.0%	0.5%	1.0%
Year 2	4.0%	1.0%	3.0%
Year 3	6.0%	1.5%	3.0%
Year 4	6.0%	2.0%	3.0%
Year 5	6.0%	2.5%	3.0%

PURCHASE PRICE ALLOCATION

Assets:	Fair Value	Years
Cash and equivalents	$0	
Accounts receivable	$0	
Inventory	$0	
Other current assets	$0	
PP&E, net	$2,500	5
Customer lists	$40,000	5

Liabilities:	Fair Value	Years
Accounts payable	$0	
Accrued expenses	$0	

GROWTH ASSUMPTIONS

Annual Changes in	Buyer	Seller
Revenue	2.5%	5.0%
Gross margins (bps)	10	20
SG&A	2.0%	3.5%
Depreciation & amortization	2.0%	7.0%
Tax rate	30.0%	N/A

A P P E N D I X   6 B

Sample Sources & Uses Table

Sources ($000s)	Amount	% of Total	Uses ($000s)	Amount	% of Total
Issue new stock	$101,750	53.2%	Buyer stock to sellers	$101,750	53.2%
Draw down on bank line	25,000	13.1%	Refinance target's debt	35,000	18.3%
Issue subordinated debt	50,000	26.1%	Cash to sellers	48,250	25.2%
Cash on hand	14,625	7.6%	Advisory fees	2,775	1.5%
			Financing fees	1,750	0.9%
			Other transaction fees	1,850	1.0%
Total sources	**$191,375**	**100.0%**	**Total uses**	**$191,375**	**100.0%**

$185 million of transaction consideration
($83.3 million in cash)

APPENDIX 6 C

Sample Synergies and Cost Savings Schedule

Synergies & Cost Savings ($000s)	Year 1	Year 2	Year 3	Year 4	Year 5
Revenue Syneries (Cross-Selling)					
Percentage of sales	2.0%	4.0%	6.0%	6.0%	6.0%
Dollar benefit	$19,749	$40,691	$62,884	$64,795	$66,771
Vendor Savings					
Percentage of cost of sales	0.5%	1.0%	1.5%	2.0%	2.5%
Dollar benefit	$3,254	$6,721	$10,413	$14,342	$18,521
SG&A Cost Savings (Admin)					
Percentage of SG&A expense	1.0%	3.0%	3.0%	3.0%	3.0%
Dollar benefit	$1,237	$3,800	$3,890	$3,983	$4,077

APPENDIX 6D

Sample Purchase Price Allocation Analysis

Purchase Price Allocation ($000s)	
Total Purchase Price:	
Total transaction uses	$191,375
Advisory fees	(2,775)
Financing fees	(1,750)
Other transaction fees	(1,850)
Total purchase price	**$185,000**
Total purchase price:	$185,000
Less: Book Value of Target's Net Assets	
Target's assets	107,614
Target's liabilties	81,950
Book value of net assets	25,664
Excess purchase price	**$159,336**
Less: Write-up of PP&E, net	(2,500)
Less: Write-up of identifiable intangible assets	(40,000)
Total goodwill created	**$116,836**

Incremental Depreciation Expense ($000s)	
Write-up of PP&E, net	$2,500
Depreciation period (yrs)	5 .0
Incremental depreciation expense	**$500**

Incremental Amortization Expense ($000s)	
Write-up of customer lists	$40,000
Amortization period (yrs)	5 .0
Incremental amortization expense	**$8,000**

APPENDIX 6 E

Sample Proforma Income Statement

Proforma Income Statement ($000s)	Actual Results		Projected Results				
Fiscal Year Ending December 31:	2014a	2015a	2016e	2017e	2018e	2019e	2020e
Revenue							
Buyer's revenue	$741,360	$763,601	$782,691	$802,258	$822,315	$842,872	$863,944
Target's revenue	180,572	195,018	204,769	215,007	225,757	237,045	248,898
Subtotal	921,932	958,619	987,459	1,017,265	1,048,072	1,079,918	1,112,842
Revenue synergies (Attrition)	–	–	19,749	40,691	62,884	64,795	66,771
% of subtotal	N/A	N/A	2.0%	4.0%	6.0%	6.0%	6.0%
Total Revenue, proforma	**$921,932**	**$958,619**	**$1,007,209**	**$1,057,956**	**$1,110,956**	**$1,144,713**	**$1,179,612**
% growth	N/A	4.0%	5.1%	5.0%	5.0%	3.0%	3.0%
Gross Profit							
Buyer's cost of sales	474,470	484,887	497,792	511,039	524,637	538,596	552,925
Target's cost of sales	135,429	145,288	152,962	161,040	169,544	178,495	187,917
Subtotal	609,899	630,175	650,754	672,079	694,181	717,091	740,842
Vendor savings	–	–	3,254	6,721	10,413	14,342	18,521
% of subtotal	N/A	N/A	0.5%	1.0%	1.5%	2.0%	2.5%
Total cost of sales	609,899	630,175	647,500	665,358	683,768	702,749	722,321
Total gross profit, proforma	**$312,033**	**$328,444**	**$359,709**	**$392,598**	**$427,188**	**$441,964**	**$457,291**
% margin	33.8%	34.3%	35.7%	37.1%	38.5%	38.6%	38.8%
EBITDA							
Buyer's SG&A	88,963	91,632	93,465	95,334	97,241	99,185	101,169
Target's SG&A	27,086	29,253	30,277	31,337	32,433	33,568	34,743
Subtotal	116,049	120,885	123,741	126,670	129,674	132,754	135,913
Cost savings	–	–	1,237	3,800	3,890	3,983	4,077
% of subtotal	N/A	N/A	1.0%	3.0%	3.0%	3.0%	3.0%
Total SG&A expense	116,049	120,885	122,504	122,870	125,784	128,771	131,835
Total EBITDA, proforma	**$195,984**	**$207,559**	**$237,205**	**$269,727**	**$301,405**	**$313,192**	**$325,456**
% margin	21.3%	21.7%	23.6%	25.5%	27.1%	27.4%	27.6%
EBIT							
Buyer's D&A expense	37,068	38,180	38,944	39,722	40,517	41,327	42,154
Target's D&A expense (historical)	9,029	9,751	10,434	11,164	11,945	12,782	13,676
Target's D&A expense (incremental)	N/A	–	8,500	8,500	8,500	8,500	8,500
Total D&A expense, proforma	46,097	47,931	57,877	59,386	60,962	62,609	64,330
Total EBIT, proforma	**$149,887**	**$159,628**	**$179,327**	**$210,341**	**$240,442**	**$250,584**	**$261,126**
% margin	16.3%	16.7%	17.8%	19.9%	21.6%	21.9%	22.1%
Net Income							
Interest expense and fees, proforma	N/A	N/A	6,727	6,402	6,077	5,752	5,427
Tax expense, proforma	44,217	49,644	51,780	61,182	70,310	73,450	76,710
% tax rate	29.5%	31.1%	30.0%	30.0%	30.0%	30.0%	30.0%
Total net income, proforma	**$105,670**	**$109,984**	**$120,820**	**$142,757**	**$164,056**	**$171,382**	**$178,989**

A P P E N D I X   6 F

Sample Proforma Debt Schedule

Proforma Debt Schedule ($000s)	Actual Results		Projected Results				
Fiscal Year Ending December 31:	**2014a**	**2015a**	**2016e**	**2017e**	**2018e**	**2019e**	**2020e**
Bank Line of Credit							
Opening balance	N/A	N/A	$25,000	$20,000	$15,000	$10,000	$5,000
Increase (decrease)	N/A	25,000	(5,000)	(5,000)	(5,000)	(5,000)	(5,000)
Closing balance	**N/A**	**25,000**	**20,000**	**15,000**	**10,000**	**5,000**	**–**
Average balance outstanding	N/A	N/A	22,500	17,500	12,500	7,500	2,500
Interest rate	N/A	N/A	6.5%	6.5%	6.5%	6.5%	6.5%
Interest expense, bank debt	**N/A**	**N/A**	**1,463**	**1,138**	**813**	**488**	**163**
Subordinated Debt							
Opening balance	N/A	N/A	$50,000	$50,000	$50,000	$50,000	$50,000
Increase (decrease)	N/A	50,000	–	–	–	–	–
Closing balance	**N/A**	**50,000**	**50,000**	**50,000**	**50,000**	**50,000**	**50,000**
Average balance outstanding	N/A	N/A	50,000	50,000	50,000	50,000	50,000
Interest rate	N/A	N/A	10.0%	10.0%	10.0%	10.0%	10.0%
Interest expense, subdebt	**N/A**	**N/A**	**5,000**	**5,000**	**5,000**	**5,000**	**5,000**
Amortization of Financing Fees							
Bank Debt Fees[1]	N/A	N/A	$50	$50	$50	$50	$50
Subordinated Debt Fees[2]	N/A	N/A	214	214	214	214	214
Total financing fees	**N/A**	**N/A**	**264**	**264**	**264**	**264**	**264**
Total Interest Expense and Fees							
Interest expense, Bank Line of Credit	N/A	N/A	$1,463	$1,138	$813	$488	$163
Interest expense, Subordinated Debt	N/A	N/A	5,000	5,000	5,000	5,000	5,000
Amortization of Financing Fees	N/A	N/A	264	264	264	264	264
Total interest expense and fees	**N/A**	**N/A**	**6,727**	**6,402**	**6,077**	**5,752**	**5,427**

[1] Fees are 1% of $25 million in borrowings, amortized over a five-year term.
[2] Fees are 3% of $50 million in borrowings, amortized over a seven-year term.

APPENDIX 6G

Target's Proforma Balance Sheet

Proforma Balance Sheet ($000s)				
Fiscal Year Ending December 31, 2015	Buyer	Target	Adjustments	Proforma
Assets				
Current Assets				
Cash and equivalents	$77,887	$20,867	($14,625)[1]	$84,129
Accounts receivable	116,831	31,300	–	148,131
Inventory	93,465	25,040	–	118,505
Other current assets	38,944	10,433	–	49,377
Total Current Assets	327,127	87,640	(14,625)	400,142
PP&E, net	74,556	19,974	2,500[2]	97,030
Customer lists	–	–	40,000[3]	40,000
Goodwill	–	–	116,836[4]	116,836
Total Assets	**$401,683**	**$107,614**	**$144,711**	**$654,008**
Liabilities & Shareholders' Equity				
Current Liability				
Accounts payable	$136,303	$36,517	$0	$172,820
Accrued expenses	38,943	10,433	–	49,376
Current portion of long-term debt	–	–	5,000[5]	5,000
Total current liabilities	175,246	46,950	5,000	227,196
Bank line of credit	–	–	20,000[6]	20,000
Other debt	–	35,000	16,750[7]	51,750
Total liabilities	175,246	81,950	41,750	298,946
Shareholders' equity	226,437	25,664	102,961	355,062
Total Liabilities & Shareholders' Equity	**$401,683**	**$107,614**	**$144,711**	**$654,008**

[1] Adjustments to cash as follows:

New bank line of credit	$25,000
New subordinated debt	50,000
Paydown of Target's debt	(35,000)
Advisory fees	(2,775)
Financing fees	(1,750)
Other transaction fees	(1,850)
Cash paid to selling shareholders	(48,250)
Total adjustments to cash	($14,625)

[2] Write-up of target's PP&E, net to fair value.
[3] Write-up of customer lists to fair value.
[4] Excess of purchase price over fair value of tangible and identifiable intangible assets.
[5] Portion of bank line of credit and subordinated debt to be repaid in 2016e.
[6] Reflects noncurrent portion of new bank line of credit.
[7] Adjustments to Other Debt as follows:

New subordinated debt	$50,000
Capitalized financing fees	1,750
Redeem target's debt	(35,000)
Total adjustments to Other Debt	$16,750

LANDMARK AND RECENT M&A LEGAL CASES IMPACTING VALUATION

The M&A field is rich with opportunity, but it also carries considerable legal risk. Any merger transaction can be second-guessed by plaintiffs. Indeed, one-fourth of all director and officer (D&O) liability insurance payouts happen because plaintiffs challenge the legality of some aspect of a merger or acquisition. In the United States, these challenges hinge on state law, federal law, or common law made through judicial decisions.

This section highlights significant cases from the U.S. Supreme Court, as well as state federal and chancery (business) courts in the United States—especially the state of Delaware, which is home to a dominant percentage of large U.S. public companies.

The following summaries of "landmark" case law have been provided by the attorneys at Seward & Kissel LLP.

CASE: *DOFT & CO. V. TRAVELOCITY.COM INC.,* 2004 DEL. CH. LEXIS 75 (DEL. CH. MAY 20, 2004), *ON REARGUMENT,* 2004 DEL. CH. LEXIS 84 (DEL. CH. JUNE 10, 2004)— *COMPARABLE TRANSACTIONS ANALYSIS IS PREFERRED WHEN IT IS DIFFICULT TO FORMULATE RELIABLE PROJECTIONS.*

Travelocity.com Inc. ("Travelocity") went public in 2000 when the online travel business was in its infancy and had an uncertain future. By early 2001, it had become "the leading online travel agency." However, the terrorist attacks on September 11, 2001, disrupted the industry, leading to slowed growth. Further, Expedia surpassed Travelocity as the leading online travel agency in early 2002 on the back of its superior business model. Specifically, Expedia utilized "the merchant model . . . in which travel agencies purchase the airline tickets, hotel rooms, or car rentals at a negotiated rate from the suppliers and then resell them directly to consumers at a higher price." This "model generate[d] higher profit margins and much higher cash flows than the traditional agency model," in which "the travel agent merely serves as a liaison between the supplier and the customer and receives a commission for the sale."

In February 2002, Travelocity's majority shareholder, Sabre Holdings Corporation ("Sabre"), initiated negotiations with the Travelocity board of directors to buy back the outstanding public stock of Travelocity not owned by Sabre. After the board rejected an offer price of $23 per share as inadequate, Sabre went directly to the shareholders with a tender offer at that price but later increased the offer to $28 per share. The board then voted to recommend the sweetened $28 offer to Travelocity's shareholders. Sabre succeeded in acquiring 95% of the outstanding stock through its tender offer, which was followed by a short-form merger cashing out the remaining minority at $28 per share to complete the going private transaction. Petitioner shareholders then brought an appraisal action seeking the fair value of their shares.

The experts for both sides utilized discounted cash flow ("DCF") and comparable transactions analyses. The court, however, found that DCF was not appropriate for this case and relied on comparable transactions analysis. Travelocity management had prepared five-year projections, which are usually "shown to be reasonably reliable and are useful in later performing a DCF analysis." However, here, the court found that neither these projections, nor the projections generated by the experts, could be relied upon, because the short financial history of Travelocity, the rapid innovation of business models in the industry, and the effects of September 11 made accurate forecasting of future financial performance impossible. Therefore, the DCF analyses were excluded from the court's determination as to whether $28 per share was a fair value.

Regarding the comparable transactions analysis, both parties agreed that Expedia was the only comparable company to Travelocity, "but disagree[d] on the appropriate discount to be applied to the multiples derived from their analyses of Expedia." Petitioner's expert relied on positive analyst reports of Travelocity's business to conclude "that Travelocity should only be at a 'moderate,' if any, discount to Expedia," which he decided should be 10%. Travelocity's expert, on the other hand, "conclude[d] that the discount to Expedia should [have been] at least 40% because Travelocity had a higher cost of capital, a lower growth rate, and a lesser ability to generate cash." The court found this 40% discount rate to be "substantially correct, albeit unduly pessimistic," and concluded that 35% was the proper discount rate. The court then concluded that firm value/EBITDA and price-to-earnings multiples were "the most important multiples in calculating Travelocity's firm value," giving them 2/3 weight and 1/3 weight, respectively, in the valuation determination. Based on this, the court found that $25.20 per share was the fair value of Petitioner's stock.

However, the court took the analysis a step further and noted that "[t]he equity valuation produced in a comparable company analysis does not accurately reflect the intrinsic worth of a corporation on a going concern basis." For this reason, the court concluded that to "correct [for] this minority trading discount," a control premium must be added. Relying on precedential cases in which the fair value determination was adjusted to account for a control premium, the court applied a 30% premium, resulting in a per-share fair value of $32.76. On Travelocity's motion for reconsideration, the court revised two computational points used previously by the court and found that the proper fair value was $30.43 per share.

CASE: *IN RE TRADOS INC. S'HOLDER LITIG.,* 73 A.3D 17 (DEL. CH. 2013)—*ZERO MAY BE A FAIR VALUE FOR COMMON SHARES IN A MERGER WHEN THE COMMON STOCK HAD NO VALUE PRIOR TO THE TRANSACTION.*

Trados Inc. ("Trados"), a desktop translation software company, received funding from several venture capital firms in exchange for preferred stock in Trados and positions on the Trados board of directors. Consequently, at the time of the disputed transaction, the venture capital firms held a $57.9 million liquidation preference, and five of the seven Trados board seats were filled by principals of the venture capital firms and other individuals nominated by the venture capital firms.

As Trados progressed under this capital structure, the venture capital firms began seeking an exit strategy with particular focus on the mergers-and-acquisitions market. To motivate the Trados officers to pursue such a sale, the board implemented a management incentive plan ("MIP"), which would provide the officers with proceeds from a sale far greater than what they would otherwise receive as common stockholders. Following the implementation of the MIP, Trados was acquired for $60 million. Under the terms of the MIP, Trados officers received the first 13% of the consideration, which amounted to $7.8 million. The venture capital firms received the remaining $52.2 million, leaving the common stockholders with nothing. But for the MIP, the preferred stockholders would have received their full liquidation preference of $57.9 million, and the common stockholders would have received the remaining $2.1 million.

A common shareholder then brought an appraisal action seeking the fair value of his shares and a second action alleging breach of the fiduciary duty of loyalty for selling the company instead of continuing to operate it to generate value for the common stock. The Delaware Court of Chancery, relying on discounted cash flow analysis, rejected these claims, explaining that, although the negotiation and sale process was severely flawed, the premerger value of the common stock was zero and it had no "reasonable prospect of generating value." Specifically, the court found that Trados needed cash to finance a business plan that would produce enough growth to create value for the common stockholders, but its venture capital investors refused to invest more, and this made it impossible to attract investments from other funds. Further, even with funding, Trados's growth rate would have to exceed the preferred shareholders' 8% cumulative dividend to create yield for the common shareholders. Thus, while Trados likely could have remained viable, it had dim prospects of adding enough value to overcome this dividend and the large liquidation preference. Therefore, in receiving no consideration for the merger, "the common stockholders received the substantial equivalent in value of what they had before, and the merger satisfie[d] the test of fairness."

CASE: *IN RE ANSWERS CORP. S'HOLDERS LITIG.,* 2011 DEL. CH. LEXIS 57 (DEL. CH. APR. 11, 2011)—*VALUATION METHODOLOGIES OTHER THAN DCF ANALYSIS MAY BE APPROPRIATE UNDER CERTAIN CIRCUMSTANCES WARRANTING THE OMISSION OF DCF.*

Answers Corporation ("Answers"), which operated Answers.com, determined that a sale of the company was in the best interests of the shareholders due to "possible competition from larger companies and the general unpredictability of its market sector." After rejecting an acquirer's initial offer, Answers retained UBS as its financial advisor for the potential transaction. After negotiations, several offer price increases, and a market check consisting of ten other companies identified by UBS as potential acquirers, UBS issued a fairness opinion in favor of the deal. However, Answers had been largely dependent on Google, as 75% of the site's revenue and 90% of its traffic came through Google in the years before the disputed transaction. Therefore, Answers' revenue and value to shareholders depended largely on the algorithms used by Google and other search engines to direct users to content, which are subject to unpredictable changes. This made valuing Answers particularly difficult. In particular, DCF analysis was not a feasible option, because the company was not able "to forecast financial performance beyond the next fiscal year" due to its dependence on Google's algorithms. Further, comparable transactions analysis was complicated by a lack of "any pure comparables because [Answers'] business [was] somewhat unique." For these reasons, UBS did not perform a DCF analysis and performed a comparable analysis using "a group of publicly traded companies which [it] believe[d] [were] most comparable to Answers.com."

Plaintiffs challenged Answers' board's reliance on UBS's fairness opinion in approving the merger because of its omission of a DCF analysis, which they argued rendered the opinion inadequate. The court rejected these claims, though, instead holding that "the Board acted reasonably in relying on UBS's analysis, which was sensibly crafted given the limited universe of information available and the unique characteristics of the Company."

CASE: *IN RE SUNBELT BEV. CORP. S'HOLDER LITIG.*, 2010 DEL. CH. LEXIS 1 (DEL. CH. JAN. 5, 2010)—*THE APPROPRIATENESS OF DIFFERENT VALUATION METHODOLOGIES DEPENDS ON THE FACTS OF THE CASE.*

Sunbelt Beverage Corporation ("Sunbelt") attempted to cash out a large minority shareholder, the Goldring family ("Goldring"), which owned approximately 14.9% of Sunbelt's stock at the time of the disputed transaction. Specifically, Sunbelt entered into a stock swap agreement with another beverage distribution company in which each company would obtain 15% of the other's stock. The Sunbelt board of directors intended to use Goldring's stock as the swap consideration and subsequently issued a call on shares owned by Goldring pursuant to Sunbelt's Shareholder's Agreement, which predetermined the call price formula. It then authorized a freeze-out merger with its own acquisition vehicle to acquire the Goldring shares at the call price. Goldring then brought both an appraisal action and an action for breach of fiduciary duty, which the court heard on a consolidated basis.

The court addressed several valuation issues in its opinion. First, Sunbelt noted that the price formula was delineated in the Shareholder's Agreement, which was the product of an arm's-length negotiation between sophisticated parties, and argued that this should be evidence of the fairness of the price. However, the court disagreed and found that the Shareholder's Agreement formula was "neither relevant to nor evidence of fair value." Specifically, the court found the Shareholder's Agreement was negotiated and agreed upon three years prior to the transaction at issue, which does not constitute evidence of fair value in the same way such an agreement might if it were negotiated immediately prior to the transaction.

Aside from this durational issue, the court found the price formula flawed, because it "relie[d] too heavily on the book value of Sunbelt, provide[d] a premium reliant solely on the company's net income in the two years preceding any Formula-based transaction, and d[id] not adequately incorporate the influence of intangibles and good will on the company's value."

Next, the court criticized and discarded the comparable transactions analysis proffered by Goldring's valuation expert. First, the court expressed "doubts about the comparability of the companies included in [the expert]'s analysis," specifically in regard to "differences in size between the comparables and Sunbelt, as well as the differences across product lines and geography, both of which stand to introduce differences across regulatory regimes." However, even assuming the comparables were adequate, the court identified other flaws in the execution of the analysis. Particularly, the court found that the expert "failed to account for important elements of specific transactions that stood to influence the accuracy of his calculations," especially "real-estate payments and post-closing price adjustments." The expert rejoined that he utilized the median multiple approach to account for these methodological flaws. The court rejected this argument, though, holding instead that "[t]he median multiple approach is at its best when it smooths out unknown or immeasurable sources of difference and error in an analysis," rather than when, as here, "there are known and measurable variations or errors in an already small sample size."

The court then addressed the inclusion of a company-specific risk premium within a discounted cash flow analysis. The inclusion of a company-specific risk premium would result in a lower valuation of the company, and thus a lower appraisal valuation. Accordingly, Sunbelt argued that "(1) the at-will termination of supplier agreements that prevails throughout the wholesale alcohol distribution industry; (2) the competition Sunbelt faces from specific players such as Southern Wine & Spirits; and (3) the level of optimism contained in Sunbelt's management projections" warranted the inclusion of a company-specific risk premium in the valuation of Sunbelt. The court disagreed, finding that Sunbelt's first two proffered justifications for a company-specific premium clearly apply to the beverage distribution industry as a whole. As for the third stated justification, the court found no indication "that it was riskier for Sunbelt to rely on its specific management projections than it is for all companies to rely on management projections." Further, accepting this as justification for the inclusion of a company-specific risk premium would allow companies "to manufacture justification for a company-specific risk premium (and all the quantitative uncertainty accompanied therewith) simply by adjusting its management projections such that there is a heightened risk in relying on those projections." Accordingly, the court rejected the inclusion of a company-specific risk premium based on the facts of this transaction.

Lastly, the court considered both parties' upward adjustments of the company valuation based on its conversion from a C corporation to an S corporation. Goldring never owned shares of the S corporation, as Sunbelt was still a C corporation at the time the shares were taken from Goldring. The court rejected the adjustment for the purposes of this case, because "[t]he basic concept of value under the appraisal statute is that the stockholder is entitled to be paid for that which has been taken from him." Therefore, because Goldring "was cashed out as a shareholder in a C corporation . . . there [was] no basis for an upwards adjustment of the per-share value of Sunbelt on the basis of Sunbelt's post-merger conversion to an S corporation."

CASE: *CEDE & CO. V. JRC ACQUISITION CORP.,* **2004 DEL. CH. LEXIS 12 (DEL. CH. FEB. 10, 2004)** *THIS COURT RETROSPECTIVELY ADDED 58 CENTS PER SHARE TO A $13 PER SHARE VALUATION BASED ON A VARIETY OF FACTORS INCLUDING THE TARGET'S LACK OF DEBT, PRE-DEAL POSSIBILITIES FOR EXPANSION, AND SMALL-CAP STATUS.*

The Rothman family ("Rothman") owned 78% of the outstanding stock of 800-JR Cigar, Inc. ("JR Cigar") and initiated an offer to purchase the remaining outstanding shares of the company. Following this offer, Rothman owned more than 90% of JR Cigar and cashed out the remaining shareholders at $13.00 per share through a short-form merger. Following this transaction, Petitioner, a significant minority shareholder, brought an appraisal action seeking a determination of the fair value of its shares. Both parties' experts performed DCF analyses, and Petitioner's expert also performed a comparable transactions analysis. The court considered each of these analyses in turn.

For his comparable transactions analysis, Petitioner's expert used a list of comparable transactions that had been used by the financial adviser to JR Cigar's special committee to evaluate and issue a fairness opinion regarding a then-proposed merger. The court noted that most of these transactions were not particularly useful because they involved change-of-control transactions, whereas a minority interest acquisition was at issue here. The expert and the financial advisor relied on one transaction in particular, which involved Swisher International and General Cigar, both cigar manufacturers, and which was also a minority-interest acquisition. However, the court discredited this comparison, because it was a merger between manufacturers, whereas JR Cigar was a retailer. Further, the court criticized Petitioner's expert's adjustment of the multiples in his comparable transactions analysis compared to the multiples used by the financial advisor, because the expert had included results for the quarters following announcement of the transactions, which inflated the multiples.

In evaluating the different results of the DCF analyses performed by the parties' experts, the court began by considering the projected growth rate used in the calculations. Based on the "declining domestic market for cigars and cigarettes" at the time of the transaction, the court determined that a projected growth rate of 3.5% was proper, as it reflected growth only slightly above the rate of inflation. The court found that this "account[ed] for the possibility, however marginal, that JR Cigar may [have been] able to expand," in the otherwise declining-industry market.

The court next reviewed the weighted average cost of capital (WACC) calculations used by the parties to determine the proper discount rate for the DCF analysis. The court explained that WACC is "the cost of equity times the percentage of equity in the capital structure plus the cost of debt times that percentage of debt." The parties disagreed on the proper percentage of debt and the proper cost of equity to use in this equation. Regarding the percentage of debt, the court concluded that, because "JR Cigar had no debt before the merger," and "[P]etitioner had introduced no evidence of non-speculative plans to incur significant debt," the proper percentage of debt was 10%. This, according to the court, "account[ed] for the probability that JR Cigar may seek to incur limited debt to pursue expansion opportunities."

Regarding the cost of equity, the parties disagreed on the appropriate level of the equity size premium to use in the calculation. The equity size premium reflects the fact that "smaller companies have higher returns on average than larger ones, i.e., small companies have a higher cost of equity." Petitioner's expert applied the equity size premium corresponding to "low-cap" companies, or those with market capitalizations between $192 million and $840 million, "because he 'determined that the value, the market capitalization, should be more at the fair value implied market capitalization.'" JR Cigar's expert, on the other hand, applied the premium corresponding to "micro-cap" companies, or those with market capitalizations below $192 million, "because its market capitalization, based on the traded price of the stock before the announcement of the merger (or based on the merger price), was well below $192 million." The court declined to find that "adjusting the equity size premium based on implied fair value is appropriate," and concluded that JR Cigar was a micro-cap company, which corresponds to an equity size premium of 2.6%. The court then entered this cost of equity and the percentage of debt into the WACC equation to complete the DCF analysis and determined that $13.58 per share was the fair value of JR Cigar's stock.

CASE: *BERGER V. PUBCO CORP.,* 2010 DEL. CH. LEXIS 110 (DEL. CH. MAY 10, 2010)—*INCLUSION OF CONTROL PREMIUMS IN VALUATION IS ONLY APPROPRIATE UNDER COMPARABLE TRANSACTIONS ANALYSIS, AND POTENTIAL CAPITAL GAINS TAXES ARE NOT AN APPROPRIATE VALUATION FACTOR WHEN NO EVIDENCE OF A SALE DATE EXISTS AT THE TIME OF VALUATION.*

Plaintiff shareholder brought an appraisal action following a short-form merger that cashed out her stock ownership of Pubco Corporation ("Pubco"). Before the court were the issues of whether a control premium was appropriate and whether it was appropriate "to reduce the value of Pubco's securities portfolio based on projected capital gain tax liability." On the first issue, the court held that the inclusion of control premiums in valuation is only warranted under comparable transactions analysis. Here, both parties' appraisers relied on discounted cash flow and book value analyses rather than on a comparable transactions methodology, making a control premium improper in valuing the company.

In regard to the second issue, the court held that it was inappropriate to reduce the value of Pubco's securities portfolio based on potential capital gains tax liability, because the likelihood of such liability was only speculative. While some of the securities held by Pubco "had market prices that exceeded their purchase prices," which would lead to a capital gains tax if the securities were sold, "[a]ll that was known and capable of proof on the merger date is the market value of the securities Pubco owned." Further, there were no indications that "any particular securities were earmarked for sale or that Pubco had a particular schedule regarding the disposition of any securities in its portfolio." The court rejected the defendants' arguments that "it had a history of selling the securities in its portfolio and that the 'operative reality' on the merger date was that all of the portfolio would be sold at some point in the future." The court instead held that "this is not evidence that a particular asset would be sold on the merger date or on any particular date thereafter and that a tax liability would necessarily be created upon such sale."

CASE: *WEINBERGER V. UOP, INC.,* 457 A.2D 701 (DEL. 1983)— *APPRAISAL AND STOCK VALUATION CASES SHOULD NO LONGER USE THE DELAWARE BLOCK METHOD, BUT RATHER A MORE LIBERAL APPROACH INCLUDING PROOF OF VALUE BY ANY TECHNIQUES OR METHODS GENERALLY ACCEPTABLE IN THE FINANCIAL COMMUNITY AND CONSIDERING ALL FACTORS RELEVANT TO THE VALUE OF A COMPANY.*

In the Delaware Court of Chancery, the class action plaintiff, a former shareholder of UOP, Inc. ("UOP") challenged the elimination of UOP's minority shareholders by a cash-out merger between UOP and its majority owner, The Signal Companies, Inc. (Signal"). After having purchased a majority stake in UOP for $21 per share in 1975, Signal now desired to purchase all the remaining shares. Signal discussed the merger with UOP's CEO, and together they relied on a fairness opinion prepared quickly to acquire a unanimous vote from the board recommending the merger. The chancellor held that the terms of the merger were fair to the minority shareholders and that the Delaware Block Method of valuation was appropriate. Under the Delaware Block Method, three elements of value are examined and assigned a weight: market value, asset value, and earnings value. The weighted average of these three elements is the value under this approach.

On appeal, the Delaware Supreme Court addressed a number of issues, including the fairness of the merger in terms of the adequacy of disclosures made to the minority shareholders, as well as the fairness of the merger in terms of the adequacy of the price paid and valuation method applied. The Court found that the record did not support a conclusion that the minority stockholder vote was an informed one, as material information had been withheld amounting to a breach of fiduciary duty, causing the court to hold that the terms of the merger did not satisfy the test of fairness.

Regarding the method of valuation and appraisal of the stock, the Delaware Supreme Court held that the Delaware Block Method, to the extent that it excludes generally accepted techniques used in the financial community, is now outmoded and applicable law must be adjusted accordingly. The court favored a more liberal approach to the valuation of fair price, requiring consideration of all relevant factors involving the value of a company, including but not limited to assets, market value, earnings, and future prospects of a company. The court found that this liberal method was not only more in tune with the realities of present-day financial affairs, but consistent with the purpose and intent of statutory law.

CASE: *IN RE 3COM S'HOLDERS LITIG.,* 2009 DEL. CH. LEXIS 215 (DEC. 18, 2009)—*UNDER DELAWARE LAW, SO LONG AS THE VALUATION WORK IS ACCURATELY DESCRIBED AND APPROPRIATELY QUALIFIED, THE RATIONALE FOR THE METHODOLOGY NEED NOT BE DISCLOSED.*

In 2009, the Delaware Court of Chancery denied plaintiff shareholders' motion for expedited discovery, holding that the shareholders failed to state colorable disclosure claims or claims for breach of fiduciary duty. Shareholders of 3Com Corporation ("3Com") sought to enjoin its acquisition by Hewlett Packard Company, claiming that management failed to make adequate disclosures in the proxy statement and the board violated its fiduciary duties by approving a merger structured to preclude competitive bids. The plaintiffs alleged there were five material disclosure violations in the proxy, the fifth being that the proxy failed to disclose why 3Com's financial advisor, Goldman, Sachs & Co. ("Goldman"), deviated from accepted practices in its valuation methodology.

3Com's shareholders believed that Goldman's DCF valuation analysis deviated from accepted practices in three ways: (1) stock-based compensation was treated as a cash expense when it is not normally treated as such; (2) Goldman's selected weighted average cost of capital was higher than 3Com's cost of equity; and (3) Goldman used an increased discount rate for this merger rather than the rate it previously used when valuing 3Com for an earlier attempted buyout. The shareholders claimed that Goldman's failure to disclose why it deviated from accepted practices was a disclosure violation.

The court held that, under Delaware law, valuation work must be accurately described and appropriately qualified, but so long as that is done, the disclosure of any discrepancies between the methodology and the Delaware fair value standard under § 262, or any other standard, is not required. Shareholders are free to exercise their appraisal rights under § 262 if they believe the company to have been undervalued, but considering the realistically limitless opportunity for disagreement on appropriate valuation methods, such disagreement cannot create the basis of a disclosure claim. The court found that Goldman's nine-page analysis, summarizing the sources of information, significant assumptions made, range of value estimates, material analyses, and important limitations, was sufficient disclosure to satisfy Delaware law. The court recommended that any additional valuation discrepancies would better be served by an appraisal action.

CASE: *ANDALORO V. PFPC WORLDWIDE,* 2005 DEL. CH. LEXIS 125 (AUG. 19, 2005)—*IN SHAREHOLDER APPRAISAL CASES, THE COURT MAY NOT RELY SOLELY ON ONE SIDE'S VALUATION, BUT MUST CONDUCT AN INDEPENDENT VALUATION ANALYSIS IN REACHING A CONCLUSION OF THE FAIR VALUE OF THE ENTITY.*

In a shareholders' appraisal action in 2005, the Delaware Court of Chancery applied both the DCF valuation method and the comparable companies method, giving the DCF method 75% weight in reaching its final value conclusion. This case arose out of a 2003 merger in which PFPC Holding Corp. acquired PFPC Worldwide, Inc. The merger was unusual, as PFPC Holding Corp. did not offer appraisal rights to the minority shareholders but rather conditioned its willingness to enter into the merger on a universal waiver by all minority shareholders of their rights to appraisal or any other claims. The plaintiffs, two stockholders, refused to waive their appraisal rights, claiming breaches of fiduciary duty, and were joined in due course by several additional minority holders, seeking appraisal damages. The appraisal and breach of fiduciary duty actions were consolidated, and the Court of Chancery tried the ultimate appraisal question first, hoping the answer would resolve the entire dispute.

With respect to shareholder appraisal cases, the court explained that it may look to the opinions advanced by the parties' experts, adopt one party's framework, create its own framework, or adopt piecemeal aspects of the expert's models, methodologies, and calculations, but the court may not rely solely on one side's valuation. The court must use its judgment and conduct an independent valuation analysis to reach its conclusion of the fair value of the entity.

The court first undertook a DCF valuation analysis as the standard that underscores the financial tenet that companies should be valued based on the expected value of their future cash flows, discounted to present value and accounting for risk. At the outset, the court briefly summarized the DCF method through the following steps: (1) estimate the value of future cash flows for a discrete period based on contemporaneous management projections; (2) determine a terminal value, or the value of the entity attributable to cash flows expected after the end of the discrete period; and (3) discount the cash flows and terminal values back using the capital asset pricing model.

The court then went on to perform a comparable companies analysis, determining it to be a common technique of real-world financial professionals and thus relevant to the present case and deserving of substantial weight. The court again briefly summarized the method as consisting of (1) finding comparable publicly traded companies that have reviewable financial information; (2) calculating the ratio between the trading price of each company's stocks and using another recognized measure reflecting income, such as revenue, EBIT, or EBITDA; (3) correcting the ratios to account for differences in capital structure; and (4) applying the average multiple to the relevant income measurement of the target company.

Through its DCF and comparable companies analyses, the court arrived at two valuation conclusions. The court chose to accord the DCF valuation method 75% weight in reaching its final value conclusion, because it deemed the DCF valuation the best technique for valuing an entity when reliable information regarding the required inputs is available. The court arrived at a fair value conclusion by combining the 75% weight of the DCF analysis with the 25% weight attributed to the comparable companies analysis.

CASE: *DEL. OPEN MRI RADIOLOGY ASSOCS., P.A. V. KESSLER,* **898 A.2D 290 (DEL. CH. 2006)**—*IN VALUING A CORPORATION PURSUANT TO A MERGER, A COURT MAY CONSIDER ALL RELEVANT, NONSPECULATIVE FACTORS, WHICH MAY INCLUDE ELEMENTS OF FUTURE VALUE THAT ARE KNOWN OR SUSCEPTIBLE OF PROOF AS OF THE DATE OF A MERGER AND NOT THE PRODUCT OF SPECULATION.*

In 2006, the Delaware Court of Chancery reviewed a combined appraisal and entire fairness action brought by petitioner minority shareholders against respondent majority shareholders, asserting that they did not receive fair value for their shares during a squeeze-out merger. Both the majority and the minority shareholders were radiologists who had formed a corporation to capture additional revenue by owning MRI centers. The majority shareholders eventually forced a squeeze-out merger using an acquisition vehicle. At the time of the merger, Del. Open MRI was comprised of three centers. There were plans, however, to open three more centers, and the projected centers were not taken into account for valuation purposes.

According to the court, however, Delaware law is clear that in valuing a corporation pursuant to a merger, a court may consider all relevant, nonspeculative factors, which may include elements of future value that are known or susceptible of proof as of the date of a merger and not the product of speculation. When a business has plans to replicate its current facilities as of the merger date, and the business plan includes specific expansion plans or changes in strategy, the court determined that such plans must obviously be considered as part of the valuation process. There is an obvious relation between the need to evaluate what the business plans of the company being valued are as of the date of the merger and the equitable corporate opportunity doctrine. The Delaware Supreme Court previously held that corporate opportunity claims can be valued in the context of an appraisal action. The court held that the "operative reality" of Del. Open MRI included the impending center expansions, and the failure of the merger to take into consideration the plans in determining fair value was improper.

CASE: *HIGHFIELDS CAPITAL, LTD. V. AXA FIN., INC.,* C.A. 804-VCL, 939 A.2D 34 (DEL. CH. 2007)—*A COURT SHOULD GIVE SUBSTANTIAL EVIDENTIARY WEIGHT TO THE MERGER PRICE TO DETERMINE FAIR VALUE IN A DELAWARE APPRAISAL ACTION IF THE MERGER RESULTED FROM AN ARM'S-LENGTH BARGAINING PROCESS AND NO STRUCTURAL IMPEDIMENTS DISTORT THE OPERATIVE MARKET REALITY.*

In a 2007 Delaware appraisal case, an institutional investor comprised of Highfields Capital–affiliated partnerships ("Highfields") petitioned the court seeking judicial appraisal of its equity holdings in AXA Financial, Inc. ("AXA"), after AXA's all-cash, all-shares merger with The MONY Group, Inc. ("MONY"). At the time of the merger, Highfields owned approximately 4.3% of MONY's outstanding common stock. In 2003, MONY's board of directors believed the company to be in a dire situation and agreed to the $31 per share price, determining the price to be fair after consultation with financial and legal advisors, as well as senior management.

The price was met with heavy criticism from institutional investors and led to immediate shareholder litigation, of which Highfields was a vocal participant. Plaintiff shareholders argued that MONY's board of directors breached its fiduciary duty to obtain the highest reasonably available value in the sale of the company. The court, however, concluded that the MONY board had ample discretion to make a good-faith and honest determination and to agree to a merger and value that was in the best interests of the corporation. Highfields was the only stockholder to move forward with the judicial appraisal demand that led to this appeal.

Based on its experts' testimony, Highfields argued that MONY's fair value was between $37 and $47 per share and that the $31 merger price was an unreliable indicator, reflecting only the value to AXA as a buyer rather than the value as a going concern. Highfields contended that without the merger, MONY was poised for success because of management's two-to-three-year plan and the increasingly receptive market. On the other hand, AXA argued that the going concern value was no more than $21 per share and that the merger price was the best indicator because of the arm's-length nature of the transaction.

After analyzing each side's valuation methods, which included DCF, comparable transactions, comparable companies, and market price methods, the court found that neither party fully satisfied its burden of persuasion regarding the valuation of MONY. It held, instead, that the court may derive fair value in a Delaware appraisal action from a sale or merger price if the sale or merger resulted from an arm's-length bargaining process and no structural impediments were to distort the operative market reality. The court found $24.97 to be the fair value of the shares and awarded that to the petitioners.

CASE: *GHOLL V. EMACHINES, INC.,* CA 19444-NC, 2004 DEL. CH. LEXIS 171 (NOV. 24, 2004), AFF'D, 2005 DEL. LEXIS 220 (JUNE 14, 2005)—*WHEN NEITHER PARTY SATISFIES ITS BURDEN OF ESTABLISHING FAIR MARKET VALUE, THE COURT MUST USE ITS OWN INDEPENDENT JUDGMENT TO DETERMINE FAIR MARKET VALUE AND IN DOING SO SHOULD CONSIDER ALL RELEVANT FACTORS THAT WERE KNOWN OR KNOWABLE ON THE MERGER DATE.*

The Delaware Court of Chancery determined in a 2004 appraisal action that neither party had met its burden of establishing the fair market value ("FMV") of eMachines, Inc. ("eMachines"), pursuant to the company's short-form merger. The court held that when neither party satisfies its burden of establishing the FMV, the court must use its own independent judgment to determine FMV. The court must determine the FMV as the going concern value, exclusive of any third-party element of value arising from the accomplishment or expectation of a merger.

After a few years of distress in a constantly evolving electronics market, eMachines contacted 55 parties in an auction but received only one bid, which was rejected without public disclosure. Following a change in management and strategy in 2001, the company began a significant turnaround. During this turnaround, one of the company's directors submitted an offer (lower than the original bid received in the auction). The prior bidder was contacted and submitted a higher bid than the director. A slightly higher bid was then offered by the director, and the offer was accepted without notification of an additional opportunity to the third-party bidder. The company argued that the price and process were fair and thorough, but the court disagreed. The court found that the auction and subsequent bidding war between the director and the third party were not inclusive of all potential bidders and were conducted too quickly to be thorough. Additionally, there was no evidence that the third-party bidder had nearly the same level of information as the director regarding the bidding process and timing, and the hasty time frame was due to the stockholders' (who were sophisticated strategic partners) desire for a timely liquidity event.

The opposing shareholders brought this appraisal action, but the court held that it must use its independent judgment to come to a fair valuation as neither party had satisfied its burden regarding valuation of the shares. The court decided that a DCF valuation was appropriate and went on to (1) project operating cash flows out to a valuation horizon; (2) determine a terminal value representing the business's value at the horizon; and (3) discount all cash flows to their present value. The court was required to consider all facts known or which could be ascertained as of the date of the merger, including contemporary premerger management projections. The court eventually determined that the value of the shares was significantly higher due to the new management's projections and strategy and accordingly awarded petitioner shareholders the value of such shares and interest.

VALUATION:
A GLOSSARY OF TERMS

Accounting rate of return (ARR). A ratio used to show the viability of an investment. It is measured as undiscounted average earnings after taxes and depreciation divided by average book value of the investment over its life. The higher the number, the better the investment. The analyst then identifies projects with an accounting return greater than a cutoff rate. By comparing this ratio among companies, an analyst can find an average multiple to use in setting a price.

Accrual accounting. A method of accounting that reports revenues in the year they are earned and deducts or capitalizes expenses in the year they are incurred, whether or not payment is received or made, unless it is a cash transaction. The alternative method of accounting, called *cash accounting*, reports revenues and expenses only when cash is received or paid. Corporations and partnerships with revenues over $5 million are required to use accrual rather than cash accounting.

Active market. A market that has enough trading activity to be able to yield information relevant for a valuation of the elements (e.g., shares of stock) being traded. Investment positions in companies that do not have an active market for their stock, particularly minority positions, have a lower value than comparable companies that do have an active market, due to inability to sell. This discount can be offset by shareholder agreements.

Algorithm.   A set of steps used to solve a mathematical problem.

Algorithmic trading.   Making buy, sell, and hold orders based on pre-defined rules expressed in one or more algorithms.

Allowance for loan and lease losses (ALLL).   A sum set aside by an entity to serve as a contingency amount in the event that there are losses from loans or leases. This is a key factor considered by the Federal Reserve Board when stress-testing bank holding companies considered to be systemically important financial institutions.

Amortization.   The allocation of the value of a balance sheet item (i.e., an asset or liability) over time to the income statement (as revenue or expense).

Annuity.   A series of annual payments made or received at intervals over a period of time, such as the life of the recipient.

Appraisal action.   A legal action forcing appraisal, such as a share-holder demand for the valuation of a company undergoing a change of control. (See the discussion of *Andaloro v. PFPC Worldwide*, 2005, in Appendix I.)

Arm's-length standard.   A standard for determining whether an amount of money paid or received was established in an objective fashion. For example, the Internal Revenue Service says that a controlled transaction (resulting from a close connection between parties) meets the arm's-length standard if the results of the transaction are consistent with the results that would have been realized if uncontrolled taxpayers had engaged in the same transaction under the same circumstances (a so-called *arm's-length result*).

This is usually determined by reference to the results of comparable transactions under comparable circumstances.

Attribution bias. Attributing an effect to the wrong cause due to some bias in judgment. Examples in valuation include assuming that a competitor's success is due to luck rather than superiority or that a company's poor performance is caused by poor management rather than by a poor business model. In valuation, attribution bias is generally associated with unfounded optimism, although undue pessimism can also occur.

Availability bias. In investment, a tendency to give more weight to information that is most readily available rather than seeking information that is most relevant. The best way to overcome this kind of bias in valuation is through a disciplined *due diligence* process.

Black–Scholes model. The name given to a formula for valuing options, developed by Fischer Black and Myron Scholes. It considers variables such as the current price of the stock, the strike price of the option, whether the option is a call or a put, expiration date of the option, risk-free interest rate, and stock volatility.

Comparable companies approach. An approach to valuation which seeks to value a company based on finding companies similar to the company being appraised and then calculating the value of the company through the use of price/earnings and other multiples.

Control. In investment, the state of being able to influence board decisions; generally considered to be any amount over 50% but also achievable at lower levels.

Control premium. An amount paid over a current equity valuation price, set by market price or by another method, which reflects the value of control.

Cost of capital. The return required to break even on an investment under certain conditions that affect the time value of money, such as inflation and interest rates. The *weighted average cost of capital* (*WACC*) is the average of these costs across a set of peer companies.

Delaware block method. Under this valuation method, a tradition in Delaware courts prior to more modern methods, three elements of value are examined and assigned a weight: market value, asset value, and earnings value. The weighted average of these three elements is the value under this approach. (For more on this method, see the discussion of *Weinberger v. UOP, Inc.* in Appendix I.)

Discounted cash flow (DCF). The present value of projected future cash flows, calculated by discounting the projected value of cash flows based on the expected *cost of capital.* DCF has gained increasing dominance as a valuation method in recent decades, despite its dependence on projections. DCF champions believe that the ability of a business to generate cash flow over a sustained period matters even more than other indicators of company value, such as accounting results or stock market performance.

Due diligence. In the M&A process, the stage at which the acquirer conducts a thorough study of the company it intends to acquire, confirming any warranties made by the seller and identifying any additional risks not covered by a seller warranty. The scope of due diligence varies by the amount of time and effort the acquirer is willing to invest, as well as the amount of risk the acquirer is willing to take on.

EBIT. Earnings before interest and taxes.

EBITDA. Earnings before interest, taxes, depreciation, and amortization.

Equity size premium. A price differential reflecting the higher cost of capital, and thus higher benchmark for returns, for companies with a smaller equity base. (See the discussion of *Cede & Co. v. JRC Acquisition Corp.* in Appendix I.)

Fair value. In general, a value generally recognized to be fair; in accounting specifically, a value measured under the FASB's Standard ASC 820, which explains how to value assets such as securities held by corporations under a range of conditions.

Going concern. Under U.S. GAAP, financial statements are prepared based on a belief that the company will be able to continue as a "going concern," that is, that the "entity will continue to operate such that it will be able to realize its assets and meet its obligations in the ordinary course of business." This is called *the going concern presumption.* Under a new FASB standard, effective 2015, management's assessment of a publicly held entity's ability to continue as a going concern should be based on relevant conditions or events known or reasonably knowable at the date financial statements are issued, and the look-forward period (how long the entity should be able to meet its obligations) should be one year from the date of issue.

Gross margin. *See* **Margins**.

Impairment. The accounting term for the reduction in value of an asset.

Inventory turnover. A ratio that tells an investor how quickly a company is selling its tangible goods. It is calculated as *total purchases divided by average inventory.*

Margins. Differences between revenues and costs, usually expressed as a ratio intended to indicate profitability and referred to as a profit margin. The basic formula is revenues minus the cost required to generate the revenues divided by the revenues. Numerators vary by extent of costs ignored or considered. *Gross profit margin* considers only the exact cost of generating the revenue; *EBIT margin* uses earnings before interest and taxes (EBIT); *net profit margin* counts earnings after interest, taxes, and preferred stock dividend; *operating profit margin* is similar to net profit margin, but it also subtracts extraordinary income (windfalls) from the earnings number. Since margins can be calculated in different ways it is important to use them in a consistent way. Margins can be calculated either aftertax or pretax.

Minority discount.   A lower valuation per share in a purchase of a non-controlling investment in a company that has no market for its shares. (For more on this topic, see the discussion of *Doft & Co. v. Travelocity.com Inc.,* 2004, in Appendix I. *See also* **Control premium**.)

Multiple.   A ratio typically applied to many companies in order to reveal patterns. Company valuation is multidimensional, so instead of comparing aspect X in Company A versus Company B, acquirers will look at *X in relation to Y* for Company A and then also for Company B, as well as additional companies within a peer group. There are many possible X/Y ratios, as they may explore various aspects:

- In the same kind of financial statement, e.g., *debt/equity* on the balance sheet and *earnings to sales* or *EBITDA to sales* on the income statement;
- Across different kinds of financial statements, e.g., *sales/ inventory* (in which the numerator comes from the income statement and the denominator from the balance sheet) or the *enterprise value–to-EBITDA* ratio, in which the numerator comes from the balance sheet (equity) and the denominator from the income statement;
- Beyond financial statements, e.g., *sales per employee* (in which the numerator comes from the income statement and the denominator does not appear on a financial statement);
- In relation to stock price, e.g., *earnings per share (EPS)*, *price/ earnings per share (P/E)*, *P/E/growth in EPS (P/E/G)*, *earnings/ equity* as return on equity (ROE), *price/book*, and *total shareholder return (TSR)*;

- In relation to the past, e.g., past growth rate for revenues and profits; and
- In relation to the future, e.g., *discounted cash flow (DCF)*.

(*See also* **Valuation multiple.**)

Net income.   The residual income left after payments to creditors, minority shareholders, and other nonequity claimants.

Net profit margins.   *See* **Margins.**

Operating profit margins.   *See* **Margins.**

Premium.   An amount paid above (or below) a particular benchmark, e.g., an amount above (or below) a stock's current trading price or prices set by a company's peer group.

See also **Control premium, Equity size premium,** and **Risk premium.**

Preprovision net revenue (PPNR).   A financial line item consisting of net interest income, fees, and other noninterest income, net of non-credit-related expenses. PPNR is one of the financial elements considered by the Federal Reserve Board in the stress-testing of bank holding companies considered to be systemically important financial institutions.

Pretax margins.   *See* **Margins.**

Profit margins.   *See* **Margins.**

R-squared (R^2).   The result of a correlation between two numbers or two series of numbers. R^2 is most commonly used to measure the movement of an individual security in relation to a benchmark, but it can express other correlations.

Return on assets (ROA).   A ratio that shows how well a company is using its booked assets. It is measured as *net profit before taxes divided by total assets*. Comparisons must be made to industry peers; asset-heavy businesses have low ROAs, whereas service companies have high ROAs.

Return on equity (ROE).   A ratio used to show how much cash is generated from existing assets. It is measured as (Net income ÷ Sales) × (Sales ÷ Total assets).

Risk-free interest rate.   The rate of return that provides the lowest possible risk for the period of investment. In the United States, this is associated with short-term Treasury bills.

Risk premium.   A negative premium calculated to reflect risk of loss in a company or industry. In securities investments, the amount a risky security must earn to be equivalent in value to a risk-free security; in company valuation, the premium a rational acquirer should be willing to pay (all else equal) over and above a comparable company, based on their differing situations. (For more on risk premiums, see the discussion of *In re Sunbelt Bev. Corp. Shareholder Litigation* (2010) in Appendix I.)

Segments.   Identifiable part of a business, such as groups of products and services, geographic locations, legal entities, and types of customer. Financial reporting standards for public companies (FASB Topic 280, "Segment Reporting") allow for diversity of reporting, with some minimum standards: for comparability purposes, sales and profit information by product or service line and by country are required.

Valuation.   The economic value of a company or of one or more of its assets or liabilities, or the process used to determine such value.

Valuation gap.   A difference between two valuations of the same object; in the cases of M&A valuation, generally a difference between the value the buyer and seller put on the same company.

Valuation multiple.   A ratio considered relevant to the process of valuing a company for the purpose of buying or selling it; thus, a means of
expressing a firm's market value relative to one or more key financial
metrics that presumably relate to that value.

SOURCES

The authors consulted a number of sources to enhance this glossary, which
is based primarily on their own knowledge and expressed in their own
words and sometimes based on their publications.

For deeper insights into the vocabulary of valuation, we recommend
the following websites:

- The Financial Accounting Standards Board: fasb.org
- The Internal Revenue Service: irs.gov
- The International Valuation Standards Council: ivsc.org

NOTES

CHAPTER 1

1   W. Buffett, Berkshire Hathaway 2008 Annual Report, February 27, 2009, available at http://www.berkshirehathaway.com/2008ar/2008ar.pdf (accessed February 1, 2015).

2   Zillow.com, "Center City West Home Prices & Values," available at http://www.zillow.com/center-city-west-philadelphia-pa/home-values/ (accessed December 5, 2014).

3   National Agricultural Statistics Services & United States Department of Agriculture, "Land Values 2013 Summary (August 2013)," available at http://www.thegreenhorns.net/wp-content/files_mf/1375739034Agri LandVa08022013.pdf (accessed July 4, 2015).

4   See, for example, *Consolidated Rock Prods. Co. v. DuBois*, 312 U.S. 510, 525-526 (1941); *Group of Institutional Investors v. Chicago, Mil., St. P. & Pac. R.R. Co.*, 318 U.S. 523, 540-541 (1943).

5   See R. A. G. Monks & A. R. Lajoux, *Corporate Valuation for Portfolio Analysis: Analyzing Assets, Earnings, Cash Flow, Stock Price, Governance, and Special Situations* (Hoboken, NJ: John Wiley, 2011).

CHAPTER 2

1   This is the main premise of the first Modigliani–Miller theorem. See F. Modigliani & M. H. Miller, "The Cost of Capital, Corporation Finance and the Theory of Investment," *The American Economic Review, 48*(3), June 1958, pp. 261–297. In this widely cited article the authors note that "the cost of capital is equal to the rate of interest on bonds, regardless of whether the funds are acquired through debt instruments or through new issues of common stock. Indeed, in a world of sure returns, the distinction between debt and equity funds reduces largely to one of terminology."

2   For more on these trends, see A. R. Lajoux, "Braving the Global Maze," *NACD Directorship*, May–June 2014, pp. 33–35.

3   *ONTI, Inc. v. Integra Bank*, 751 A.2d 904, 916 (Del. Ch. May 26, 1999). See this case in the "Landmark Cases" section, available at http://law.justia.com/cases/delaware/court-of-chancery/1999/14514-3.html (accessed July 4, 2015).

4   "Counterclaim Defendants further believe that PRN and AOR are not comparable because they also perform medical oncology, which is far less equipment intensive than radiation oncology, the only type performed by the Eight Centers, and because they derive significant amounts of revenues and profits from pharmaceuticals. Both of these facts make the financials of these two companies significantly different from those of the Eight Centers, according to Counterclaim Defendants." *Onti v. Integra Bank* (op. cit. note 3, supra).

5   *In re Radiology Assoc., Inc. Litigation.* 611 A.2d 485 (1991).

6   C. D. Kirkpatrick, *Time the Markets: Using Technical Analysis to Interpret Economic Data,* Revised Edition (Upper Saddle River, NJ: Pearson/Financial Times Press, 2011). Chapter "Using Technical Analysis to Interpret Economic Data" available at http://www.ftpress.com/articles/article.aspx?p=1809118&seqNum=5 (accessed July 4, 2015).

7   These durations are given as examples in L. Tuller, *Finance for Nonfinancial Managers and Small Business Owners* (Avon, MA: Adams Media, 2008).

8   See P. Suozzo, S. Cooper, G. Sutherland & Z. Deng, "Valuation Multiples: A Primer," UBS Warburg, November 2001, available at http://pages.stern.nyu.edu/~ekerschn/pdfs/readingsemk/EMK%20NYU%20S07%20Global%20Tech%20Strategy%20Valuation%20Multiples%20Primer.pdf (accessed July 4, 2015).

9   See "Leases—Joint Project of the FASB and the IASB," Financial Accounting Standards Board, June 25, 2014. See also, "Boards Continue Their March Toward New Leases Standard," Ernst & Young, June 19, 2014. For an overview of global accounting convergence, see A. R. Lajoux, "Accounting Convergence: What in the World Is Happening?" *NACD Directorship*, May–June 2014.

10 See "Leases—Joint Project of the FASB and the IASB," Financial Accounting Standards Board, June 25, 2014, available at http://www.FASB.org (accessed July 4, 2015).

11 This requirement matches the concept in the lessor accounting guidance of what constitutes a sale with the same concept in the new FASB revenue recognition standard, which evaluates whether a sale has occurred from the customer's perspective. See "Revenue Recognition—Joint Project of the FASB and IASB," June 3, 2014, available at http://www.fasb.org/revenue_recognition.shtml (accessed July 4, 2015).

12 For a discussion of bias in corporate valuation, see R. A. G. Monks & A. R. Lajoux, "Antivaluation! Human Valuation and Investment Foibles," in *Corporate Valuation for Portfolio Investment: Analyzing*

Assets, Earnings, Cash Flow, Governance, and Special Situations (Hoboken, NJ: John Wiley, 2011), available at http://onlinelibrary.wiley.com/doi/10.1002/9781118531860.app11/pdf (accessed July 5, 2015).

13   The "e" in 2014e and 2015e stands for "expected."

14   For more on the "real option" approach, see K. Smith & A. R. Lajoux, *The Art of M&A Strategy: A Guide to Building Your Company's Future through Mergers, Acquisitions, and Divestitures* (NY: McGraw-Hill Education, 2011). See also R. Bruner, "Real Options and Their Impact on M&A," in *Applied Mergers & Acquisitions* (Wiley, 2011). See also T. E. Copeland & V. Antikarov, "Real Options: Meeting the Georgetown Challenge," *Journal of Applied Corporate Finance, 17*(2), 2005, pp. 32–51.

15   *In re Sunbelt Beverage Corp. Shareholder Litigation*, Del. Ch. Consol C.A. No. 16089-CC, February 15, 2010.

16   T. F. Cummins, *"In Re Sunbelt Beverage Corp. Shareholder Litigation: A Delaware Fair Value Case Analysis,"* 2010, available at http://www.srr.com/article/re-sunbelt-beverage-corp-shareholder-litigation-delaware-fair-value-case-analysis (accessed July 4, 2015).

17   For a study showing outcomes for various M&A rationales, see KPMG in conjunction with Steven Kaplan, University of Chicago, "Determinants of M&A Success: What Factors Contribute to Deal Success?" 2010, available at http://www.kpmg.com/NZ/en/IssuesAndInsights/Articles Publications/Documents/Determinants-of-MandA-Success-report.pdf. (accessed July 4, 2015). For a more recent discussion of M&A rationale, see KPMG, "2014 M&A Outlook Survey," available at http://www.kpmgsurvey-ma.com/pdf/2014%20MA%20Outlook%20Survey.pdf?pdf=2014-MA-Outlook-Survey (accessed July 4, 2015).

18   For anecdotal evidence, see quarterly earnings releases in the first year following a merger. See, for example, "United Continental Posts Wider Loss as Revenue Weakens," Reuters, April 24, 2014, available at http://www.reuters.com/article/2014/04/24/unitedcontinental-results-idUSL2N0NG0KQ20140424 (accessed July 4, 2015).

19   Electronic Code of Federal Regulations, current as of July 1, 2015, available at http://www.ecfr.gov/cgi-bin/text-idx?SID=55a854cf58f 3a66228e5d48c885ec447&node=17:3.0.1.1.8&rgn=div5 (accessed July 5, 2015). The full title of the part is "Part 201–Form and Content of and Requirements for Financial Statements, Securities Act of 1933, Securities Exchange Act of 1934, Investment Company Act of 1940, Investment Advisers Act of 1940, and Energy and Policy and Conservation Act of 1975."

20   Id.

21   [45 FR 63671, Sept. 25, 1980, as amended at 46 FR 43412, Aug. 28, 1981; 47 FR 29837, July 9, 1982; 50 FR 25215, June 18, 1985; 50 FR 49533, Dec. 3, 1985; 59 FR 65636, Dec. 20, 1994; 74 FR 18615, Apr. 23, 2009].

CHAPTER 3

1   On January 29, 2014, the FASB voted 5–2 not to add the segments topic to its technical agenda. This means that the previous recommendation stands for the moment.

2   Ernst & Young, "Global Corporate Divestment Study: Strategic Divestments Drive Value," 2014, available at http://www.ey.com/Publication/vwLUAssets/EYGlobalCorporateDivestmentStudy/$FILE/EY-Global-Corporate-Divestment-Study.pdf (accessed February 1, 2015).

3   Duff & Phelps, *Valuation Handbook—Industry Cost of Capital*, 2015, available for ordering at http://www.duffandphelps.com/expertise/Pages/Cost_of_Capital.aspx (accessed July 4, 2015).

4   Historically, a common way of arriving at a defensible small company premium was to use the *Ibbotson SBBI Valuation Yearbook*, as shown in Figures 3-11 and 3-12. The *Ibbotson* tables, published by Morningstar, contain historical capital markets data that include, among other things, total returns and index values for stocks dating back to 1926. However, Morningstar recently discontinued the *Ibbotson SBBI Valuation Yearbook* after the 2013 edition. The last edition of the yearbook will likely remain relevant for a few more years. However, its usefulness will probably fade over time, as market conditions change. As a result, we have seen an increasing number of references to the "Duff & Phelps Risk Premium Report" for third-party support of a size premium.

5   In fact, the lead author of this book remembers his pre-law professor during freshman year of college asking him to think of the most dominant businesses he knew. For the lead author, it was McDonald's and Microsoft. The professor said that any business we thought of will eventually go bankrupt. At the time, it seemed impossible. Today, given the trends toward healthier eating and Apple's dominance in technology, it seems within the range of possible outcomes over the long run.

CHAPTER 4

1   American Bar Association Business Law Section, Mergers and Acquisitions: Market Trends Subcommittee, "2013 Private Target Mergers & Acquisitions Deal Points Study." (2013).

2   Duff & Phelps, "2012 Contingent Consideration Study," p. 10, available at http://www.duffandphelps.com/SiteCollectionDocuments/Reports/DUF_0008_Contingent%20Consideration%20Study8%2020.pdf (accessed December 28, 2014).

3   Id.

4   R.E. Spatt, "Selected Legal Issues Related to the Selection and Implementation of Differing Forms of Consideration in M&A Transaction," March 14, 2014, available at http://www.stblaw.com/content/publications/pub1723.pdf (accessed December 28, 2014).

5   Id.

6   Note: If the buyer assumes liabilities this is considered a form of transaction consideration under § 1.338–1(a)(1) of the U.S. Tax Code; also, § 483 could apply even if the agreement itself does not explicitly refer to contingent consideration. The benefit relates mainly to the buyer, as the seller would have to recognize interest income when the contingency has been resolved for amounts that might otherwise be characterized as capital gain. In many circumstances, a portion of the amount that is nominally considered part of the purchase price in the agreement, when and if paid to the seller, is required to be recharacterized by the buyer as interest expense under the imputed interest rules of § 483. The result to the buyer is typically favorable in that the resulting unstated interest expense may be currently deducted in the year paid rather than capitalized as part of the purchase price of the assets of the business. Source: C. Conjura & K. Milone, "Consider the Consideration," KPMG, September 2013.

7   The following discussion of contingent consideration treatment under U.S. Generally Accepted Accounting Principles versus International Financial Reporting Standards is adapted from "IFRS and US GAAP: Similarities and Differences," PricewaterhouseCoopers, October 2014, available at http://www.pwc.com/en_US/us/issues/ifrs-reporting/publications/assets/ifrs-and-us-gaap-similarities-and-differences-2014.pdf (accessed February 1, 2015).

8   This clause is still under review by IFRS, as is the entire topic of contingent consideration. See report by Deloitte "IASB completes post-implementation review of IFRS 3," June 17, 2015, accessible at http://www.iasplus.com/en-us/news/2015/06/pir-ifrs-3 (accessed July 5, 2015).

9   The Interpretations Committee of IFRS has observed that an arrangement in which contingent payments are automatically forfeited if employment terminates would lead to a conclusion that the arrangement is compensation for postcombination services rather than additional consideration for an acquisition, unless the service condition is not substantive. The Interpretations Committee reached this conclusion on the basis of the conclusive language used in paragraph B55(a) of IFRS 3. See IFRIC Update, January 2013, available at http://media.ifrs.org/2013/IFRIC/January/IFRIC-Update-January-2013.html (accessed February 1, 2015). For expert commentary, see also http://www.ifrs.org/Meetings/MeetingDocs/Interpretations%20Committee/2012/September/041209AP04%20-%20IFRS3%20Continuing%20employment.pdf (accessed February 1, 2015).

10 Note: On December 19, 2011, the IRS finalized prior temporary regulations and issued additional proposed regulations regarding the valuation of stock-based consideration packages for the purposes of the "continuity of interest" requirement applicable to most tax-free reorganizations under § 368 of the Internal Revenue Code. See 26 U.S.C. § 368, "Definitions Relating to Corporate Reorganizations," available at http://www.law.cornell.edu/uscode/text/26/368 (accessed July 4, 2015).

For current rules, see 26 Code of Federal Regulations 1.338 –3, available at http://www.law.cornell.edu/cfr/text/26/1.338-3 (accessed July 4, 2015). For a table showing correspondence of the U.S. Code and the Code of Federal Regulations, see http://www.gpo.gov/help/parallel_table.pdf (accessed July 5, 2015).

11 11 U.S.C. § 363, "Use, Sale, or Lease of Property," available at http://www.law.cornell.edu/uscode/text/11/363 (accessed July 5, 2015).

CHAPTER 5

1 KPMG, Corporate Tax Rates Table, available at http://www.kpmg.com/global/en/services/tax/tax-tools-and-resources/pages/corporate-tax-rates-table.aspx (accessed July 5, 2015).

2 U.S. Government Accountability Office, "Corporate Income Tax: Effective Tax Rates Can Differ Significantly from the Statutory Rate," May 2013, available at http://www.gao.gov/assets/660/654957.pdf (accessed January 1, 2015).

3 Nontaxable pass-through entities, such as partnerships, LLCs, S corporations, and sole proprietorships, generally do not pay federal income taxes on their entity-level earnings; rather, the taxes are paid by the individual owners on their own tax returns. Therefore, unlike a C corporation, there is no double taxation when previously taxed entity-level earnings are distributed as dividends to the individual owners. In addition, and more importantly, these pass-through entities provide an increase in basis to their owners for all earnings retained in the business, in turn reducing the tax when the business is later sold.

4 KPMG, Corporate Tax Rates Table, op. cit, note 1.

5 Burger King Investor Relations, "World's Third Largest Quick Service Restaurant Launched with Two Iconic and Independent Brands: Tim Hortons and Burger King," available at http://investor.bk.com/conteudo_en.asp?idioma=1&tipo=43682&conta=44&id=166086 (accessed January 3, 2015).

6 U.S. Department of the Treasury, "Fact Sheet: Treasury Actions to Rein in Corporate Tax Inversions," available at http://www.treasury.gov/press-center/press-releases/Pages/jl2645.aspx (accessed January 3, 2015).

7 TCM, 1999-254 (July 29, 1999).

8 898 A.2d 290 (Del. Ct. Ch. 2006).

9 *Bernier v. Bernier*, 449 Mass. 774 (2007) (*Bernier I*); *Bernier v. Bernier*, 82 Mass. App. Ct. 81, June 29, 2012 (*Bernier II*).

10 Relevant cases in this area include *Gross v. Commissioner*, 2001, U.S. App. Lexis 24803 (6th Cir., November 19, 2001); *Wall v. Commissioner*, TCM, 2001-75 (March 27, 2001); *Adams v. Commissioner*, TCM, 2002-80 (March 28, 2002); *Heck v. Commissioner*, TCM, 2002-34 (February 5, 2002);

Dallas v. Commissioner, TCM, 2006-212 (September 28, 2006); *Bernier I*; *Giustina v. Commissioner*, TCM, 2011-141 (June 22, 2011). For a discussion, see Russo, C. J., Mertins, L. & Martin, C. (2012), "Business Valuation Transaction Prices and Tax-Affecting S Corporations," *Advances in Taxation*, Revised and Resubmitted, June 2013, available at http://russophdcpa.com/uploads/3/1/2/9/3129429/bus_valuation_premiums_s_corporations_2012.pdf (accessed January 1, 2015).

11　One of the laws limiting the reach of state income taxes was broadened in early 1992 when the U.S. Supreme Court declared a *de minimus* exception to a 1959 law establishing a federal limitation on state income taxes. This exception, set forth in *Wisconsin Department of Revenue v. William Wrigley, Jr., Co.*, found that certain activities were "not entirely ancillary to requests for purchases" and, therefore, not exempt from state income tax.

12　As of the date this book was written, dividends were subject to a maximum federal tax rate of 20% provided that they were deemed "qualified." In order to be taxed at the qualified dividend rate, the dividend must be paid by a U.S. corporation (or one that meets certain tax treaty requirements), and the shareholder must have held the stock for more than 60 days.

13　This statement assumes that the fair market value of the assets sale is higher than their tax basis.

14　For an excellent article on this subject, see S. Hoffer & D. A. Oesterle, "Tax-Free Reorganizations: The Evolution and Revolution of Triangular Mergers," *Northwestern University Law Review*, *108*(3), 2013, pp. 1083–1114, available at http://papers.ssrn.com/sol3/Delivery.cfm/SSRN_ID2487866_code1468587.pdf?abstractid=2269838&mirid=1 (accessed July 4, 2015).

15　See 26 U.S.C. § 338, "Certain Stock Purchases Treated as Asset Acquisitions." Under § 338 of the Code, a stock acquisition can be treated as an asset acquisition so the tax basis of the assets held by the target company gets stepped up to the purchase price. Treasury rules under § 338(b)(5) identify classes of assets.

16　Of course, as noted multiple times in this text, the buyer should know what it's willing to pay in an asset deal versus a stock deal, with the spread being the present value of the depreciation tax shield created by the asset deal.

17　Note that the "hypothetical" intermediary corporation in fact never exists, but rather is a fiction created by the Code. For the purposes of historical background, the Code's purpose behind the hypothetical intermediary corporation is to address the fact that an acquirer "theoretically" could (1) set up a new corporation to acquire the stock of the target, and then (2) liquidate the newly acquired corporation and absorb the assets. Under this transaction structure, the seller effectively would be selling stock of the target, whereas the acquirer essentially would be buying the assets of the target. According to old tax case law (*Kimbell-Diamond Milling Company v. Commissioner*, 14 T.C. 74 [1950], *aff'd per curiam*, 187 F.2d 718 [5th Cir. 1951]), the tax treatment of the liquidation to the acquirer would depend on the acquirer's intent—that is, if the liquidation was intended to be part of an overall plan to acquire the target's assets. This subjective approach proved difficult for the IRS to administer, and as a result, § 338 evolved in order to establish an objective standard to determine whether a stock purchase would be taxed as an asset purchase.

CHAPTER 6

1   The full rules are included in Financial Accounting Standards Board (FASB) Accounting Standards Codification (ASC) topic 805, *Business Combinations* (ASC 805). ASC 805 became effective for business combinations with acquisition dates during financial reporting periods beginning on or after December 15, 2008. Outside the United States, International Financial Reporting Standards (IFRS) 3R, *Business Combinations*, outlines similar financial reporting requirements.

2   The requirements for purchase price allocations for tax purposes are covered by §§ 1060 and 338 of the Internal Revenue Code. As with many other GAAP-versus-tax processes, the output from a purchase price allocation for financial reporting purposes may differ from an allocation conducted for tax reporting purposes.

3   ASC topic 820, *Fair Value Measurement*.

4   A potential exception would be a write-down of accounts receivable if it turns out the target had an undisclosed problem with bad debt expense.

5   As an aside, AOL's stock price soared 45% the day Microsoft announced this $1 billion asset purchase, as investors realized the value of the patents AOL continued to own after the deal but which were not reflected in the company's financial reports.

6   Both buyer and seller can often agree on one thing, though: neither wants much consideration allocated to a seller noncompete. The amount allocated to a noncompete is generally ordinary income to the seller, whereas the buyer will be required to amortize the sum over 15 years, irrespective of the actual term of the agreement.

INDEX

ABA (American Bar Association) survey, 105
Accounting practices, effect on valuation, 31–35
Accretion/dilution analysis, 232–237
  determining accretive and dilutive
    transactions and, 232–234
  factors influencing whether transactions are
    accretive or dilutive and, 234–235
  incorporating into transaction analysis,
    236–237
  steps in building, 235–236
Accretive transactions. *See* Accretion/dilution
    analysis
Acquisition date, 168
Acquisitions, unsuccessful
  taxes and, 142
Acquisitive transactions, tax-free, 177
Adjusted basis, 134
Alcoa, 36
America Online (AOL), 207
American Bar Association (ABA) survey, 105
Amortization, PPA and, 214–215
Andaloro v. PFPC Worldwide, 263–264
Annual reports, 25
  for transactions details, 52
AOL (America Online), 207
*The Art of M&A: A Merger/Acquisition/Buyout
    Guide*, vii
*The Art of M&A Structuring: Techniques for
    Mitigating Financial, Tax, and Legal
    Risk*, 132
The Art of M&A Valuation and Modeling, vii
Asset purchases, 150, 151–153
  benefits of, 158–159
  diagram of, 153
  disadvantages of, 152–153
  double tax and, 160–161, 162
  justifiable for tax purposes, 162
  for legal purposes, 151–152
  purchaser's cost basis and, 159
  stock purchases compared with, 161
  tax implications of, 153, 155, 156, 159–160
  for tax purposes, 143–144
  taxable. *See* Taxable acquisitions
  transaction types and, 158
  types of, 155, 156
  when to use, 152
Assumptions tabs, 196–200
  best practices for creating, 198–200
  building transaction model and, 218, 219
  key assumptions and, 197–198
  sample, 244
Attribution analysis, for DCF analysis, 71

Balance sheet
  elements of, 58–60
  proforma. *See* Proforma balance sheet
Balance sheet contingencies, earnouts and, 112
Bankruptcy, contingent consideration and, 129
Bankruptcy transactions, tax-free, 177
Bargain hunting, 17
Bargain purchases, 211
Barriers to entry, constant growth rate and, 95
Behring, Alex, 139
Berkshire Hathaway, 39
Bernier v. Bernier, 141, 260–261
Beta, 85, 86
Biotech industry, rules of thumb and, 7
Bond Yield Plus Risk Premium, 84
Boot relaxation rules, 189
Bottom-line earnouts, 111–112
Bottom-up approach to free cash flow, 74,
    76, 77–78
Buffett, Warren, 3, 5
Burger Chef, 95
Burger King, 138–139
Burlington National, 39
Business units
  DCF analysis for, 72–73
  earnouts when buying, 111

C corporations, 146, 147–148
  double tax and, 160–161
Canadian National, 38–43
Canadian Pacific, 38–43
Capital, cost of. *See* Weighted average cost of
    capital (WACC)
Capital asset pricing model (CAPM), 84–90
  calculating inputs for, 86–87
  estimating cost of common equity
    using, 84–86
  illiquidity premium in, 89–90
  size premium in, 87–89, 90
Capital structure, changes in, WACC and, 83
Carryover basis, 156, 163. *See also* Stock
    purchases
  cost basis vs., 159
Carve-outs, 111
Cash flow reconciliation, in transaction models,
    231–232
Cash flows. *See also* DCF analysis
  accounting practices for, 34–35
  free. *See* Free cash flow
  in Type B transactions, 186
Cede & Co. v. JRC Acquisition Corp., 258–260
Chandler, William B., 47

ABOUT THE AUTHORS

H. Peter Nesvold, Esq., CFA, CPA, is a managing director and chief operating officer of Silver Lane Advisors, an M&A investment bank that specializes in the financial services industry. His diverse background in law, finance, and accounting offers unique perspective and depth of expertise into the structure of highly complex corporate transactions. He is a graduate of the University of Pennsylvania and Fordham Law School, and serves on the board of the New York Society of Security Analysts, a founding member of the CFA Institute.

Elizabeth Bloomer Nesvold is the founder and managing partner of Silver Lane Advisors. She has advised on more than 150 M&A, valuation, and strategic advisory assignments over her 25-year career. A member of Young Presidents' Organization, Liz is a graduate of Binghamton University and Fordham Business School.

Alexandra Reed Lajoux is chief knowledge officer of the National Association of Corporate Directors in Washington, D.C., a member of the Global Network of Director Institutes. She has authored numerous publications on a variety of business topics, including books in *The Art of M&A* series, which she co-founded nearly 30 years ago. A graduate of Bennington College, she holds an M.B.A. from Loyola University in Maryland and a Ph.D. from Princeton University.

Lightning Source UK Ltd.
Milton Keynes UK
UKHW021254260119
336202UK00003B/89/P